Henscratches and Flyspecks

BY PETER SEEGER

How to Play the Five-String Banjo
The Caroler's Songbag (with the Weavers)
The Goofing Off Suite
American Favorite Ballads
The Steel Drums of Kim Loy Wong
The Folksinger's Guitar Guide (with Jerry Silverman)
The Folksinger's Guide to the Twelve String Guitar (with Julius Lester)
The Bells of Rhymney and Other Songs and Stories
Bits and Pieces
Hard-hitting Songs for Hard-hit People (with Alan Lomax and Woody Guthrie)
How To Make A Chalil
Oh, Had I a Golden Thread (New Songs)
The Incompleat Folksinger

Henscratches and Flyspecks

How to read melodies from songbooks
in twelve confusing lessons

PETER SEEGER

FOUNDED 1838
GPPS

G.P. PUTNAM'S SONS
New York

Published simultaneously in Canada
by Longman Canada Limited, Toronto.

SBN: 399-11091-7

Library of Congress Catalog Card Number: 72-90805

PRINTED IN THE UNITED STATES OF AMERICA

Acknowledgments

This list will acknowledge and thank the following publishers for allowing their songs to be printed in this book:

ALMANAC MUSIC, INC., "Last Night I Had the Strangest Dream"

ATLANTIC MUSIC CORP., "The MTA Song"

BERANDOL MUSIC LIMITED, "The Squid Jigging Ground"

IRVING BERLIN MUSIC CORPORATION, "Blue Skies," "We Saw the Sea"

BOOSEY & HAWKES (CANADA) LIMITED, "I'se the B'ye That Built the Boat"

BOOSEY & HAWKES, INC., "Colonel Bogey"

CAMPBELL CONNELLY & CO. LTD., "Brownskin Gal"

CHERRY LANE MUSIC CO., "What Did You Learn in School Today?"

FALL RIVER MUSIC, INC., "(The Ring on My Finger Is) Johnny Give Me," "King Henry," "Where Have All the Flowers Gone?"

FAMOUS MUSIC CORP., "I'm Popeye the Sailor Man"

LEO FEIST, INC., "Yes, My Darling Daughter"

FOLKWAYS MUSIC PUBLISHERS, INC., "Black Girl," "Bring Me Li'l Water, Silvy," "Cotton Fields," "Ev'rybody Loves Saturday Night," "The Frozen Logger," "Kisses Sweeter Than Wine," "Riding in My Car," "Rock Island Line," "So Long, It's Been Good to Know Yuh," "Wimoweh," "(The Wreck of the) *John B*"

FRANK MUSIC CORP., "Oh Brandy, Leave Me Alone"

MICHAEL H. GOLDSEN, INC., "Philadelphia Lawyer"

T. B. HARMS COMPANY-ANNE-RACHEL MUSIC CORP., "Carioca"

HOLLIS MUSIC, INC., "Anna," "Charlie Is My Darling"

HOLT, RINEHART AND WINSTON, INC., "Oh, Watch the Stars"

LEEDS MUSIC CORPORATION, "Now Is the Hour"

LUDLOW MUSIC, INC., "All the Pretty Little Horses," "Another Man Done Gone," "Cowboy's Lament," "Dink's Song," "Go Down, Ol' Hannah," "Goodnight, Irene," "Hard, Ain't It Hard," "If I Had A Hammer," "Leatherwing Bat," "Lolly Too-Dum," "Mary Ann," "New York Town," "Pastures of Plenty," "Roll on Columbia," "Sweet Rosyanne," "This Land Is Your Land," "Tom Dooley," "Tom Joad," "We Shall Overcome," "When I First Came to This Land," "Why Oh Why"

EDWARD B. MARKS MUSIC CORP., "Lilli Marlene," "Yours (Quiereme Mucho)"

MCA MUSIC, "Joe Hill," "The Sinking of the *Reuben James*"

MELODY TRAILS, INC., "Get Up And Go," "I Never Will Marry," "Putting on the Style," "Turn! Turn! Turn!"

MILLER MUSIC CORP., "Once in a While"

MILLS MUSIC, INC., "Sly Mongoose," "Tzena, Tzena"

ROBBINS MUSIC CORPORATION, "Ballad for Americans"

ST. NICHOLAS MUSIC, INC., "Rudolph the Red-Nosed Reindeer"

SANGA MUSIC, INC., "House of the Rising Sun," "Michael, Row the Boat Ashore," "The 1913 Massacre," "Wasn't That a Time"

G. SCHIRMER, INC., "Black Is the Color," "I Wonder As I Wander," "Lulloo Lullay"

SCHRODER MUSIC COMPANY, "Little Boxes," "There'll Come a Time"

SHAPIRO-BERNSTEIN & CO., INC., "By the Beautiful Sea," "Casey Jones," "School Days"

SHARI MUSIC PUBLISHING CORP., "Jamaica Farewell"

STORMKING MUSIC, INC., "I Come and Stand at Every Door," "Oh, Had I a Golden Thread," "Peat Bog Soldiers," "River of My People," "Shoals of Herring," "Union Maid," "Viva La Quince Brigada," "Which Side Are You On?"

WARNER BROS. MUSIC, "Begin the Beguine," "Bei Mir Bist Du Schön," "Blowin' in the Wind," "California, Here I Come," "Mack the Knife," "Oh, Lady Be Good," "Sweet Georgia Brown"

WAROCK CORPORATION, "In a Shanty in Old Shanty Town"

WILLIAMSON MUSIC, INC., "Oh, What a Beautiful Mornin'," "Some Enchanted Evening"

WYNWOOD MUSIC CO., INC., "Candy Man Blues"

Thanks to a friend of four decades, composer Herbert Haufrecht, who read through the manuscript of this book and helped me from making too many mistakes. And thanks to the most long suffering editors, Janet Kramer and Karen Levine, for seeing it through.

Thanks above all to the songwriters of the world, the rewriters, the arrangers, and the joiners without whose songs this book would be useless. Thanks to them all, known and unknown, living and dead.

Contents

This book got an ironclad copyright in the U.S. Library of Congress.

Anyone caught copying or repeating parts of this book and passing them on to others . . . will sure be a good friend of mine, 'cause that's what I wrote it for in the first place.*

(Don't let the publisher catch you.)

*Thanks to Woodrow Wilson Guthrie for this thought.

Introduction

Do you like to sing? If you are fortunate enough to live in a musical community, or in a singing family, there may be little need for you to learn to read music. You can learn songs in the same way that folk music has always been learned: by ear.

However, if you are a member of one of our deprived twentieth-century industrial societies, with more gadgets than your grand-parents ever had, but deprived of the traditions which enriched their lives, and if you would like to bring back into your life and your children's lives the custom of making music, perhaps you can use the help of this book.

Music teachers sometimes *over*emphasize the importance of learning to read music early. Would you teach a baby to read before it could talk? Should a teen-ager study dance notation before learning to dance? Musicians need, in the beginning, to train their ears, their vocal cords, or their hands, and to develop the sense of music that tells them when to sing what.

This book is written for people who like to sing folk songs and find themselves hampered by their inability to decipher the hen scratches and flyspecks on the pages of a songbook. Perhaps you have sometime heard a song which has caught your heart. You approach the singer afterward and ask where you could learn it.

"Why, it's in such-and-such a songbook," comes the reply.

"Not on any recording?"

"No, not recorded that I know of."

So now you're stymied.

The fact is, if you can carry a tune, if your eyes can focus on a page, you can probably learn within a few weeks or months to pick average tunes out of a songbook. Here's wishing you luck.

P.S. This whole book is a case of the blind leading the blind. The author is a self-taught, half-trained musician who still learns songs better by ear than by eye. Still, you know, a half-blind person is often better to lead a totally blind person. He takes less for granted.

How to Use This Book

Leaf through it quickly first. Learn roughly what ground it covers.

Then work your way through slowly.

If you come to some song that stumps you, don't waste time on it. Skip it for the moment, go on. Return and try it again later.

The tunes I've used as examples are mostly old-fashioned ones, some good, some junky. If they are not to your taste, just be patient. It's hard to find interesting songs which are simple enough to start learning on (and not copyrighted). Furthermore, it's impossible to suit every taste and still find songs familiar to all. When you have finished struggling through the book, then you can get hold of songs you really want to learn.

Lesson 1
A Few Simple Tunes to Read, Melodies and Rhythms

Ignore, for a moment, ninety-five percent of the hieroglyphics that European musicians have invented over several centuries, to try to describe the music they want to play:

D.C.
D.S.
D.C. al Fine
mp
pp.
8va
f
ff
1
2

For now, consider several things:

1) A "noise" is a vibration that can be heard.

2) A "musical tone" has a regular vibration.

3) When we sing a song, usually each syllable has a separate musical "note," high or low.

4) The usual "note" lasts from a fraction of a second, to several seconds, in length of time.

Here is a “note”—
a most common kind of note:

It’s called a *quarter note.* No need to ask why.
You’ll find out later.

This is a staff (always five lines):

Now, put the note on one of the lines or spaces, and you can tell if it is

a higher note: 

or a lower note: 

Some voices can sing high notes like these:

Altos and baritones and other low voices feel more comfortable singing notes like these:

The tails (stems) of the notes usually point down when the note is on or above the middle line. Usually up when the note is below the middle line.

*When notes get too high or too low for the staff, they are put on (or between) little short lines called *ledger lines.*

At the left end of a staff is usually a spiral thingummy:

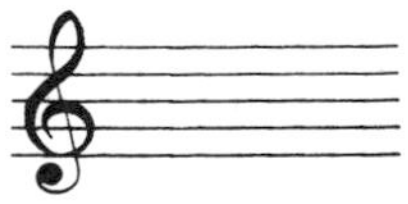

It's called a *G clef* sign. (There is also an *F clef* used by bass singers in a chorus, or for the left-hand part of a piano, and there are a couple other rarely used clef signs, but you don't need to bother with them now.)

The 𝄞 actually was an old-fashioned way of writing the letter *G*, and it always encircles the second line from the bottom of the staff. Each line and space on the staff is given a letter of the alphabet. After seven notes, start the alphabet over.

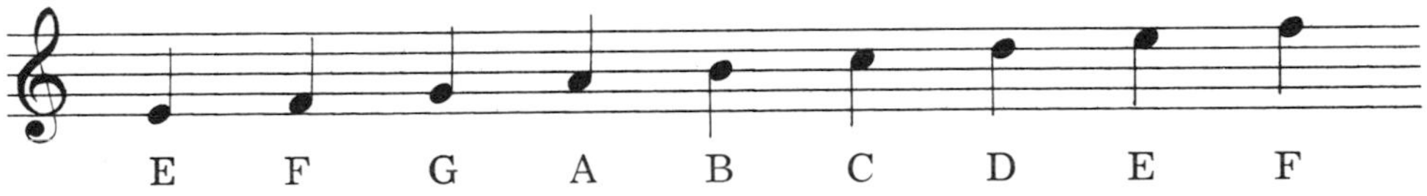
E F G A B C D E F

And naturally, with ledger lines you could continue repeating the same seven notes up as far as you want to squeak, or down to growl.

etc.
G A B C D E F G A B C D E F G A B C

Can you sing a scale? A scale is a row of notes going up or down. The Christmas carol "Joy To The World" starts with a descending scale:

Joy to the world the Lord is come

Next, an *as*cending scale. You can sing the old "do, re, mi" names, or you can sing "One, two, three, etc."

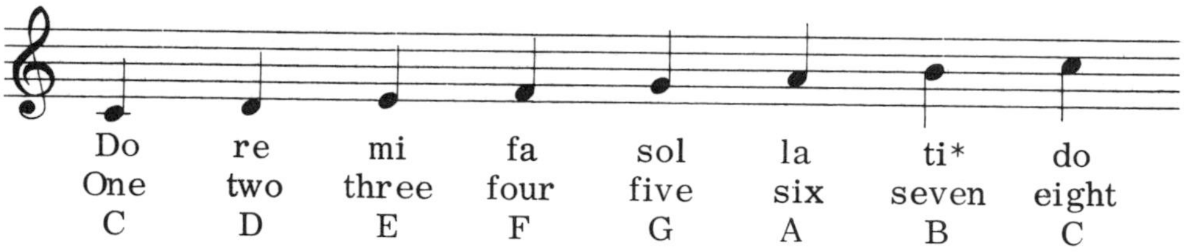
Do re mi fa sol la ti* do
One two three four five six seven eight
C D E F G A B C

This scale is called a *C scale* because it starts and ends on a C note. Notice that the first and last notes sound alike, except that one is high and one is low. They are one *octave* apart—eight notes. The high note's vibrations are twice as fast as the low note's.

*Some say *si* instead of *ti*. Don't blame mi.

Of course, you can sing a scale high or low, anywhere you want. Here is a scale starting and ending on G, so it's called a *G scale*:

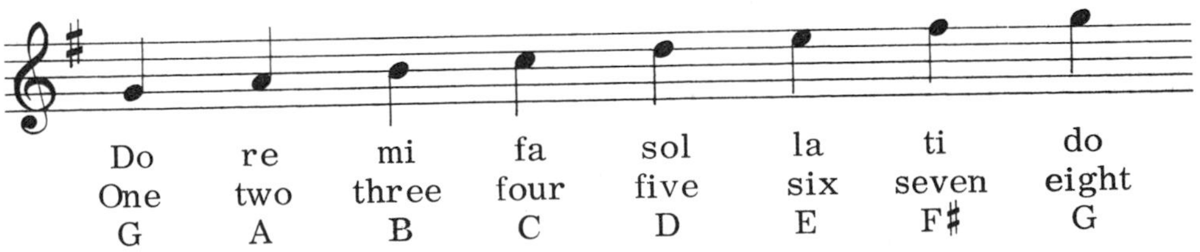
Do One G
re two A
mi three B
fa four C
sol five D
la six E
ti seven F♯
do eight G

Songs in the key of G need a *sharp* sign (♯) on the line of the staff. You'll find out why in Lesson 8.

Only a tenor or soprano could sing that G scale, though. Maybe a real low voice could sing *down* from G:

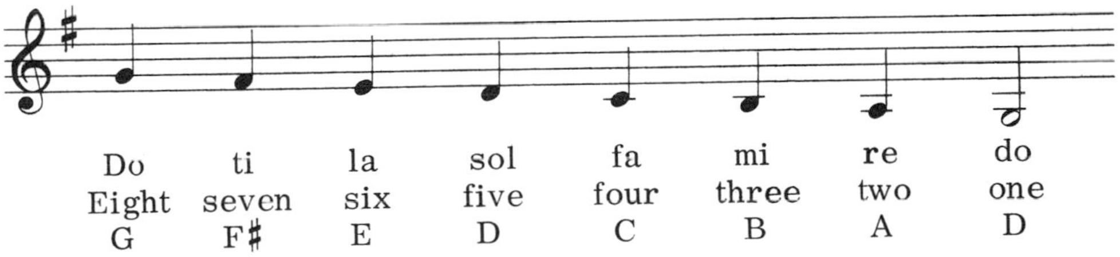
Do Eight G
ti seven F♯
la six E
sol five D
fa four C
mi three B
re two A
do one D

You notice that last note is hollow?

Something new: 𝅗𝅥

This is called a *half note*: 𝅗𝅥

It is held twice as long as a quarter note.
In other words

♩ plus ♩ = 𝅗𝅥

Now we're almost ready to read and sing some melodies. But first I better explain some things about

RHYTHM

Because

Rhythm

is

everyone's

stumbling

block

Here is a tune you know, a tune with strong rhythm:

Yan-kee Doo-dle went to town Rid-ing on a po - ny

1. The vertical lines on the staff are called *bar lines* and mark off the main rhythm. The space between each bar line is called a *measure.* The first note in each measure is accented, and the third note is also.

2. Since each measure in this song has four quarter notes in it (or the equivalent), we call this *four-four time* (or four-four meter) and put a *time signature* at the beginning of the song: 4/4

3. Even the last measure has four beats, because each half note equals two beats. Tap out the beats, four to a measure, while you sing it.

Is everything clear so far?

OK, here's the first confusion. For a group of instrumental musicians it may be very important to all play notes in "concert pitch." If a violinist's A had 440 vibrations per second and the saxophone player had an A note which was higher—vibrating 450 times a second—that wouldn't do.

But you are singing a song to yourself or to some friends. The book may have it written in the key of C, *but you can and you should sing it in whatever key you think best, higher or lower.*

Your eyes can read the notes on the page in the C scale but the sounds can come out of your mouth in any key you damn please.

That is what I call a *MOVABLE DO*—that is, "do, re, mi" can be sung high or low. It doesn't matter.

"Wha-a-at!??" I hear someone exclaim. "Why the heck bother printing songs in a lot of different keys, if people can sing them in any key they want?"

Let me explain again:

People playing in orchestras *have* to play in the correct pitch to sound right together. Instruments are manufactured to hold "concert pitch"—an A above middle C is 440 vibrations per second. Some people are born with "perfect pitch." You could turn to them any time and say "Whistle me a concert A," and they'd be able to.*

Songs are usually put in songbooks in what the editor of the songbook thinks is a convenient key to sing. But small children, tenors, or sopranos might want to sing it higher than it is written. This writer, with a middle-aged voice, finds it convenient to sing *all* the songs in this book several notes lower than they are written.

Women's voices are higher than men's, but usually not a full octave higher. Thus women will often prefer to sing a song in a *lower* key

*It doesn't mean they are necessarily good musicians. Scientists have discovered that horses have perfect pitch.

than men. Get it? Men might prefer the song in C or D, but the women might prefer it in G or A.

Get used to the idea of a movable "do." That is, be able to sing "do, re, mi, fa, sol, la, ti, do" high or low, as it feels comfortable for your voice. The songs in the first half of this book will all be written in either the key of G or the key of C. But you sing 'em where your voice feels it right.

We'll end up the first lesson with parts of some old songs. With each song, do the following three things:

1. First get the feel for the rhythm. Notice the *time signature.* Beat time with your foot, tap with your fingers—anything. Notice the long and the short notes. Keep the rhythm regular.

2. Next, check what key the song is in. In the next few lessons I'll just give songs in the key of G or C. Make sure you know which note of the scale the song starts at. Sing up or down the scale till you come to the right note to start.

3. Now sing through the song several times, until it goes smoothly. Notice how the notes go up and down on the staff, which notes are accented, which are long or short. Keep the rhythm regular.

Yankee Doodle

Go through the three steps mentioned above. First, check the rhythm, 4/4. Second, notice it's the key of G. This song starts on "do," the first note of the scale.

Do do re mi

You know that the song is in the key of G because you see the ♯ at the left. Of course the same song could be written higher; for example the key of C could be used:

or lower:

Third, try singing the song in whatever pitch is comfortable for your voice.

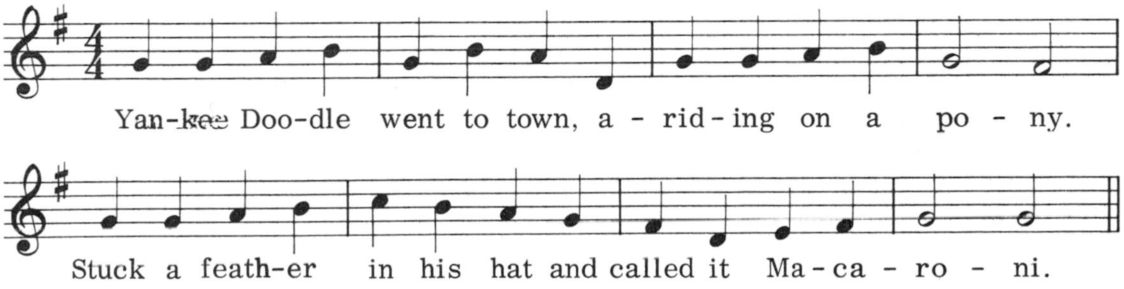
Yan-kee Doo-dle went to town, a - rid-ing on a po - ny.
Stuck a feath-er in his hat and called it Ma-ca - ro - ni.

(The refrain you'll get in a later lesson, see page 42).

Frère Jacques

This song also starts on the first note of the scale, but take a look at the time signature: 2/4. For this song there are only two beats in each measure. Why? If you really want to discuss it, see page 47.

Frè - re Jac - ques, Frè - re Jac - ques
Dor - mez vous? Dor - mez vous?

("Brother Jack, Brother Jack, are you sleeping, are you sleeping?" Don't let the French pronunciation throw you: "Fre-ruh Zhakuh, dor-may voo." OK? The rest of the song is on page 39.)

Jingle Bells

This song starts on the third note of the scale. Sing a scale to yourself, high up: "Do, re, *mi* - - -!"

Do re mi

Now start singing up there, on "mi."

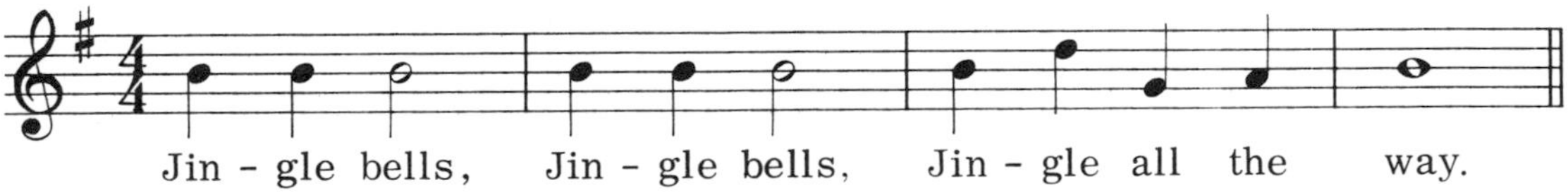
Jin - gle bells, Jin - gle bells, Jin - gle all the way.

(Rest of the song on page 57.)

Mary Had A Little Lamb

This song also starts on the third note of the scale, but it's written in the key of C. So sing it lower down.

Do re mi

Ma - ry had a lit - tle lamb lit - tle lamb, lit - tle lamb,

Ma - ry had a lit - tle lamb, its fleece was white as snow.

Again, something new has been added: a *whole note* 𝅝. It equals four beats. In other words:

and
plus

Also the rhythm of this song may not seem quite right to you. You'll find out why in the next lesson.

Go Tell Aunt Rhody*

Another song in C, which also starts on the third note of the scale:

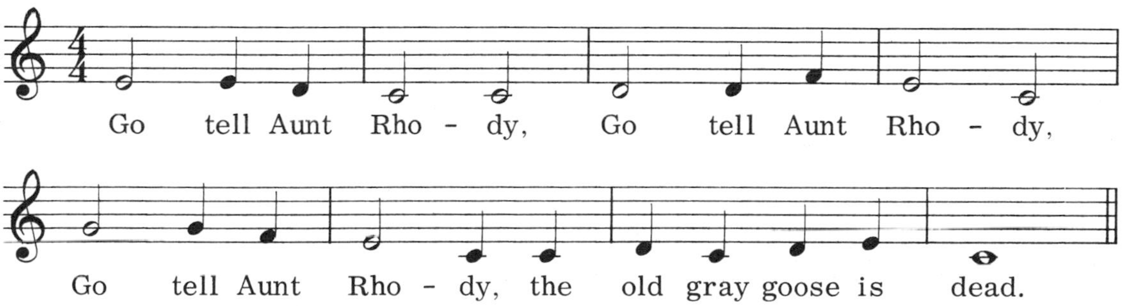
Go tell Aunt Rho - dy, Go tell Aunt Rho - dy,
Go tell Aunt Rho - dy, the old gray goose is dead.

This also ends with a whole note. And since both the last two melodies have been given complete, they end with a double bar line ‖. This usually means the end of the song. Funny, but it's usual to end a song like this with a whole note, while in actual singing, the voice pronounces "dead" briefly and then rests for the remaining four beats of the measure. But you're not supposed to learn *rests* until Lesson 7.

OK, OK, you'll be able to graduate from kindergarten soon. Stick around. This next song makes some bigger jumps in the melody. It starts on the first note of the scale, but goes right up to the fifth note in the scale, and later to the top "do." You'll recognize the tune; it's almost the same as "Twinkle Twinkle Little Star."

*Don't worry if you know a different version of the words or notes of any song in this book. Just say to yourself, "Seeger's got this wrong here," and pass on. No sweat.

When I First Came To This Land

Do re mi fa sol
One two three four five

The song is in C.
Sing your scale.

Adapted from a
Pennsylvania Dutch Song

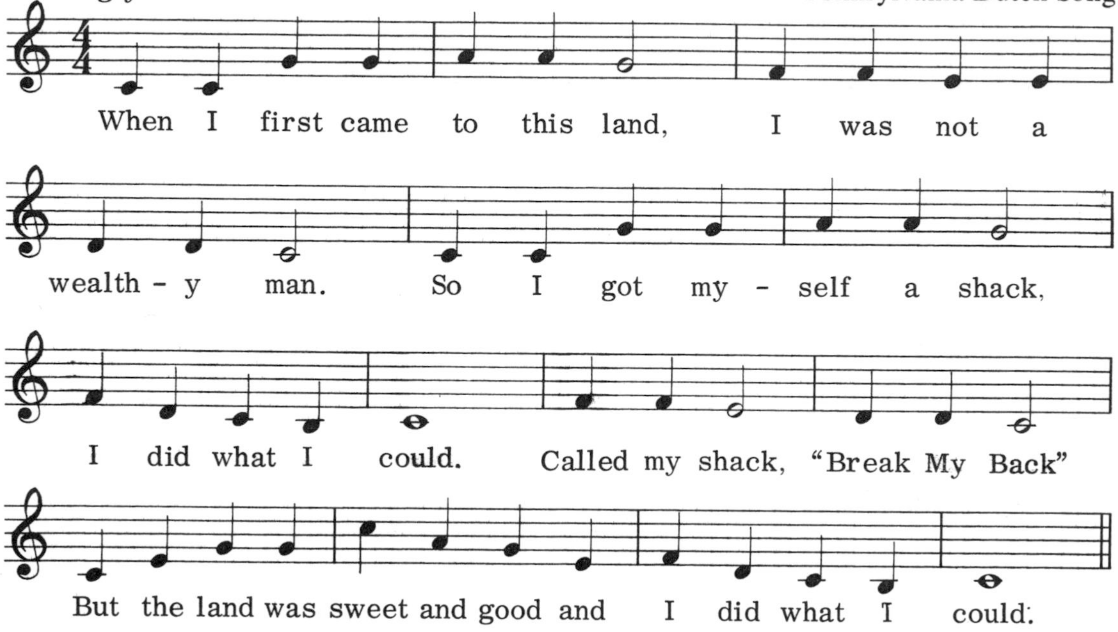
When I first came to this land, I was not a
wealth - y man. So I got my - self a shack,
I did what I could. Called my shack, "Break My Back"
But the land was sweet and good and I did what I could.

2. When I first came to this land
I was not a wealthy man
So I got myself a cow
I did what I could.
(melody repeats) { Called my cow, "No Milk Now"
Called my shack, "Break My Back"
But the land was sweet and good
And I did what I could.

3. When I first came to this land
I was not a wealthy man
So I got myself a duck
I did what I could.

(three repeats, get it?)

Called my duck, "Out Of Luck"
Called my cow, "No Milk Now"
Called my shack, "Break My Back"
But the land was sweet and good
And I did what I could.

4. . . . got myself a wife . . . "Run for Your Life"

5. . . . got myself a son . . . "My Work's Done"

Often a melody starts below "do." In the next song, sing your way down, to locate the right note to start on:

Do ti la sol
Eight seven six five

And watch the rhythm; the accent (the *downbeat*) comes on the second note; the first note comes on the *upbeat*:*

The Riddle Song

I gave my love a cher - ry that has no stone.

(Complete song on page 58)

similarly in the next song.

Caisson Song

The opening note is on the fifth note of the scale. Sing up to it:

Do re mi fa sol
One two three four five

*If the first note of a measure is the downbeat, the beat just before it is the upbeat.

Watch. This song is not only faster, but the downbeat does not come till the *third* note of the song.

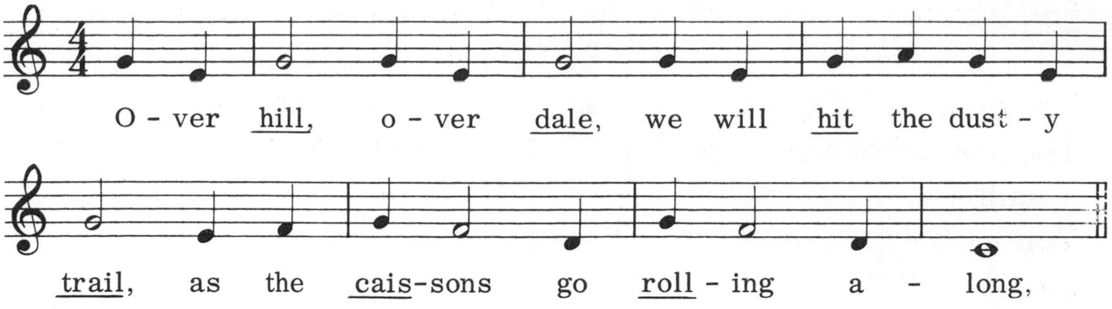
O - ver hill, o - ver dale, we will hit the dust - y
trail, as the cais-sons go roll - ing a - long,

Got that syncopated rhythm in the last three measures? More about this in a future lesson. In Lesson 4 you'll get the whole song.

By now you should be watching closely to see if a melody makes little jumps (as when you sing a scale), or bigger jumps, as in a bugle call. Gradually your ear should be able to tell you if the melody has jumped three notes of a scale, or four, or five, or more. But don't expect this skill to come right away.

Meanwhile, here's a nice little test. See if you can recognize this melody. And put the bar lines in the right place. It's in 4/4 time. This is the first line of a well known song:

Answer below.

No, don't look until you have to.

Oh, the sun shines bright on my old Ken-tuck-y home

(at this point we must break down and weep)

Score yourself. Were you right?

QUESTION: *HOW LONG IS A MUSICAL PHRASE?*

No matter how many measures are squeezed into one line, you'll find it easier to learn a song one phrase at a time.

The phrase might be two measures long, or four measures, or more. The musical phrase might have a phrase of words under it, such as a sentence, but usually it is shorter, sometimes only a few words. You have to decide for yourself. (Usually a phrase is sung in one breath.)

In later Lessons you'll be able to read all kinds of melodies. Right now we have to stick to pretty simple ones. But here's a famous theme from Beethoven's Ninth Symphony.

(Starts on the third note of the scale: "do, re, *mi.*")

Ode To Joy

You'll have to get the rest of it later. It's a little too complicated for now.

I would have liked to use in this book more of America's great pop tunes and show tunes, but they are copyrighted and the publishers would sue the b'jeezus out of anyone who printed more than a handful of notes of them. Some of these songs are great melodies. I'll occasionally sneak in a few. You can write for the complete sheet music from the publishers.

Sweet Georgia Brown

Rhythm simplified
see page 229.

By BERNIE-PINKARD-CASEY

TEST for Lesson 1

Here are all the melodies you supposedly learned in this lesson. Put the bar lines in the right places and write the title of the song. If you are a demon for punishment, try copying out some of the tunes in a higher or lower key. If it is in C, write it in G; if it is in G, write it in C.

1.

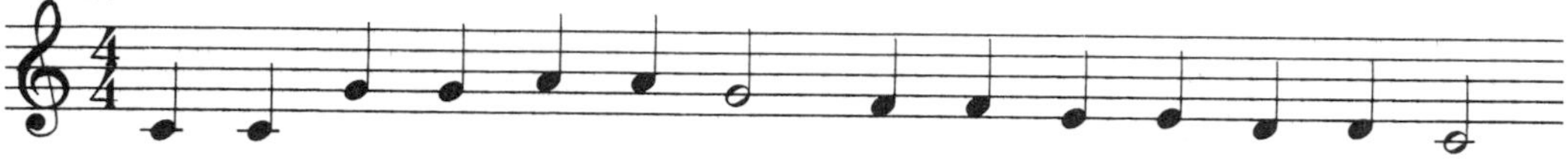

2.

3.

4.

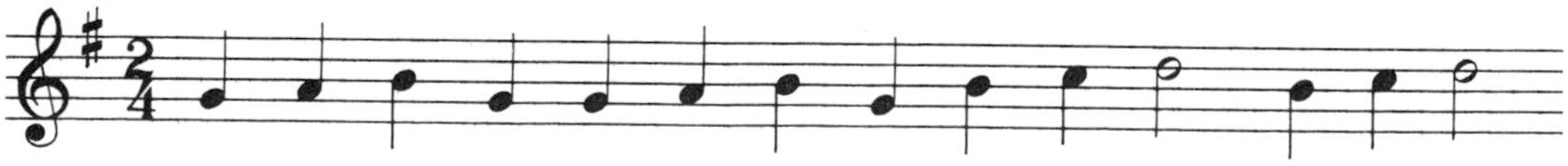

5.

6.

7.

8.

9.

10.

And four songs you didn't get in this lesson but probably know. The first is the chorus of America's most famous ditty. It starts on the *fourth* note of the scale: "do, re, mi, *fa*."

Answers upside down at bottom of page.

1.

2.

3.

4.

Answers: 1. "O Susanna"
2. "Little Old Sod Shanty"
3. "A Tisket, A Tasket"
4. "O Come all Ye Faithful"

And a review of all you've learned in the first lesson:

quarter note ♩

staff 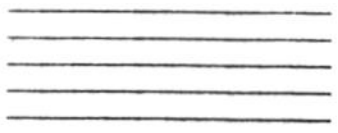

ledger lines 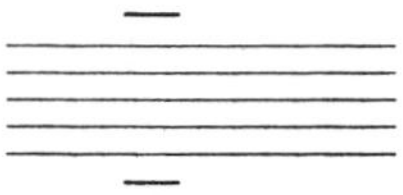

treble clef sign 𝄞

names of notes 
A B C D E F G A B C D E F G A

sharp sign ♯

half note 𝅗𝅥

bar lines 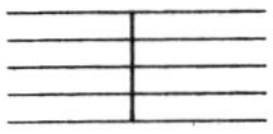

a measure 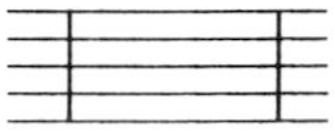

time signature $\frac{4}{4}$ *four-four time*

time signature $\frac{2}{4}$ *two-four time*

whole note 𝅝

double bar line 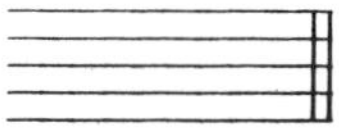

On to the
next lesson!

Notes

Lesson 2
Dotted Notes, and More Old-Fashioned Tunes

If you put a dot to the right of a note, you lengthen it by 50%.

Thus: 𝅗𝅥. lasts as long as 𝅗𝅥 + ♩

and 𝅗𝅥. plus ♩ = 𝅝

or ♩ + ♩ + ♩

(two dots after a note lengthen it 75%: 𝅗𝅥.. = ♩ + ♩ + ♪)

All clear?

Tap out the four beats in each measure as you sing this:

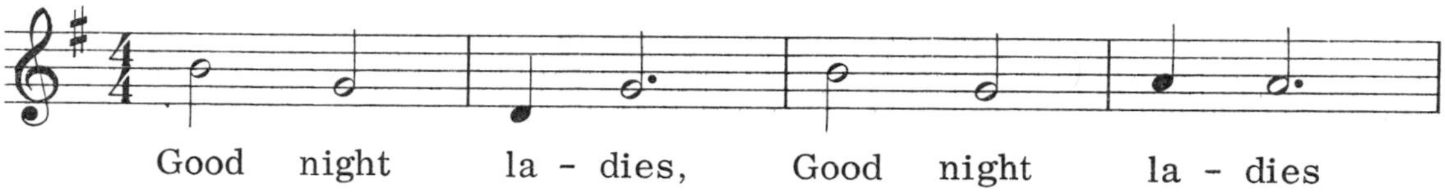
Good night la - dies, Good night la - dies

Or this:

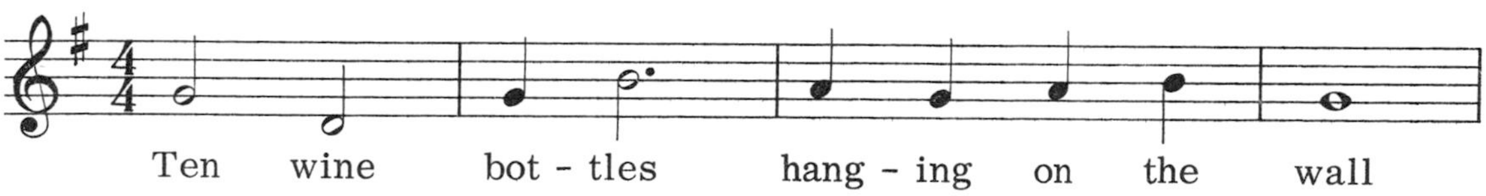
Ten wine bot - tles hang - ing on the wall

Or this:

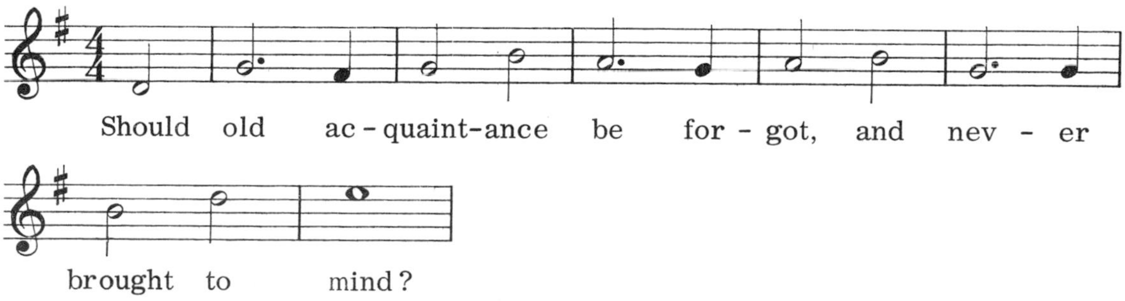
Should old ac - quaint-ance be for - got, and nev - er
brought to mind?

So now here's some songs you may want to go through.

Jacob's Ladder

Remember:

1. What rhythm is it in?
2. What key? And what note of the scale does it start on?
3. Sing through it slowly, keeping it regular.

Negro spiritual—the
version of it I like best

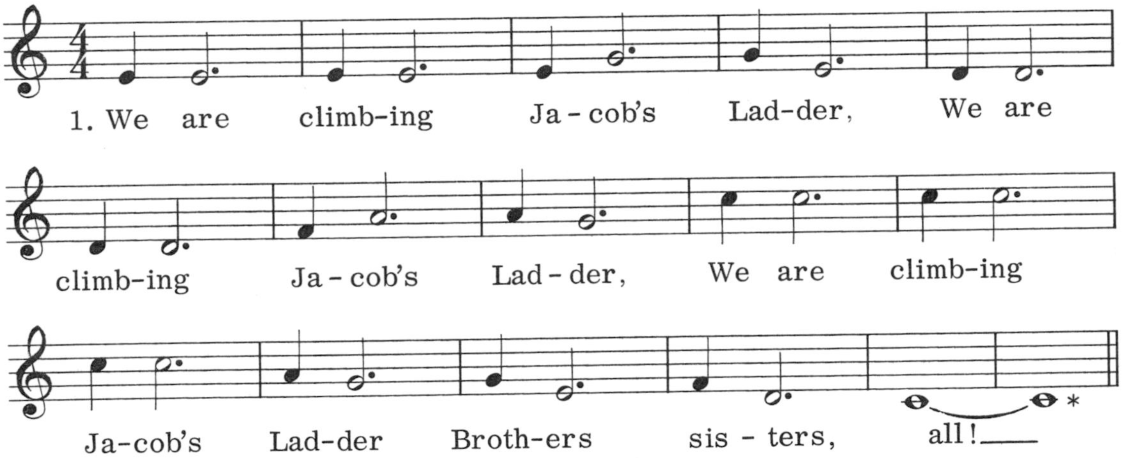

1. We are climb-ing Ja-cob's Lad-der, We are
climb-ing Ja-cob's Lad-der, We are climb-ing
Ja-cob's Lad-der Broth-ers sis-ters, all!
*

Some other verses:

Ev'ry rung goes higher, higher, (3 times)
Brothers, sisters all.
Ev'ry new one makes us stronger, (3 times)
Brothers, sisters, all.
We are black and white together, (3 times)
Brothers, sisters, all.

Again, tap out the four beats per measure.

*Something new: The curved line ‿ between the last two notes is called a *tie*. In effect it makes the two notes into one very long note. Here it extends the length of the note four more beats, making the two notes into one very long note of eight beats. A tie can also connect three or more notes together. See how it is used in the next few songs.

All Through The Night

trad. Welsh

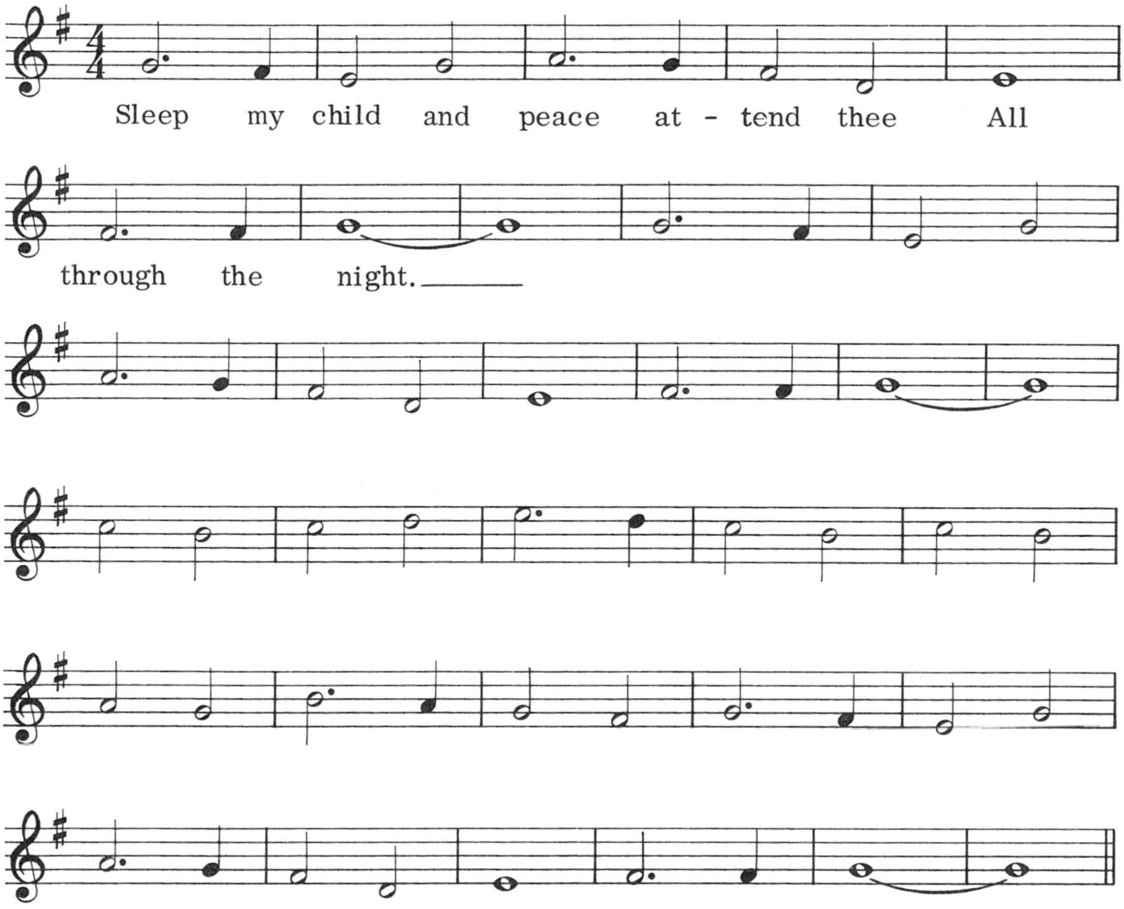
Sleep my child and peace at - tend thee All
through the night.

Richard Strauss was once conducting a rehearsal of his new symphony when he stopped abruptly and said to the trombonist, "That is a half note, not a dotted half note."

The trombonist peered carefully at his part, then smiled and nodded. "I'm sorry, maestro. It was a fly speck and I misread it."

They started over again, but now Strauss stopped the orchestra when they passed the same place. "No," he said thoughtfully. "The fly was right."

Bury Me Beneath The Willow

A fine old hollering country song. It starts on the fifth note of the scale. Count up. Then start. Tap with your fingers or your feet, so you keep track of half notes, and dotted half notes.

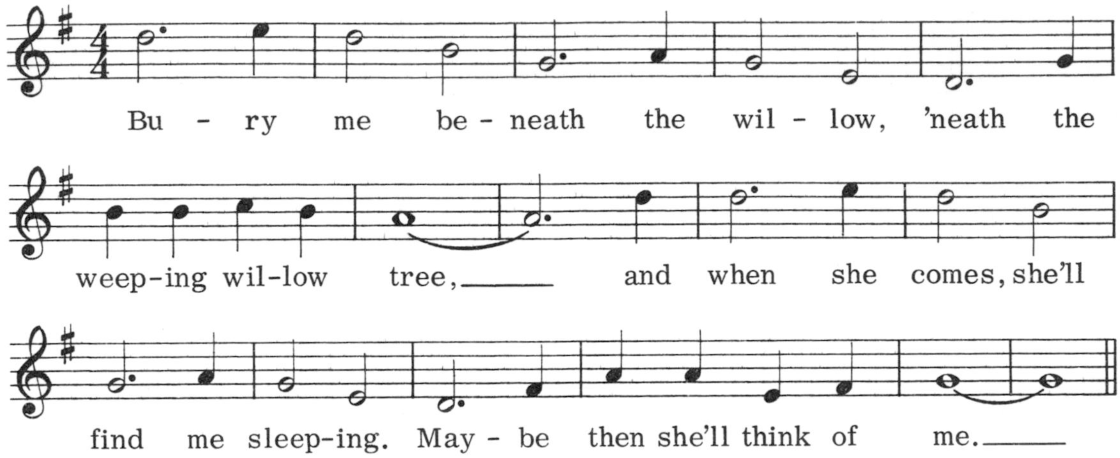
Bu - ry me be - neath the wil - low, 'neath the
weep-ing wil-low tree,___ and when she comes, she'll
find me sleep-ing. May - be then she'll think of me.___

Maybe this is as good a time as any to point out that the note written on the staff cannot tell exactly what a singer may want to sing, any more than cold print on a playwright's script can tell an actor exactly how to pronounce the words.

The notes are like the bare skeleton of a melody. The subtle changes and shadings usually have to be added by the singer. This is especially true of Afro-American music such as spirituals, blues, etc., but it's true of other idioms as well.

Before I give you a batch more songs to try out, learn a new kind of note:

an *eighth-note*  (It's half as long as a quarter-note.)

Two or more together sometimes have their stems joined like this:

In old days the individual tails looked so confusing. Nowadays they are more often joined together. It's called "beaming" a note.

Also now see 
plus

and 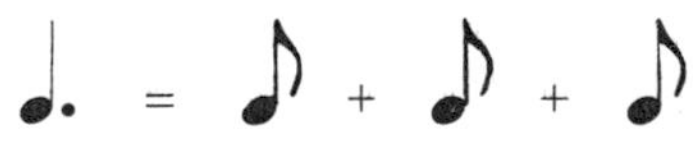

and 
plus

All clear?

Now is the time to point out that I really wrote out "Mary Had A Little Lamb" (p. 24) incorrectly.

I wrote it as this:

Mar - y had a lit - tle lamb

But it should have been this:

Mar - y had a lit - tle lamb

The first two notes (Ma-ry) are *not* equal in length. The first is strongly accented. The second note is shorter. Right?

* * *

In case you are getting dizzy from trying to remember too much at once, here's some rhythm practice. After a while you will get so used to these patterns, you'll hardly remember how confusing they once were.

Sing through each of the measures below many times. Sing out the words in capital letters. But when you come to the words in parentheses, pat your feet on the floor, or tap your fingers on the table, to keep a steady beat.

"ONE TWO THREE (Four)"

Sing it over and over, in rhythm.

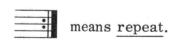

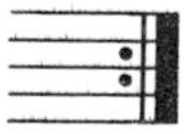 means repeat.

Now try this

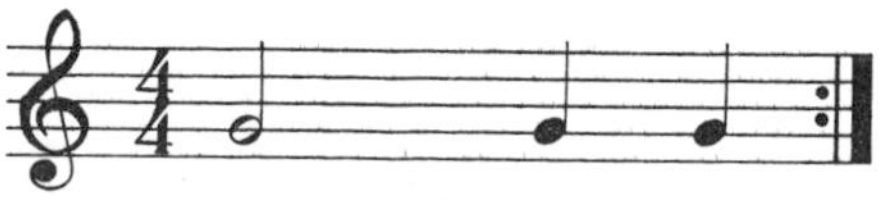

ONE (two) THREE FOUR

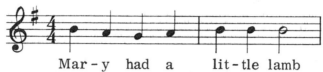

Here's more difficult patterns. Sing through each many times, till your ear recognizes them easily.

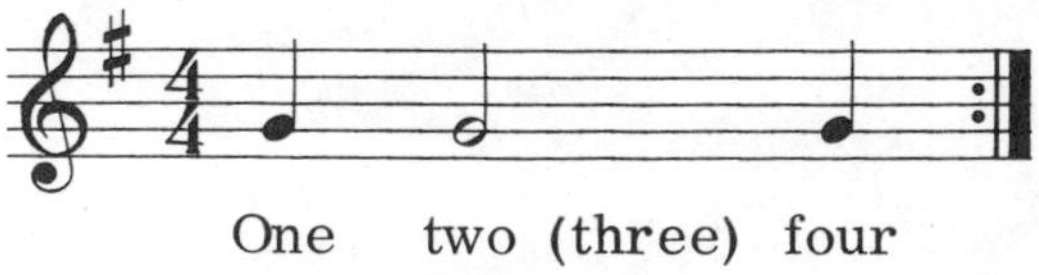
One two (three) four

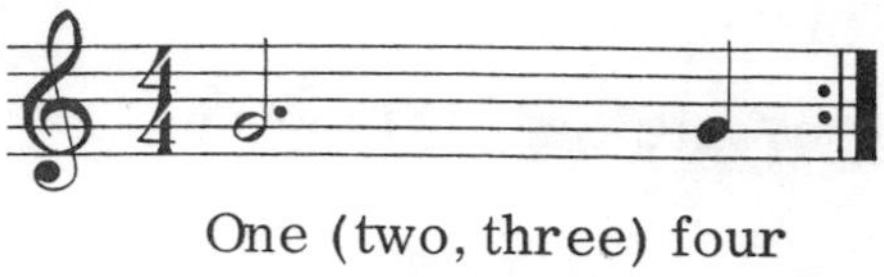
One (two, three) four

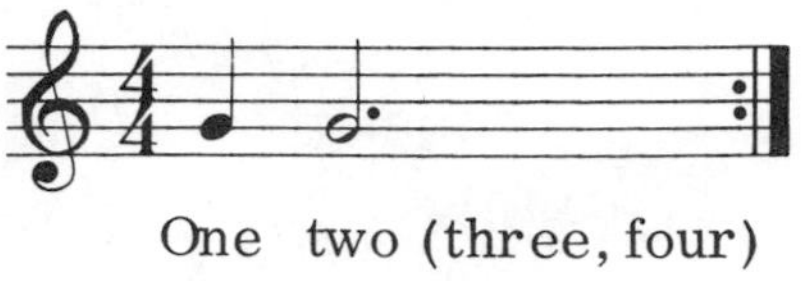
One two (three, four)

Here's a double measure pattern: "ONE (two, three, four, one) *TWO THREE FOUR!*"

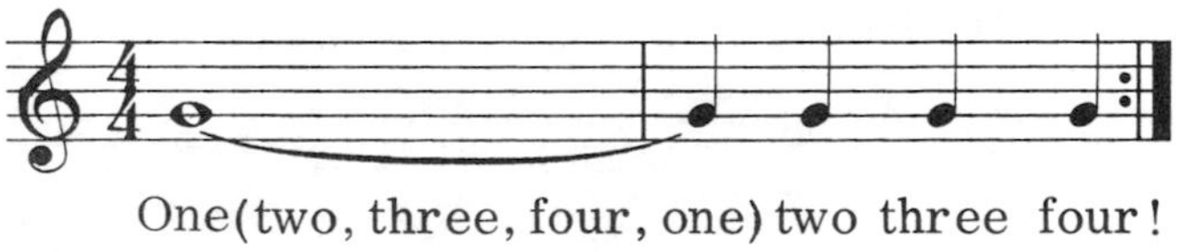
One(two, three, four, one) two three four!

Here's the same rhythm patterns, using quarter-notes and eighth-notes. Sing them with the word *and* to indicate the short eighth-note:

One and two

over and over

One two and

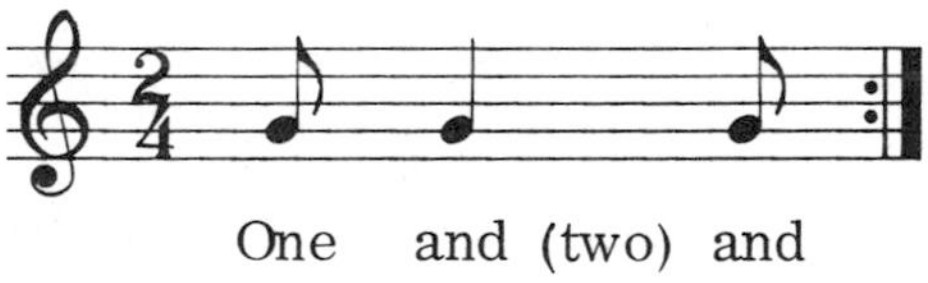
One and (two) and

That's pretty tricky. We'll go into it more thoroughly in Lesson 4.

And the double measure pattern can now be put into one measure. (It's the same as "When the Saints Go Marching In," page 75.)

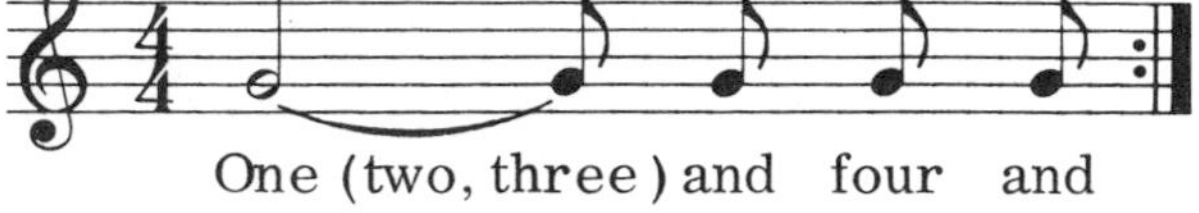
One (two, three) and four and

If that's too tricky for now, don't let it discourage you. Sing through the next few practice measures; then we'll have more songs.

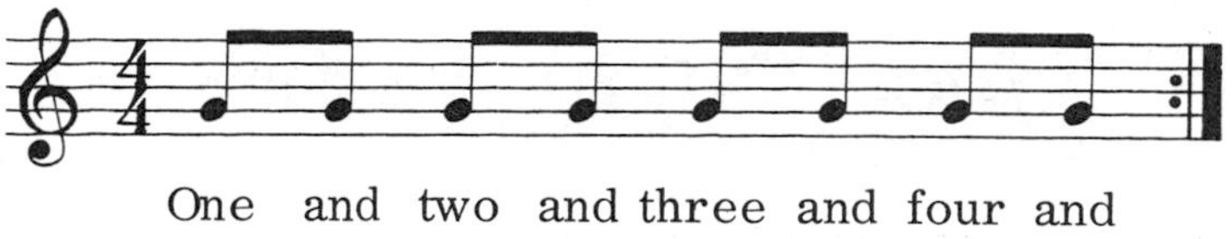
One and two and three and four and

One two and three four

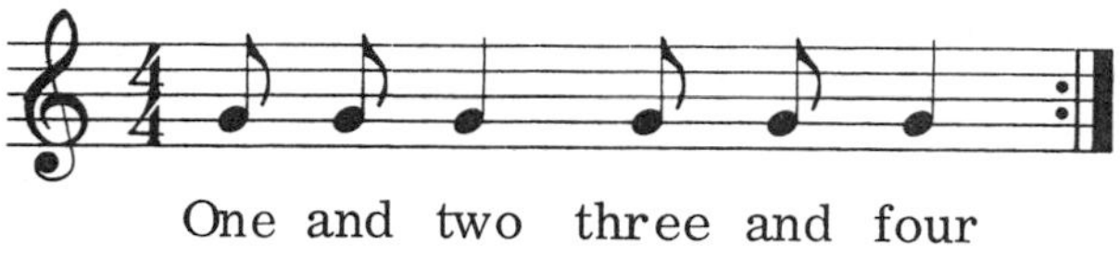
One and two three and four

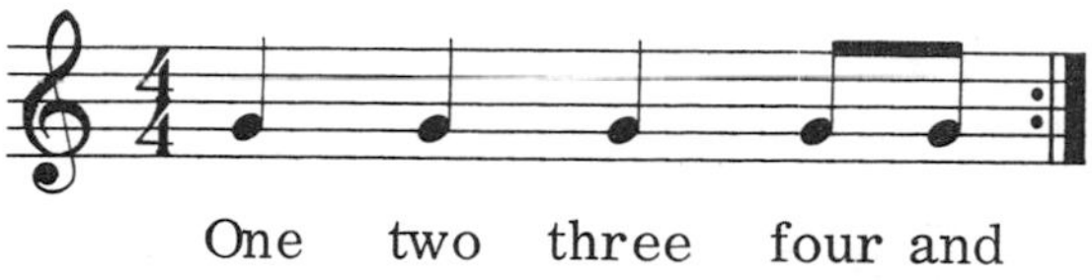
One two three four and

More old fashioned tunes. Take 'em *slowly,* slowly as necessary at first. But keep the beat regular. Then when you have the rhythm and tune right, speed it up as much as you want.

Ten Little Indians

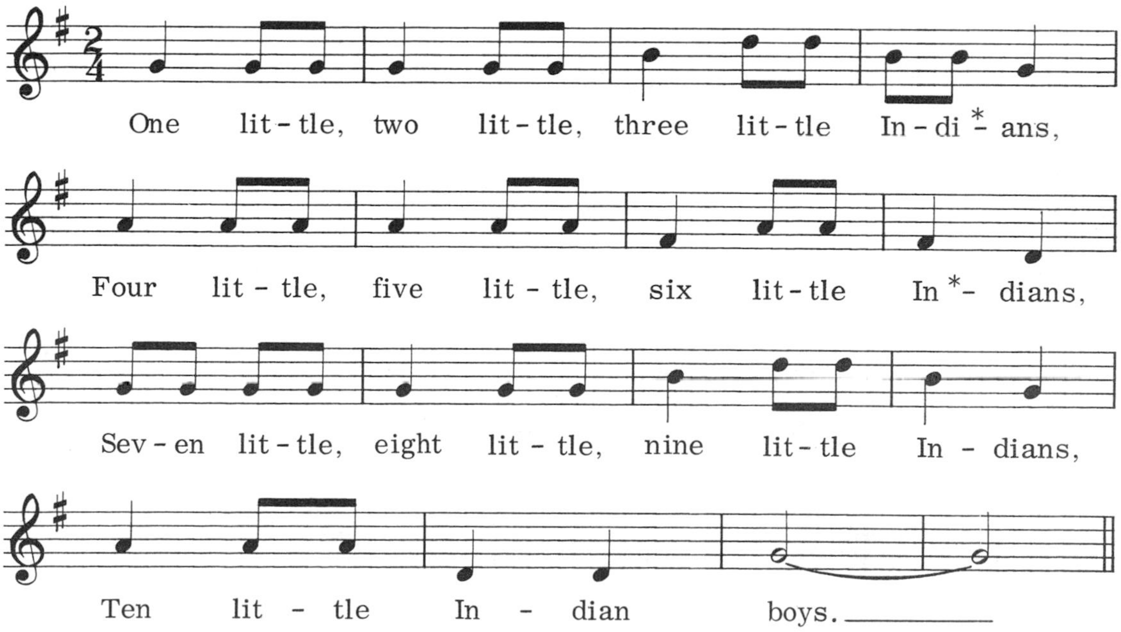
One lit-tle, two lit-tle, three lit-tle In-di*-ans,
Four lit-tle, five lit-tle, six lit-tle In*-dians,
Sev-en lit-tle, eight lit-tle, nine lit-tle In-dians,
Ten lit-tle In-dian boys.

*It's illogical to write this word in two different ways. But it shows to go you: there's different ways of writing the same song.

Good Night Ladies

Two different kinds of dotted notes in one song:

Good night, la-dies! Good night, la-dies! Good night,
la-dies, we're bound to leave you now. Mer-ri-ly we
roll a-long, roll a-long, roll a-long.
Mer-ri-ly we roll a-long, O'er the deep blue sea.

Here's more songs you started to learn in the first lesson, but couldn't finish. Now you can. (PROGRESS!)

Yankee Doodle

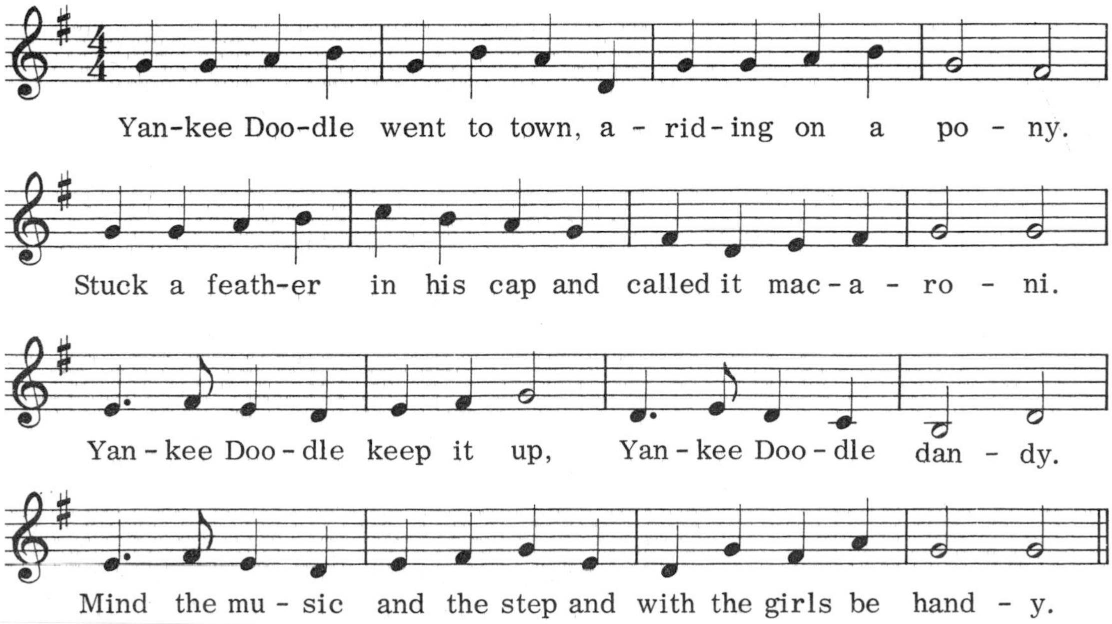

Yan-kee Doo-dle went to town, a-rid-ing on a po-ny.
Stuck a feath-er in his cap and called it mac-a-ro-ni.
Yan-kee Doo-dle keep it up, Yan-kee Doo-dle dan-dy.
Mind the mu-sic and the step and with the girls be hand-y.

Frère Jacques

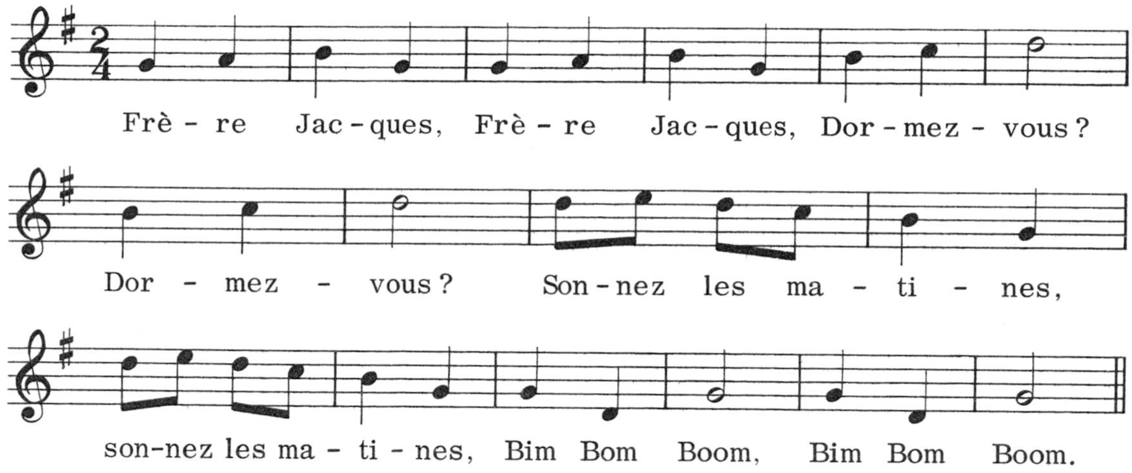
Frè - re Jac - ques, Frè - re Jac - ques, Dor - mez - vous?
Dor - mez - vous? Son - nez les ma - ti - nes,
son-nez les ma - ti - nes, Bim Bom Boom, Bim Bom Boom.

("Brother Jack, Brother Jack, are you sleeping? Are you sleeping? Morning bells are ringing, morning bells are ringing, ding ding dong, ding ding dong.")

Ode To Joy

(You don't need to sweat about these German verses if you don't want to. Just "da-dee-da" your way through it.)

Music: LUDWIG VAN BEETHOVEN
Words: WILHELM SCHILLER

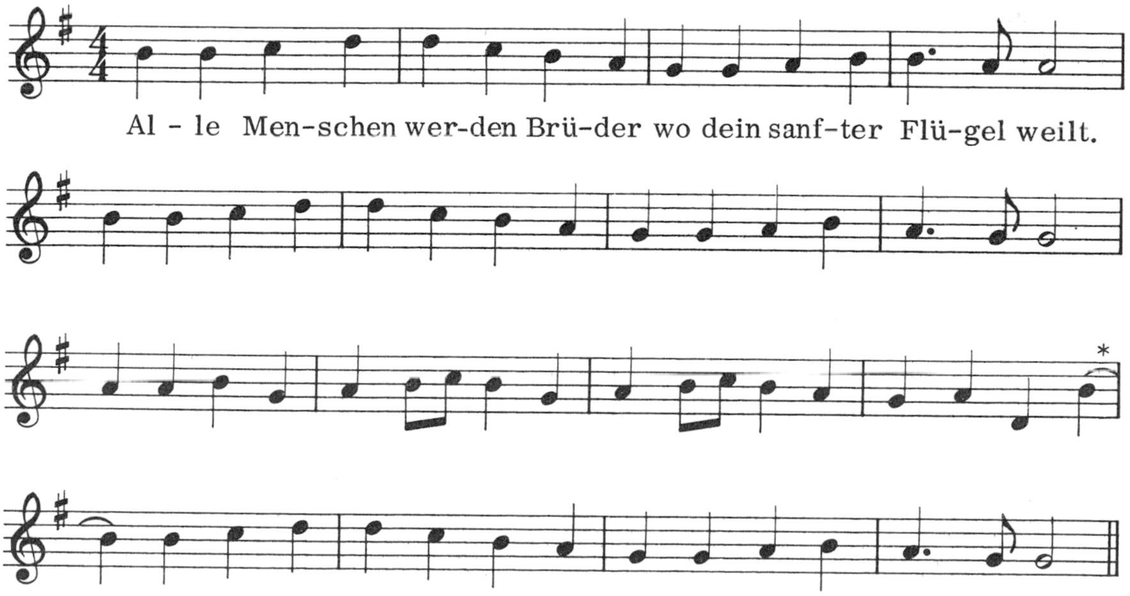
Al - le Men-schen wer-den Brü-der wo dein sanf-ter Flü-gel weilt.
*

*If you can master this tie, you'll be doing good. Beethoven brings in the first note of the new phrase a whole beat earlier than it would be expected. It is a syncopation effect he is aiming at; the downbeat comes halfway through the note. (Literal translation of the above German words: "All men will be brothers . . .")

Joy To The World

Here's the old Christmas carol with the right time value for each note. (On page 18 it was written incorrectly.)

Joy to the world, the Lord is come, Let earth re -
ceive her King, Let

Uh oh, better learn the rest of this in the next chapter, after all.

Old MacDonald Had A Farm

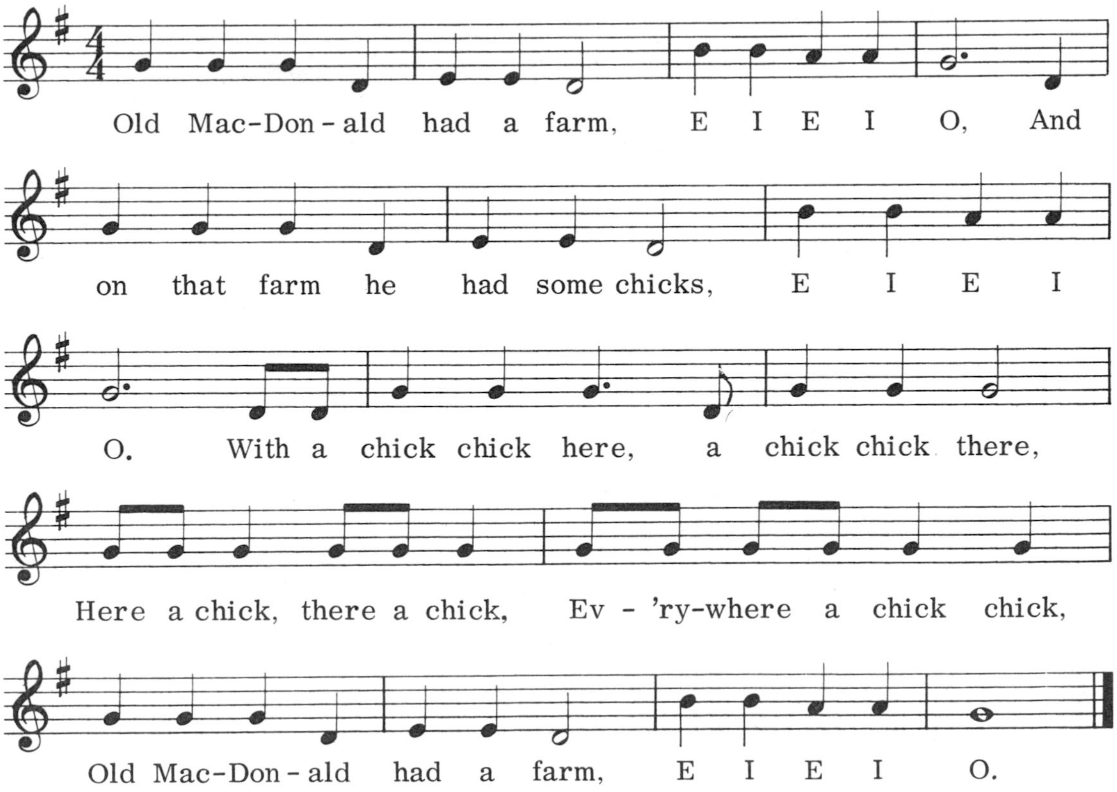
Old Mac-Don - ald had a farm, E I E I O, And
on that farm he had some chicks, E I E I
O. With a chick chick here, a chick chick there,
Here a chick, there a chick, Ev - 'ry-where a chick chick,
Old Mac-Don - ald had a farm, E I E I O.

She'll Be Coming Round The Mountain

A whole song full of eighth-notes. Remember, two foot taps per measure here.

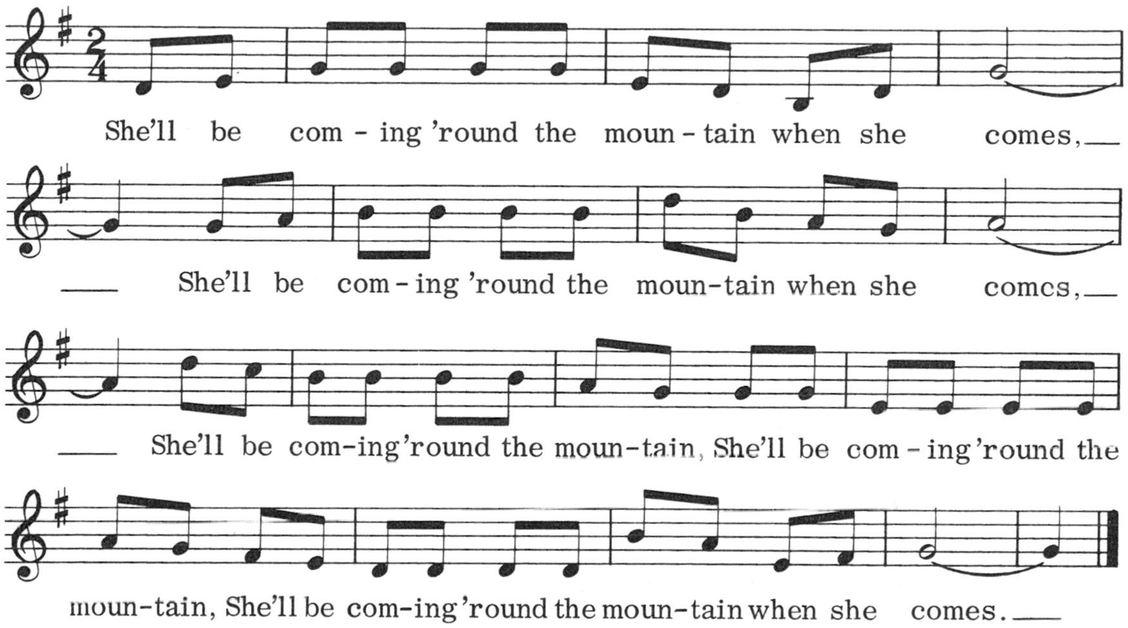
She'll be com - ing 'round the moun - tain when she comes,___
___ She'll be com - ing 'round the moun-tain when she comes,___
___ She'll be com-ing 'round the moun-tain, She'll be com - ing 'round the
moun-tain, She'll be com-ing 'round the moun-tain when she comes.___

This Land Is Your Land

Words and Music by
WOODY GUTHRIE

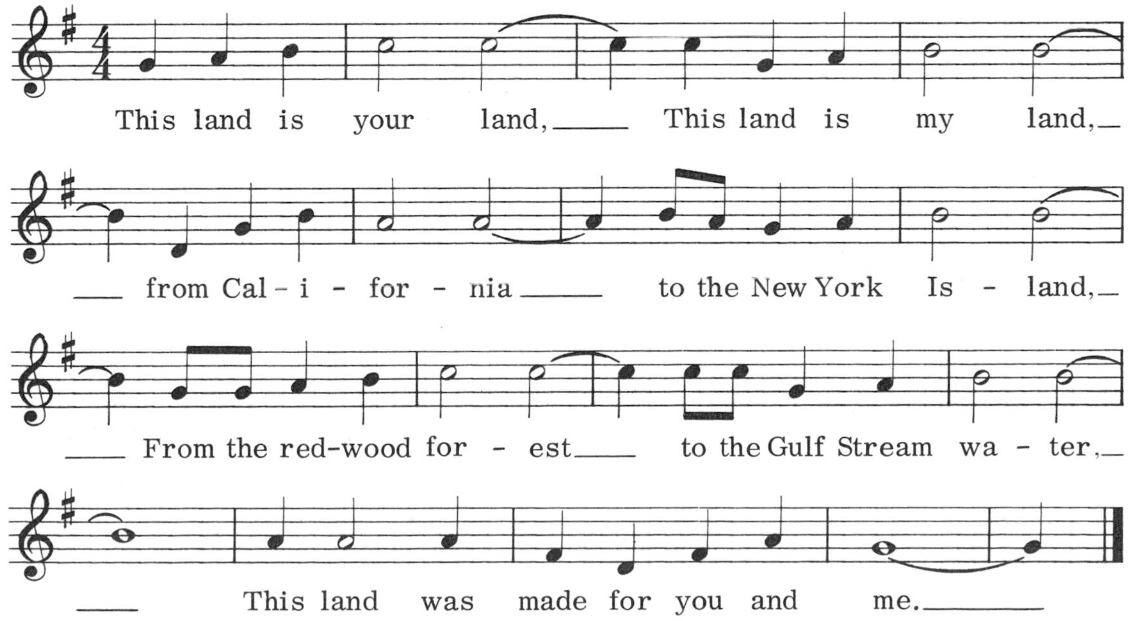
This land is your land,___ This land is my land,__
___ from Cal - i - for - nia ___ to the New York Is - land,__
___ From the red-wood for - est___ to the Gulf Stream wa - ter,__
___ This land was made for you and me.___

Now, just to show you something—the previous song could be written down like this:

*
*
This land is your land,— This land is my land,— from Cal - i-

or this:

This land is your land,— This land is my land,— from Cal - i -

You see, it's possible to write down any melody several different ways. Two musicians might argue about whether to put it in 2/4 or 4/4 time, faster or slower, in a higher or lower key, and so on. Here's the song you saw on page 38.

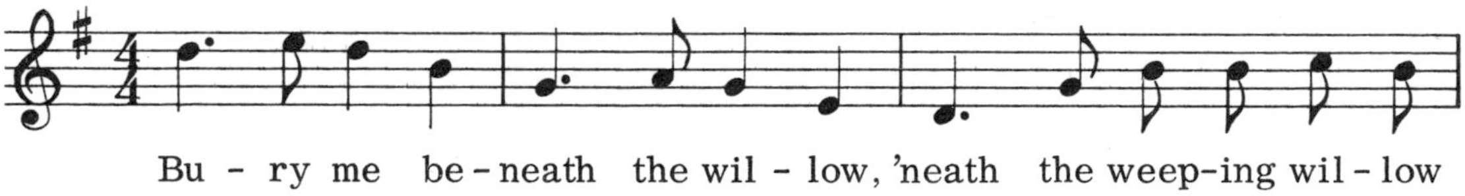
Bu - ry me be - neath the wil - low, 'neath the weep-ing wil - low

It's usual to think of a quarter-note as one march step or dance step. So "Yankee Doodle" would usually be written:

Yan-kee Doo-dle went to town a - rid - ing on a po - ny

Question: How long is a beat? Answer: Usually one tap of the foot.

*A tie is needed here because the note crosses a main beat, at the half measure.

But this answer is confused by a custom used by modern sheet music, of indicating 4/4 time in two ways:

"C" means *common time* and is the average 4/4 time, tempo of a march, or slower.

₵ means *cut time* and might be most accurately translated as 2/2 time.

Strictly speaking, most of the 4/4 songs you've had so far should have had ₵ as a time signature, to indicate that the four-four time goes at a faster speed, but compared to 2/4, simpler to look at.

Examples: "Caisson Song," "Yankee Doodle."

What *is* the difference between 2/4 time and 4/4 time anyway? Answer? Strictly speaking, the two accents* below are supposed to be exactly equal. Your foot taps are equal in strength, the two accented notes sung with equal loudness:

loud
soft
loud
soft

The two accents next are *not* equal, supposedly. The first is stronger than the second.

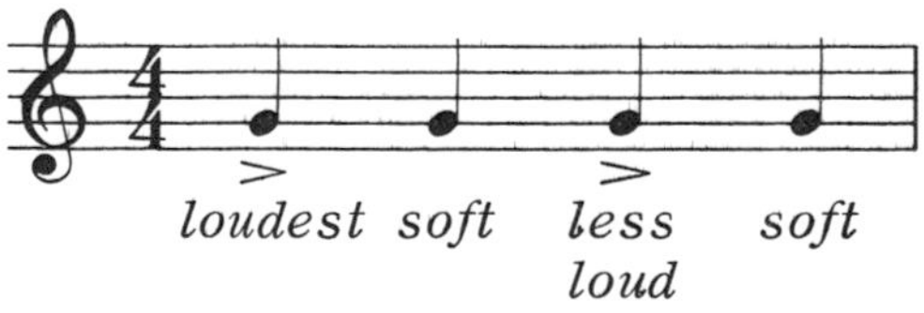
loudest
soft
less loud
soft

*An accent sign > above or below a note means that this note is emphasized.

But this ruling was handed down to us by European musicians, for European art music. With a lot of Afro-American music, it's a foolish distinction. What do you do about a rock-and-roll song with a strong offbeat handclap?

— Clap! — Clap!

Or what would you do with a song, such as a banjo ballad, which is really in a kind of 1/4 time, with no strong accents at all?

Or with this?

(two loud beats) (two soft beats)

Or this?

(one loud) (and three soft)

Moral: Don't depend on a book alone to teach you a song; know the character of the song. For example, know if it is supposed to be a blues or a march. Also figure that the songbook may have got it down wrong.

Reviewing Lesson 2, I see you only officially learned a couple of new things:

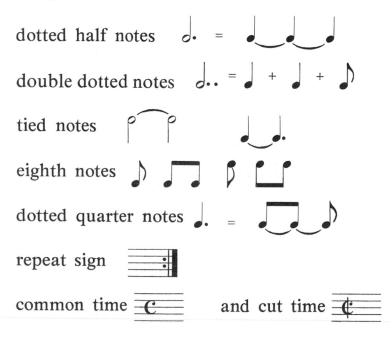

dotted half notes 

double dotted notes 

tied notes 

eighth notes 

dotted quarter notes 

repeat sign 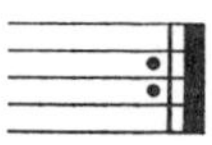

common time  and cut time 

But I hope you are a lot better at reading rhythms. If not, go through the lesson again, preferably with someone who knows how to read music already.

Practice, practice! In years past, Americans learned note reading from church hymnbooks. If you missed out on this, find songbooks with songs you like, and dig in.

A reminder: some of the world's greatest melodies are triumphs of simplicity:

A La Claire Fontaine

TEST: Copy out the two melodies below in a faster rhythm, as shown:

All Through the Night (refer to p. 37)

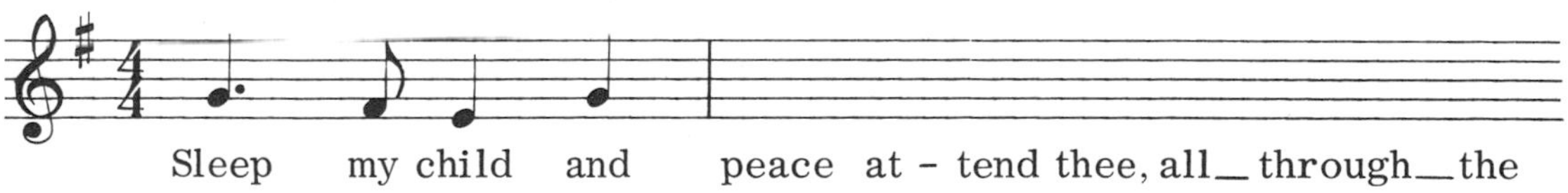
Sleep my child and peace at - tend thee, all — through — the

night...

When I First Came To This Land

(p. 26)

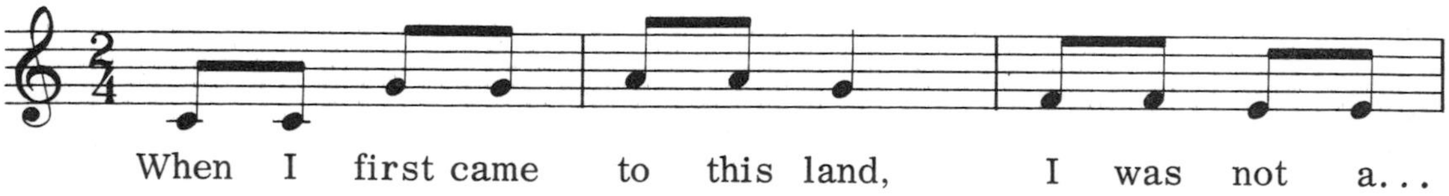
When I first came to this land, I was not a...

And now, hoping you can make a game out of it and not a chore, I give you again the first lines of a lot of songs. See how many you can identify—even if you don't know the name of the song, or if you know a different version of the song.

Throughout the book you'll find these quizzes. I've included good songs and bad songs, marches, old pop songs, themes from opera and symphony, children's street songs, men's gutter songs, barroom favorites, and hymns, all thrown together in profane juxtaposition.

Answers upside down, p. 53.

1.

2. (Downbeat comes on the 4th note)

3.

4.

5. A British Army parody, from WW I

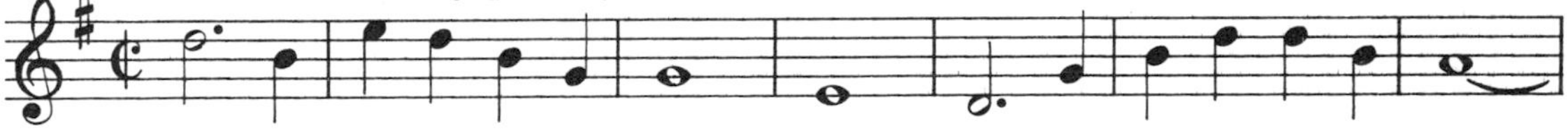

6.

7.

8.

9.

10. (Chorus only)

11.

12.

13.

14. The melody is on the bottom. Anyone like to sing high harmony?

15.

Answers

1. "Careless Love"
2. "O Sole Mio"
3. "Anchors Aweigh" by Capt. Alfred H. Miles, U.S.N. (Ret) and Charles A. Zimmerman
4. "Lolly Toodum"
   Collected, adapted and arranged by John A. Lomax and Alan Lomax
5. "When This Bloody War Is Over
   No more soldiering for me . . ."
   (Tune: "Take It to the Lord in Prayer)
6. "What Did You Learn in School Today" (Tom Paxton)
7. "Joe Hill" by Earl Robinson and Alfred Hayes
8. Theme of "Ballad For Americans"
   Text by John LaTouche, music by Earl Robinson
9. "This Old Man He Plays One"
10. "In the Sweet Bye and Bye (Pie in the Sky)"
11. "Aloha Oe" by Princess Liliokalani
12. "Kumbaya"
13. "The Gypsy Rover"
14. "Skip to My Lou, My Darling"
15. "Rock of Ages, Cleft for Me" by Thomas Hastings

Notes

Lesson 3

Slurs, Big Jumps, Faster Rhythms

When a curved line, like a tie, connects several notes of different pitches; it is called a *slur.* All the connected notes are sung on one syllable.

Do you remember the opening notes of the "Volga Boatmen" song?

Ay___ yukh - neym

And here's another slur you'll recognize:

The Marine's Hymn

Music by JACQUES OFFENBACH
Author unknown

etc.
From the halls of Mon - te - zu - ma to the shores of

And still another:

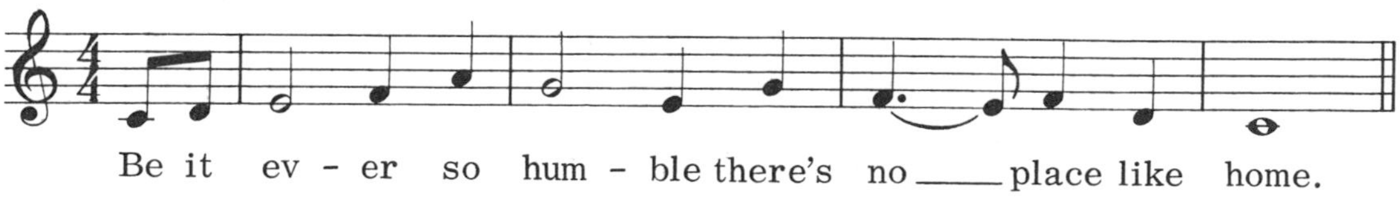
Be it ev - er so hum - ble there's no ___ place like home.

And you all know the slur at the end of the following verse:

Jin-gle bells, jin-gle bells, jin-gle all the way,
Oh what fun it is to ride on a one horse o-pen
sleigh,

And this:

He's got the whole world in his hands

(The rest of this song on page 225.
Too syncopated to learn just now.)

And this:

Blowin' In The Wind

Words and Music by
BOB DYLAN

In singing a slurred note, keep in mind that the human voice is like a trombone. I don't know about you, but I like to hear a voice that moves around easily and smoothly, without yoo-hooing. You know what I mean by a "yoo-hooer"? It's the kind of singer who sings,

"He's got the whole wur-hurld
In his hands"

Maybe some like it. You make up your own mind about it.

Now you can do this all the way through.

The Riddle Song

Old English, collected by Cecil Sharp
in the southern Appalachians

1. Rhythm. The song starts on the upbeat.

2. Key. Starts on the sixth note of the scale, but *below* "do." Count down:

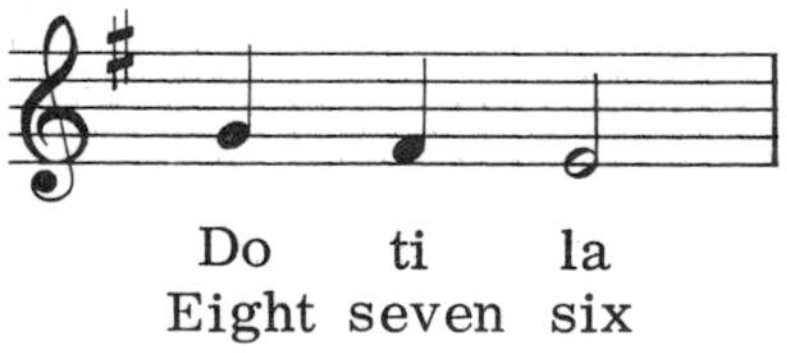

Do ti la
Eight seven six

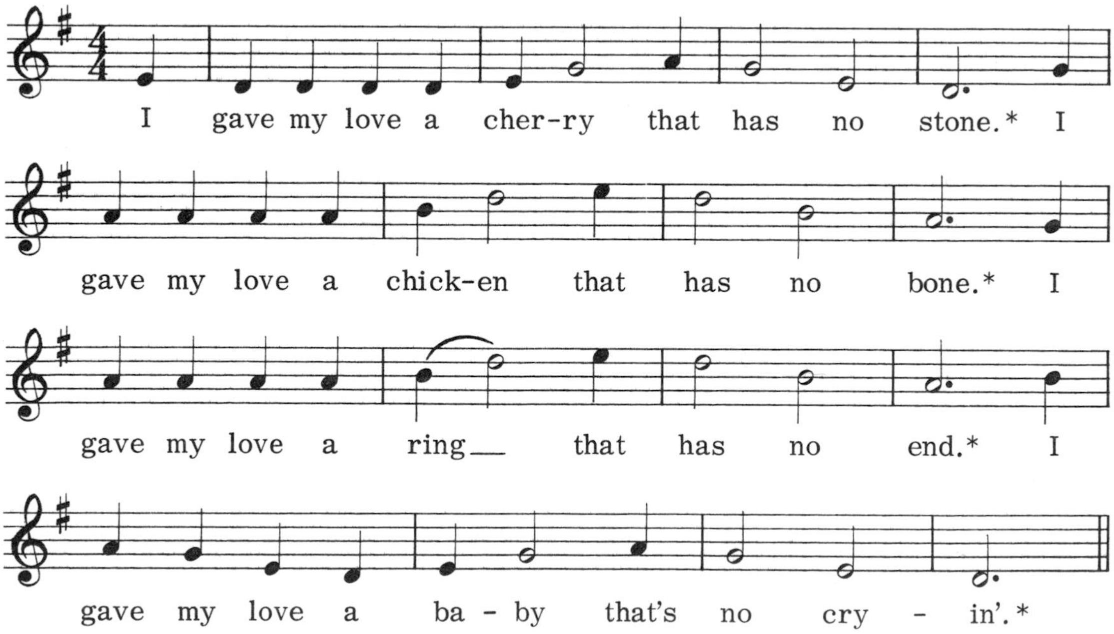

I gave my love a cher-ry that has no stone.* I
gave my love a chick-en that has no bone.* I
gave my love a ring__ that has no end.* I
gave my love a ba - by that's no cry - in'.*

*These are the logical places to take a breath. Unless you are intentionally singing the song in a very free, unrhythmical way, watch that you don't lose track of the rhythm at this point.

How can there be a cherry
  that has no stone?
How can there be a chicken
  that has no bone?
How can there be a ring
  that has no end?
How can there be a baby
  that's no cryin'?

A cherry when it's blooming
  it has no stone.
A chicken when it's pippin'
  it has no bone.
A ring when it's a-rolling
  it has no end
And a baby in the making
  it's no cryin'.

Huddie Ledbetter, known as Leadbelly, one of the greatest folksingers of all time, used to put beautiful strong slurs in his songs. Here are fragments of three of his songs:

Cotton Fields
(THE COTTON SONG)

Words and Music by HUDDIE LEDBETTER

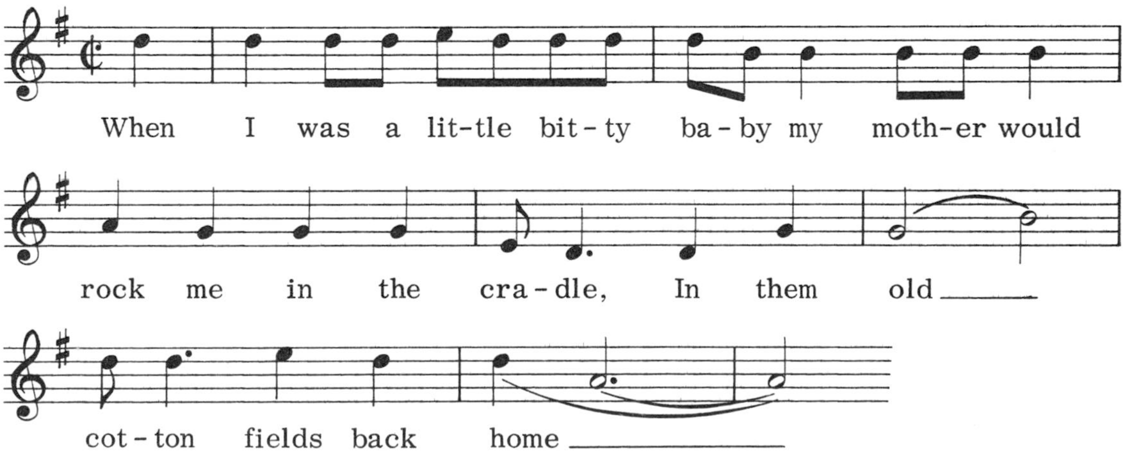
When I was a lit-tle bit-ty ba-by my moth-er would
rock me in the cra-dle, In them old
cot-ton fields back home

And Leadbelly's version of this old prisoner's lament is surely one of the greatest. "Old Hannah" was their nickname for the sun.

(Count the beats in each measure. It's a great song.)

Go Down, Ol' Hannah

Words and Music by HUDDIE LEDBETTER
Collected and adapted by
John A. Lomax and Alan Lomax

Slowly*

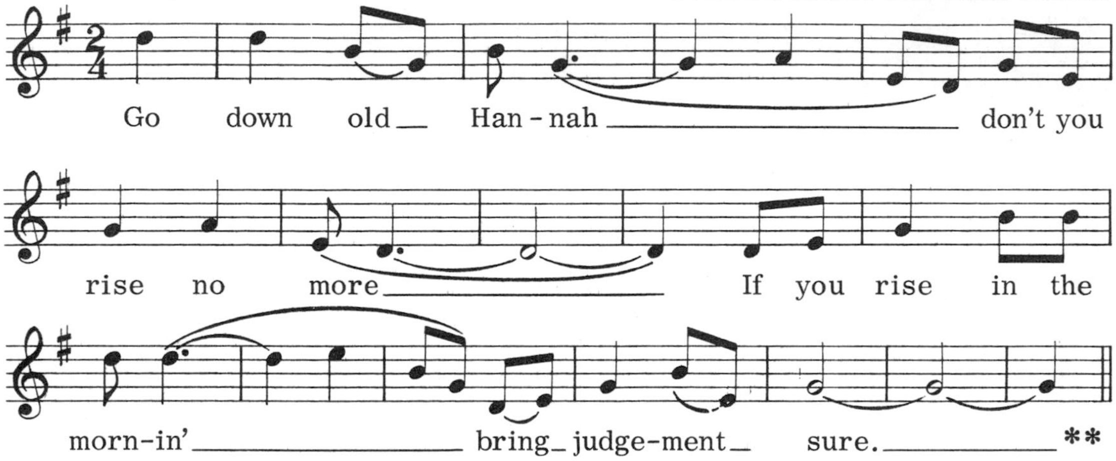
Go down old_ Han-nah ______ don't you
rise no more ______ If you rise in the
morn-in' ______ bring_ judgement_ sure. ______ **

I looked at old Hannah———she was turnin' red
I looked at my partner———he was almost dead.

I said, "Wake up, old dead man———help me carry my row."
I said, "Wake up, old dead man———help me carry my row."

Well, if you get lucky———and make it back home
Go down by Julie's———tell her, I won't be along.

Well I was a good man———but they drove me down
Well, I made up my mind———I'm going to head on.

*Directions for how to sing a song are usually given at the left, above the first staff—"Allegro," etc. (See Appendix.)

**When a song starts on an upbeat, as this one does, and has several verses, as most songs do, it is customary to have fewer beats in the last measure, just before the double bar line. The last measure is completed by singing the upbeat of the next verse.

Bring Me Li'l' Water, Silvy

Words and Music by HUDDIE LEDBETTER
Collected and adapted by John A. Lomax and Alan Lomax

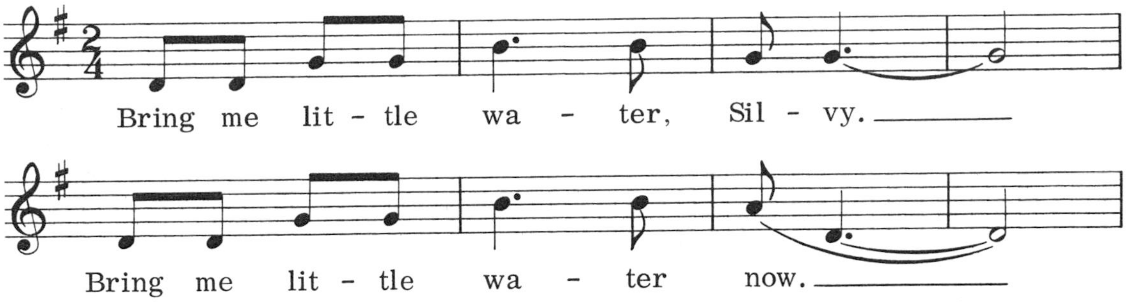
Bring me lit - tle wa - ter, Sil - vy.
Bring me lit - tle wa - ter now.

A fine old English sailor song, probably unknown to most of you. Did you know Kidd was a New Yorker? His wife and daughter continued living there after he was hanged. (The year was 1701, the city's population less than 10,000.)

Captain Kidd

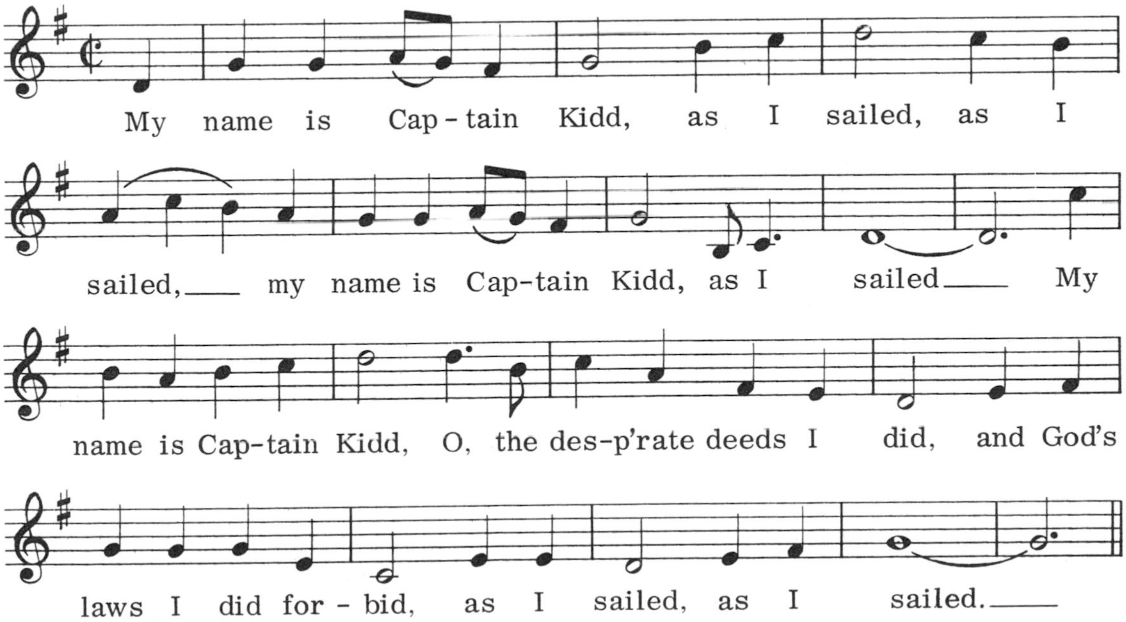
My name is Cap - tain Kidd, as I sailed, as I
sailed, my name is Cap-tain Kidd, as I sailed My
name is Cap-tain Kidd, O, the des-p'rate deeds I did, and God's
laws I did for - bid, as I sailed, as I sailed.

My parents taught me well,
As I sailed, as I sailed,
My parents taught me well,
As I sailed.

My parents taught me well
To shun the gates of hell
But against them I rebelled
  As I sailed, as I sailed.

I murdered William Moore, etc.
And left him in his gore
Forty leagues from the shore, etc.

And being cruel still, etc.
My gunner I did kill
And his precious blood did spill, etc.

And being nigh to death, etc.
I vowed with every breath
To walk in wisdom's way, etc.

My repentance lasted not, etc.
My vows I soon forgot,
Damnation was my lot, etc.

Now to execution dock,
  I must go, I must go,
Now to execution dock,
  I must go.
Now to execution dock
Lay my head upon the block
No more the laws I'll mock
  As I sailed, as I sailed.

Some old church music and opera really went in heavy for this singing of many notes for one word.

Angels We Have Heard On High

French Christmas Carol

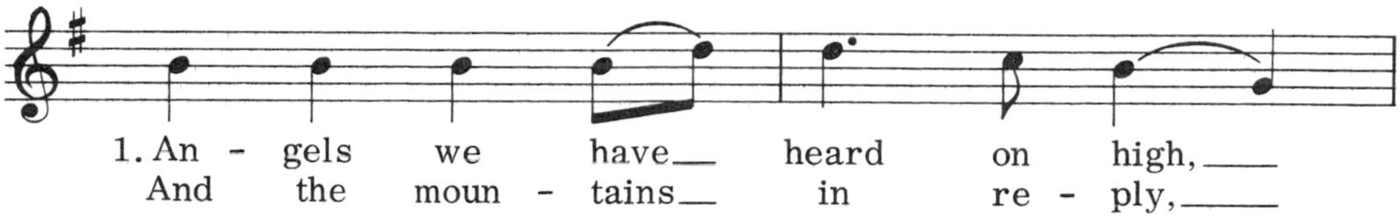
1. An - gels we have___ heard on high,____
And the moun - tains___ in re - ply,_____

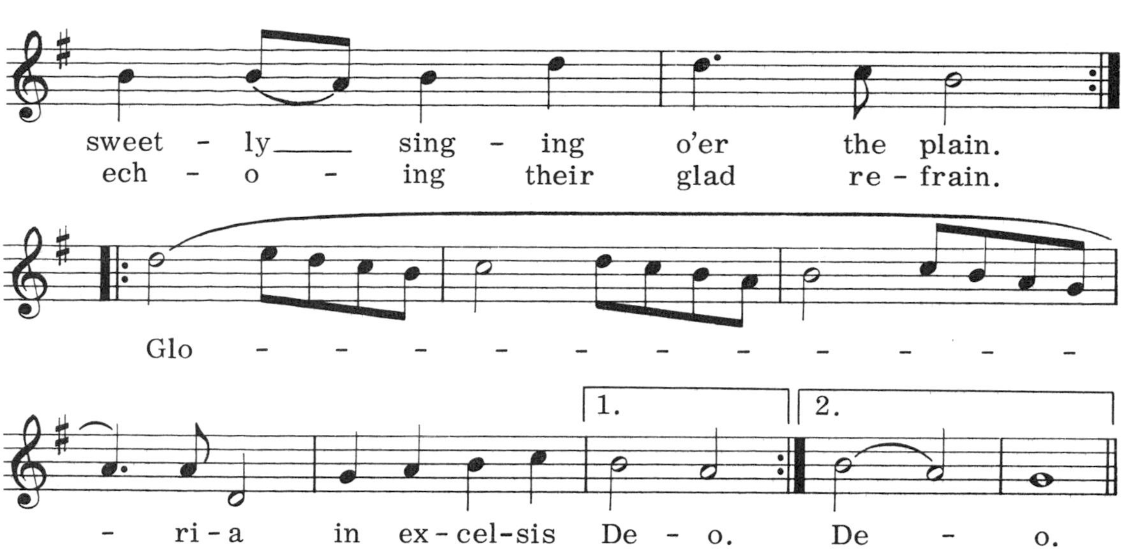
sweet - ly___ sing - ing o'er the plain.
ech - o - ing their glad re - frain.
Glo - - - - - - - - - - -
- ri - a in ex - cel - sis De - o. De - o.
1.
2.

To save space in songbooks, lots of repeat signs are often used. It makes things a little difficult to read. Here's how the above song would go:

1. When the singer comes to the first he returns to the beginning of the song and sings the words on the lower line, to the same melody: "And the mountains . . ."

2. The singer continues right through the double bar this time and sings the chorus, "Glo-o-ria," etc.

3. On coming to the second double bar line, the singer should return just to the previous double bar and repeat the chorus "Glo-o-ria!"

4. The second time through the chorus he skips the measure with 1. above it, and goes past it and sings the measures with 2. above it. Got it?

Incidentally, not everybody thinks highly of this style of song. The down-to-earth Benjamin Franklin wrote a letter from London in 1765:

> A modern song . . .neglects all the beauties and proprieties of modern speech, and in their places introduces its defects and absurdities as so many graces. . . . Here is the first song I lay

> my hand on. It happens to be a composition of one of our greatest masters, the ever-famous Handel . . . is admired by all his admirers and is really excellent in its kind. . . .Now I reckon among the defects . . . drawling, or the extending of syllables beyond their natural length, stuttering, or making many syllables of one . . . The words might be the principal part of an ancient song, they are of small importance in a modern one . . . only a pretence for singing. Your affectionate brother, etc.

Maybe this next one is what old Ben was referring to. Don't be dismayed if you can't read it yet. You'll get sixteenth notes explained on page 72.

from the oratorio "The Messiah" G. F. HANDEL

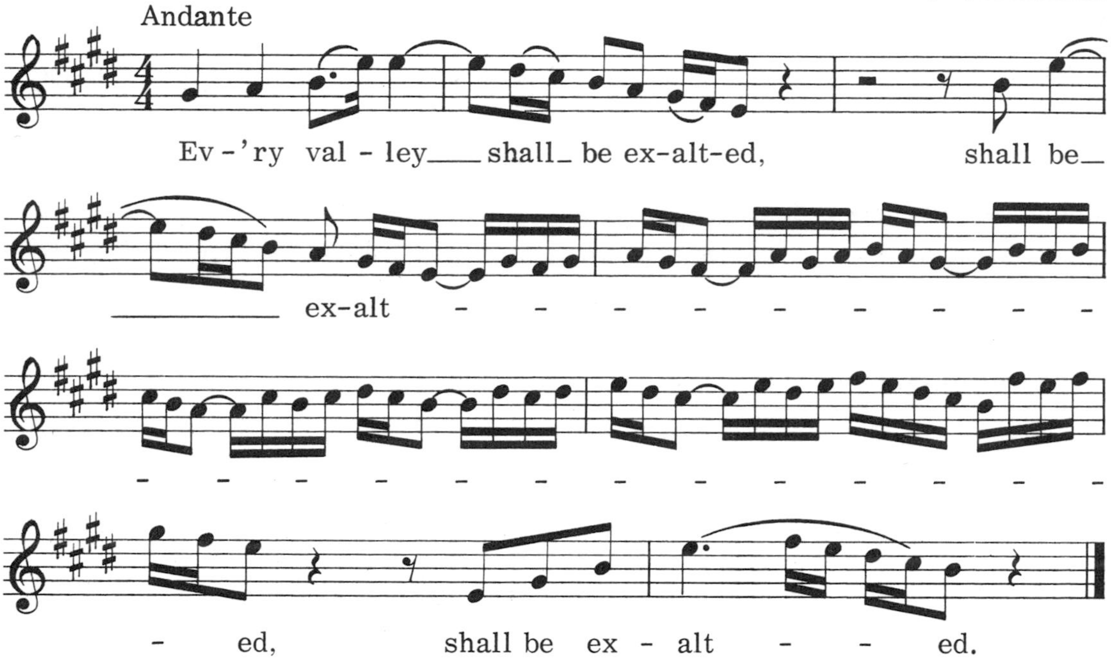
Andante
Ev-'ry val-ley___ shall_ be ex-alt-ed, shall be_
___ ex-alt - - - - - - - - -
- - - - - - - - - - - - - - -
- ed, shall be ex - alt - - ed.

In the last chapter we started on the song "Joy to the World" but had to quit, because the refrain had a lot of slurs in it. Here's the complete song now.

Joy To The World

Joy to the world, the Lord is come! Let earth re-ceive her
King!___ Let ev - 'ry__ heart___ pre-pare_ Him_

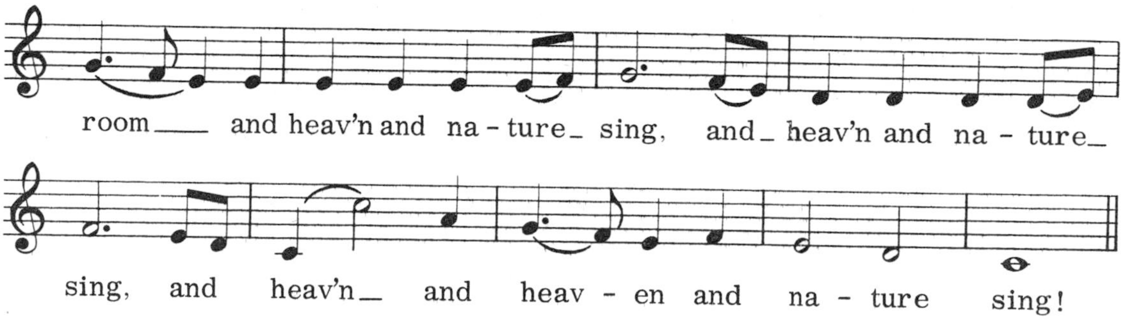
room___ and heav'n and na - ture_ sing, and_ heav'n and na - ture_
sing, and heav'n_ and heav - en and na - ture sing!

As you see, in this lesson you have to get used to reading melodies with bigger jumps in them. Whenever you find yourself stumped by this, count up or down the lines and spaces of the staff, singing a scale as you go, till you come to the right note.

The next few songs will be in the key of C, and the melody keeps jumping up to the high C. Get your ear used to hearing that octave jump, as in the word "heav'n" in the fourth measure from the end of "Joy to the World."

A real oldy, with some big jumps in the melody, especially that jump to a high C.

Annie Laurie

Max - wel - ton's braes are bon - nie___ where
ear - ly falls_ the dew___ and 'twas there that
An - nie Lau - rie___ gave me her prom - ise true,_
___ Gave me her prom - ise true,___ which ne'er for -

got shall be___ and for bon - nie An - nie
Lau - rie___ I'd___ lay___ me doon and dee.___

For all good union members, a song out of history. The tune was written at the time of the Civil War. In the late nineteenth century striking English transport workers gave it new words and it became a favorite U.S. union song.

Hold The Fort

Music by PHILLIP B. BLISS

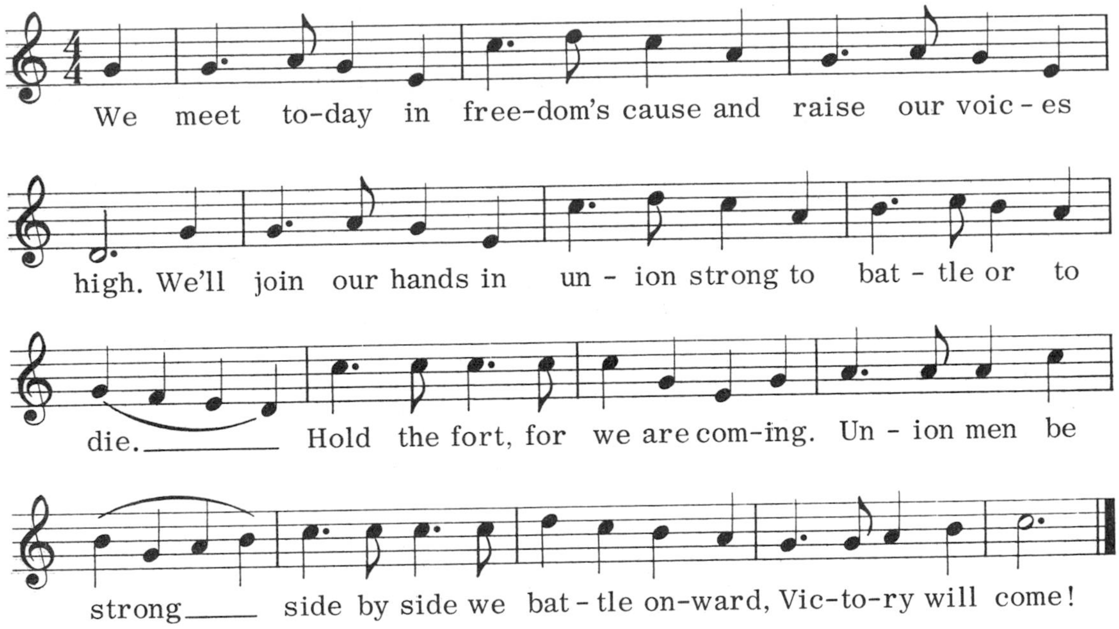
We meet to-day in free-dom's cause and raise our voic - es
high. We'll join our hands in un - ion strong to bat - tle or to
die.___ Hold the fort, for we are com-ing. Un - ion men be
strong___ side by side we bat - tle on-ward, Vic-to-ry will come!

(This was originally a hymn tune. People throughout the centuries put new words to old tunes. It's like putting an old building to new uses. Of course, the person who loves the old song is rarely happy about it. He says, "Hey, that building is still occupied."
It's also common to put new variant tunes to old words. Here's a f'rinstance: though hardly anyone but me sings it this way nowadays, I originally wrote the last line of "If I Had A Hammer" with a long slur.)

If I Had A Hammer

(The Hammer Song)

Words and Music by
LEE HAYS and PETE SEEGER

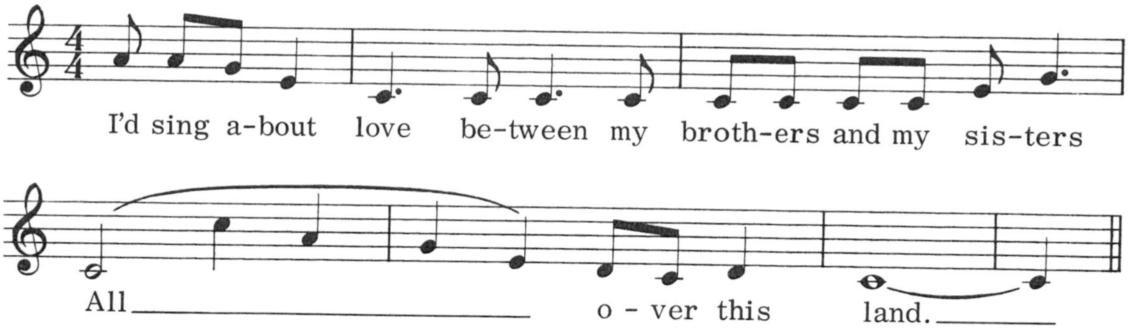
I'd sing a-bout love be-tween my broth-ers and my sis-ters
All ___ o - ver this land. ___

Another song with that jump to a high C. It's one of the most beautiful melodies in all American folk music, learned by old John Lomax from a black woman who died soon after singing him her song.

Dink's Song

Collected and adapted with new music by
BESS B. LOMAX and JOHN A. LOMAX

If I had wings ___ like No-rah's dove, ___ I'd fly up the
riv - er ___ to the one I love, ___ fare thee
well ___ O hon - ey ___ fare thee well. ___

That man I love, he's long and tall
He moves his body like a cannonball
  Fare thee well, O honey, fare thee well.

Remember that night, was a drizzling rain?
'Round my heart came an aching pain,
  Fare thee well, O honey, fare thee well.

One of these days and it won't be long
You'll call my name and I'll be gone,
  Fare thee well, O honey, fare thee well.

If I had wings like Norah's dove,
I'd fly up the river to the one I love,
  Fare thee well, O honey, fare thee well.

(You can change "Norah" back to "Noah" if you wish. I think the folk pronunciation sounds better with the slur here. But *make up your own mind*–life's hardest job. In the end, I guess most songs have to be sung in the singer's own dialect, folk or fancy.)

The distance between any two notes is called an "interval."

The distance between the first and the third note of the scale is called an interval of a third. The interval between the first and the fourth is called an interval of a fourth. Etc. Complicated?

Here's four examples of thirds.

Here's some fourths.

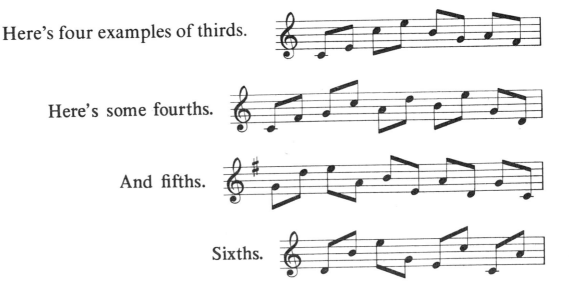

And fifths.

Sixths.

Sevenths.
(a hard one to hear
at first)

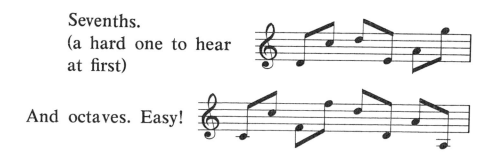

And octaves. Easy!

Test yourself: Write the name of the interval above each of these pairs. (Answers below.)

hey it's a tune

Caution: On paper you may score 100%. But the important thing is to train your ear to *hear* these intervals and identify them. Then you'll be able to read 'em and sing 'em.

Yodelers like to jump a sixth, when they break into falsetto:

Freely—no rhythm
O lay dee oh lay dee hoo!

Here's a reverse yodel I've sung for years, this high solo of the South African song "Wimoweh":

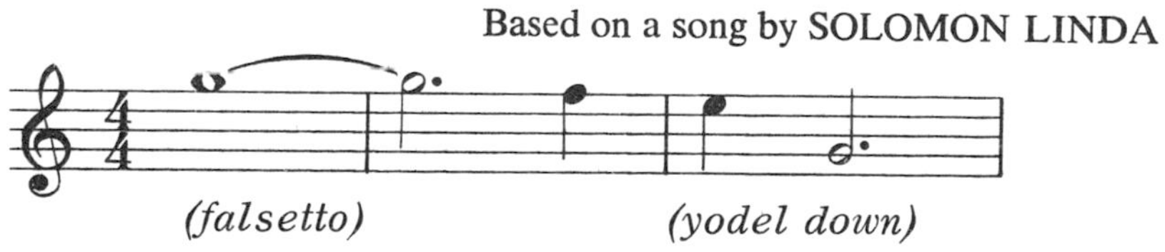
Based on a song by SOLOMON LINDA
(falsetto)
(yodel down)

Answers: fourth, fourth, sixth, third, third, sixth, fifth, octave.

The German song, "Lilli Marlene," has a striking jump of a sixth. This is just the last line:

Lilli Marlene

Music by NORBET SCHULTZE
German words by HANS LEIP
English words by TOMMIE CONNOR

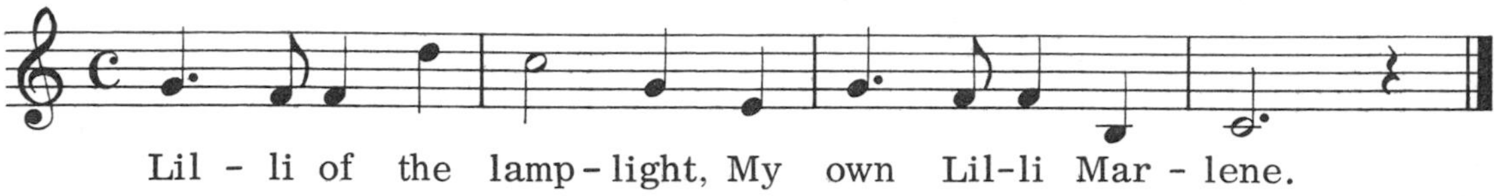
Lil - li of the lamp-light, My own Lil-li Mar - lene.

Another well-known British army song picked up by U.S. troops. Notice the high, shouted note, and an octave jump down.

I've Got Sixpence

Roll-ing home (Roll-ing home) Roll-ing home (Roll-ing home) by the
light of the sil - ver-y moon, Hap-py is the day when the
ar - my gets its pay, as we go rol - ing, roll-ing home.

Russian melodies also have a liking for jumping up a sixth:

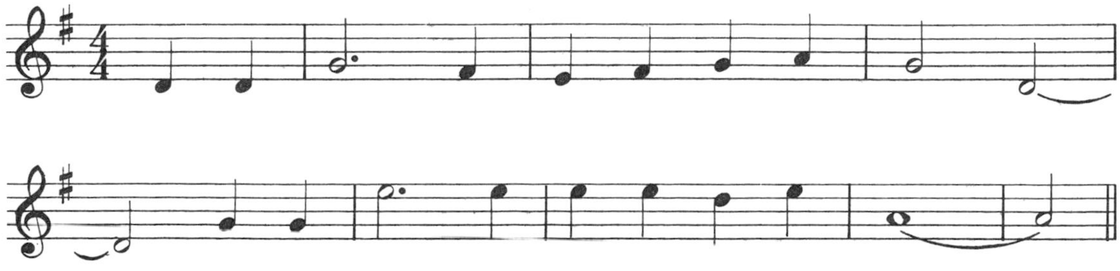

Here's another song which jumps up to that high C. I was with Woody when he wrote it. We had just finished singing at a little union meeting in Oklahoma City, 1940. Local vigilantes had threatened to break it up, but didn't, because the meeting was a real family affair, with many women present, and some children, and we got 'em all singing.

Union Maid

By WOODY GUTHRIE

There once was a un - ion maid, she nev - er was a - fraid of
goons and ginks and com-pa-ny finks and the dep-u - ty sher-iffs that
made the raids. She went to the un - ion hall when a
meet - ing it was called, and when the com - pa - ny
boys came 'round, she al - ways stood her ground:"Oh you can't scare
me I'm a-stick-ing to the un - ion,___ I'm a-stick-ing to the
un - ion,___ I'm a-stick-ing to the un - ion.___ Oh you

can't scare me, I'm a-stick-ing to the un - ion,

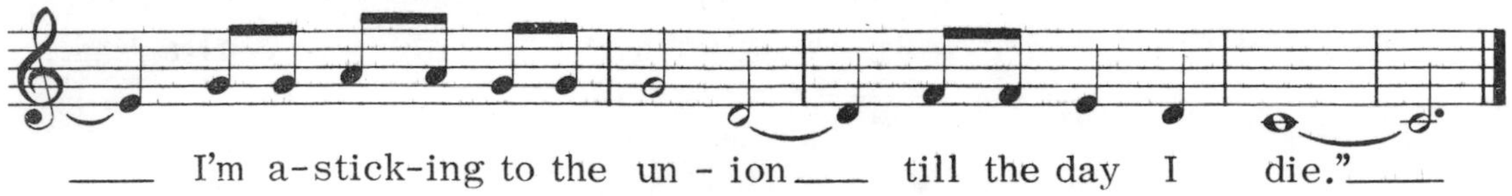
I'm a-stick-ing to the un - ion till the day I die."

I suppose you know where Woody swiped the tune.

O the moon shines bright on pret - ty Red - wing

(The tune was used earlier by Schumann, "The Happy Plowboy."

In 1947 I had a job singing in a New York night club. Woody came down to listen and see how I was doing. For him I started singing "Union Maid." A drunk near Woody started banging his glass on the table, "You can't scare me, I'm a capitalist, I'm a capitalist." Woody started swinging an empty beer bottle and shouting, "It's bastards like you stayed home making money while we was out fighting the fascists." (Woody had been torpedoed twice in World War II.)

Maybe I shouldn't have waited so long to give you one more kind of note: a sixteenth note. Four of them equal a quarter note:

and 

and 
plus

and 

and 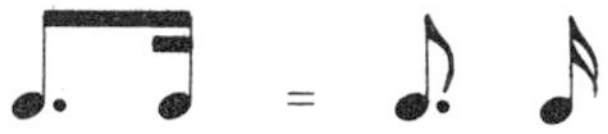

All clear?

This is all the kinds of notes you'll use. (Some symphony composers even go in for thirty-second notes, I've heard:  Ugh.)

To hear the difference between  and  sing the next chorus.

When "Yankee Doodle" is written out, with  = one step, you need some sixteenth-notes:

Yan - kee Doo-dle keep it up, Yan - kee Doo-dle dan - dy

Same way with "Jingle Bells":

Jin - gle bells, Jin - gle bells, Jin - gle all the way

(Why some eighth notes  and others  ? No logic. Some songbooks do it one way, some another. Now hear this: It has been customary to beam the notes for instrumental music. In recent years vocal music does this too.)

Dixie

by DANIEL EMMET

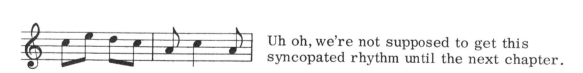

Uh oh, we're not supposed to get this syncopated rhythm until the next chapter.

(Did you know that before this song became the anthem of white supremacists it was simply one of America's pop tunes? Came out of the minstrel show era of the 1850's—and was written by a man who was a strong Northern Union man throughout the Civil War. After Appomattox, Lincoln had it played at the White House. "We won the war, didn't we recapture the song?" said he. I'm afraid he was wrong.)

I found one of the handiest ways to become a facile note reader was to try a batch of fiddle tunes. I used to tootle them on a recorder.

Devil's Dream

Arkansas Traveler

Perhaps you've been trying to grope your way through a lot of unfamiliar songs. Here's one you do know. (The rhythm pattern of the second measure is the same as one we analyzed on p. 40.)

Saints Go Marching In

1. O when the saints go march-ing in, O when the
saints go march-ing in. O Lord I want to be in that
num-ber when the saints go march-ing in. *

O when the moon drips red with blood (2 times)
O Lord, I want to be in that number
When the saints go marching in.

O when the trumpet sounds a call, etc.

O when they crown Him Lord of all, etc.

*Don't forget: The reason this last measure has not got a full four beats, is that the next verse has three eighth-notes to start with, before the first downbeat.

Review of Lesson 3

Slurs

Repeat

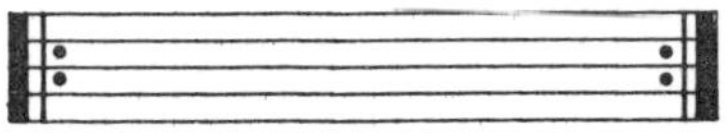

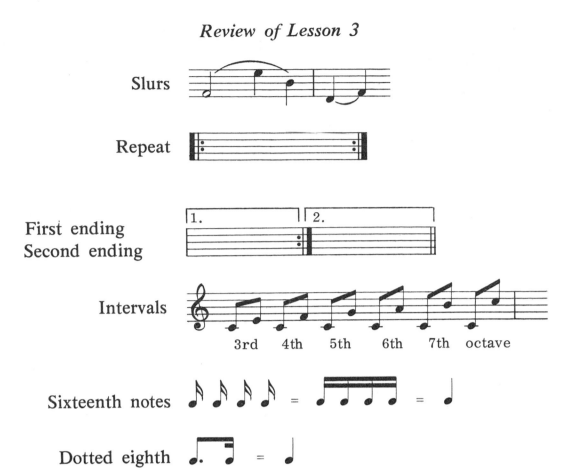

First ending
Second ending

1.
2.

Intervals

3rd
4th
5th
6th
7th
octave

Sixteenth notes

Dotted eighth

I really don't expect you to memorize all this at once. But you can check these review pages from time to time. If you feel that there are a lot of subtleties in music that don't seem possible to put into notes—you're absolutely right. Our system of music writing was developed by European ecclesiastical musicians, and works much less well for folk music, and not well at all for music of Asia and Africa.

However, as with the food we eat, the clothes we wear, or the spelling of the English language—all more a matter of custom than logic—we get along with it. It's the most generally understood system handy just now.

More songs to guess. Answers page 78.

1.
2.
3.
4.
5.
6.
7.

8.
9.

10.

11.

12. **Any Canadian readers?**

13.

Answers

1. "Little Brown Jug"
2. "William Tell Overture" (G. Rossini) ("Lone Ranger" theme)
3. "Twelve Days of Christmas"
4. "Green Grow the Rushes O"
5. "Onward Christian Soldiers" (Sir A. Sullivan)
6. "Jimmy Crack Corn and I Don't Care"
7. "Anna"
   English lyric by William Engvick, original lyric by F. Giordano, music by R. Vatro
8. "Minstrel Boy"
9. "Girl I Left Behind Me"
10. "Oh Shenandoah"
11. "Ave Maria" (Schubert)
12. "Viva la Canadienne"
13. "Ah, Si Mon Moine"

Notes

Lesson 4

A Little Syncopation

Here's a string of notes ♪ ♩ ♪ ♪ ♩ ♪ ♪ ♩ ♪ ♪ ♩ ♪

Do you know that if you repeated them over and over, they could sound three very different ways? It depends on which note you accent. Just as with words, try putting the emPHAsis on the wrong sylLAble.
If you put the accent on the second note, and sang them over and over, you'd get a kind of galloping banjo rhythm:

*
Bump - dit-ty, Bump - dit-ty, Bump-dit - ty.

If you put the accent on the third note and sang them over and over, the rhythm would sound like this:

Pat - a-cake, pat - a-cake, (Baker's Man)

But if the accent was placed on the first note, you'd find yourself singing a sort of syncopated rhythm:

Bos-ton, Chi - ca-go, St. Lou-is, To - pe-ka.

Too difficult? Turn the page. Before the end of the lesson you'll have it down cold.

*Remember, > means "give a strong accent to this note."

You've actually seen this pattern before when we've given it with half notes and quarter notes:

when the cais-sons go roll - ing a - long:

and

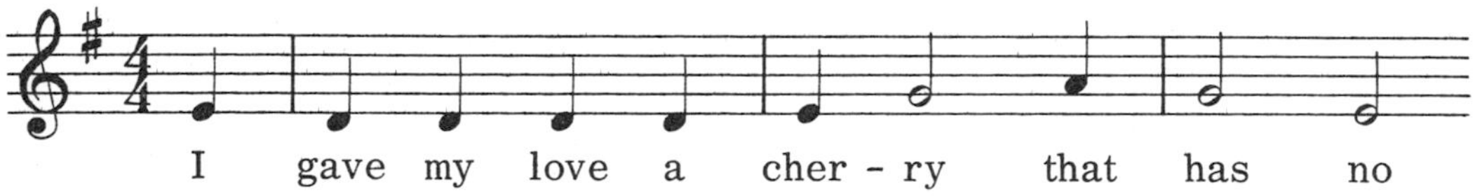
I gave my love a cher - ry that has no

and

Good - night, la - dies, we're going to leave you now.

 is the same rhythm pattern as —twice as fast.

This lesson is about a little syncopation. The word *syncopation* describes what happens when your foot keeps tapping a regular beat, but the accented notes of a song fall between the foot taps.

Here's "Tom Dooley," with arrows showing where the foot beats would come down.

Tom Dooley

Hang down your head, Tom Doo-ley, Hang down your head and cry,
Hang down your head, Tom Doo-ley, Poor boy, you're bound to die.

Your foot comes down half a beat after your lips have already started singing the syllable.

In this chapter are a lot of songs using this rhythmic device, fast or slow:

a short note, accented. ♪ >
a longer note, with the beat coming halfway through it. ♩
one more short note. ♪

Sing through the following songs till your ear can recognize the pattern easily. Later on we'll have much more complicated syncopation. It's a common feature of American songs.

So here's that famous army song up to tempo, as it usually would be written:

The Caisson Song

by EDMUND GRUBER

O-ver hill, o-ver dale, we will hit the dust-y trail as the
cais-sons go roll-ing a - long.
For it's Hi hi hee! in the
field ar - til - ler - y. Shout out your num-bers loud and
strong. (One, two) And wher - e'er you go you will ·al-ways

know that the cais-sons are roll-ing a - long.

× Indicates shouted or spoken words or handclaps, footstamps, etc.

A not-so-martial soldier song—the version I sang in basic training, World War II.

Around Her Neck She Wore A Yellow Ribbon

*
A - round her neck she wore a yel - low rib - bon she
wore it in De - cem - ber and in the month of
May, Hey! hey! And if you asked her why the hell she
wore it, she wore it for a sol-dier who was far, far a -
Chorus:
way. Far a - way, far a - way, far a - way, far a -
way. She wore it for a sol-dier who was far, far a - way.

*Note ♩. ♬ sounds different from ♫: Agreed?

The same pattern shows up in the opening of "The Hammer Song."

If I had a ham - mer, ___ I'd ham-mer in the morn - ing ___

Hard, Ain't It Hard

Words and Music adapted by
WOODY GUTHRIE

There is a house in this old town That's where my true love hangs a-
round. He takes oth-er wom-en right down on his knee, and
tells 'em a tale he don't tell me. Well, it's
hard and it's hard and it's hard to love one that nev-er did love
you. It's hard and it's hard and it's hard, Great God, to
love one that nev - er will be true.

This infamous little ditty uses the same pattern:

Rudolph The Red-Nosed Reindeer

by JOHNNY MARKS

John Jacob Jingleheimer Schmidt

John Ja - cob Jin-gle-heim-er Schmidt, His name is my name
too, And when - ev - er we go out the peo-ple al-ways shout:
*f
"John Ja - cob Jin-gle-heim-er Schmidt, da da da da da da da."

*The letter *f* stands for the Italian word *forte* which means "loudly." The glossary (p. 241) gives such abbreviations. *ff* means "very loud."

The Sinking of the *Reuben James*

by WOODY GUTHRIE

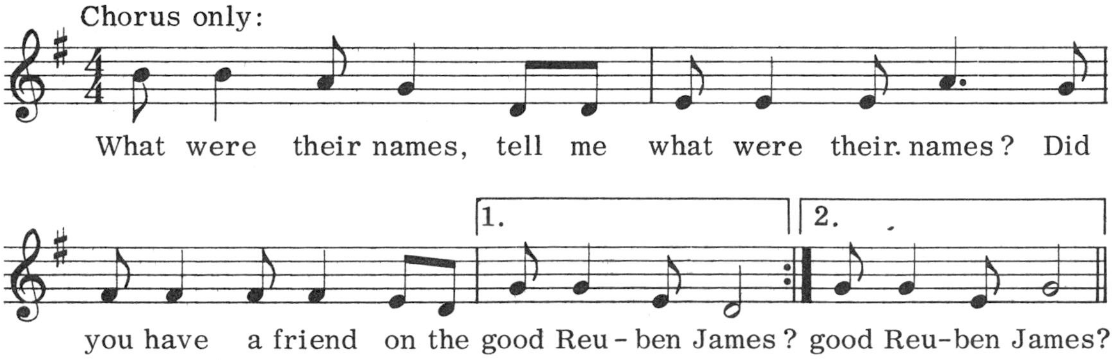
Chorus only:
What were their names, tell me what were their. names? Did
1.
2.
you have a friend on the good Reu - ben James? good Reu-ben James?

Jesse James

Jes-se James was a lad that killed man-y a man.
He robbed the Glen-dale_ train._____ He stole from the
rich and he gave to the poor. He'd a hand and a
heart and a brain._____ O Jes-se had a wife, to
mourn for his life. Three chil-dren they were brave.___
___ But that dir-ty lit-tle cow-ard that shot Mis-ter
How-ard, has laid poor Jes-se in his grave._____

It's customary to beam eighth-notes and sixteenth-notes in groups totalling one beat. Makes it easier to read the total number of beats per measure.

All the measures below would usually be considered *incorrect* (see Lesson 11).

This same syncopated pattern can be done at faster speeds. After all:

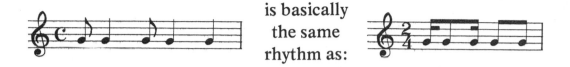

is basically the same rhythm as:

Right? . . . it's usually liable to sound faster.

Turkey In The Straw

(Chorus)

And do you know this one?

Old Dan Tucker

by DAN EMMETT

Get out the way for old Dan Tuck-er, You're too late to
get your sup-per

Or this?

Buffalo Gals

Buf-fa-lo gals won't-cha come out to-night, come out to-night,

come out to-night! Buf-fa-lo gals won't-cha come out to-night and
dance by the light of the moon.

Here's a variant of the pattern. Instead of 
we have 

Here's a chorus of an old song recently repopularized. In the 1880's ladies corsets were so tight, they said, "Let's take the agony out of putting on the style."

Putting On The Style

New words and new music adaptation by
NORMAN CAZDEN

Chorus:

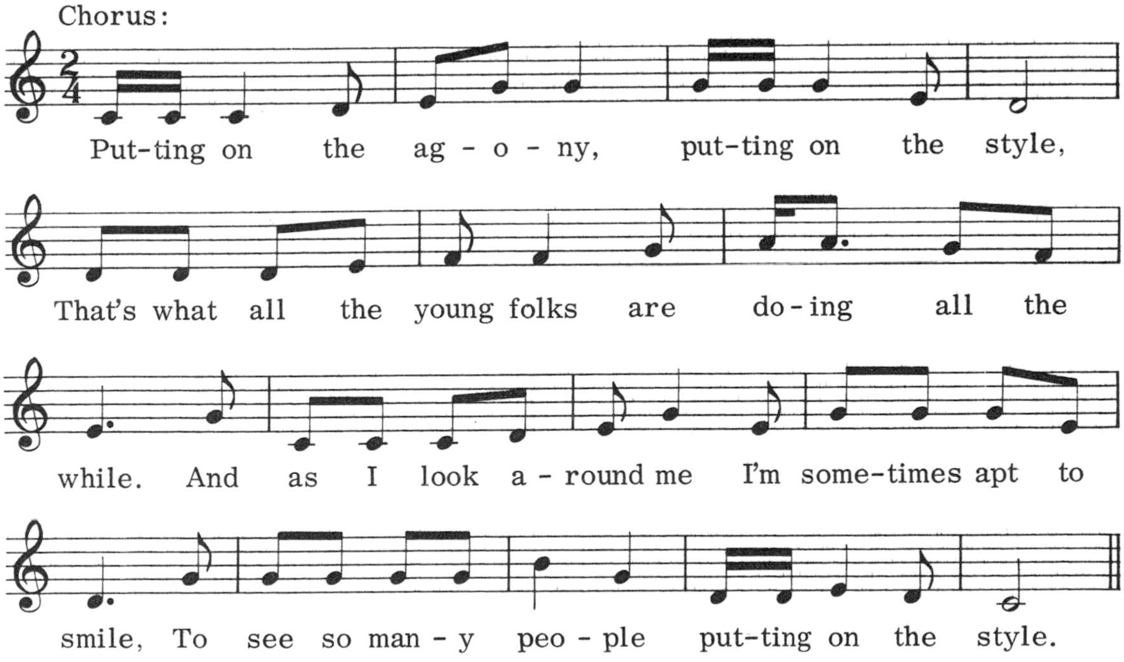
Put-ting on the ag - o - ny, put-ting on the style,
That's what all the young folks are do - ing all the
while. And as I look a - round me I'm some-times apt to
smile, To see so man - y peo - ple put-ting on the style.

A chorus of an old Mississippi riverboat song, as sung by the one and only Uncle Dave Macon, uses the same pattern:

Rockabout My Saro Jane

Chorus:
Rock-a-bout my Sa - ro Jane! O rock-a-bout my Sa - ro
Jane, Oh, there's noth-ing to do but__ set down and sing and
rock - a - bout my Sa - ro Jane!

And the most unforgettable verse of the old railroad song:

Wreck Of The Old '97

Music by HENRY C. WORK

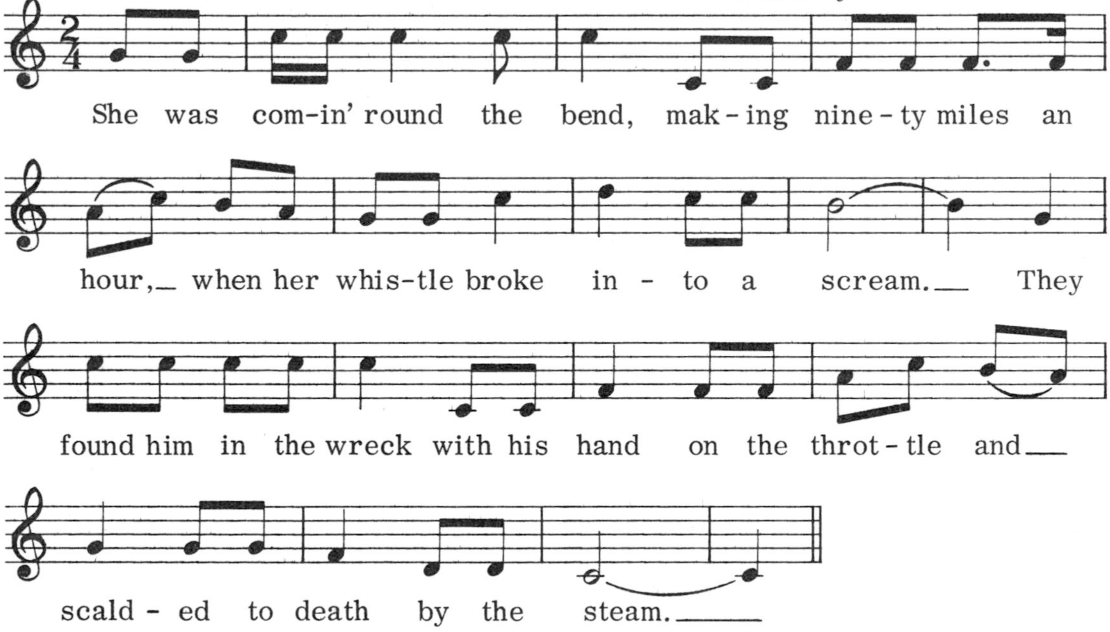
She was com-in' round the bend, mak - ing nine - ty miles an
hour,__ when her whis-tle broke in - to a scream.__ They
found him in the wreck with his hand on the throt - tle and__
scald - ed to death by the steam.____

Now hear this: What would this rhythm sound like?

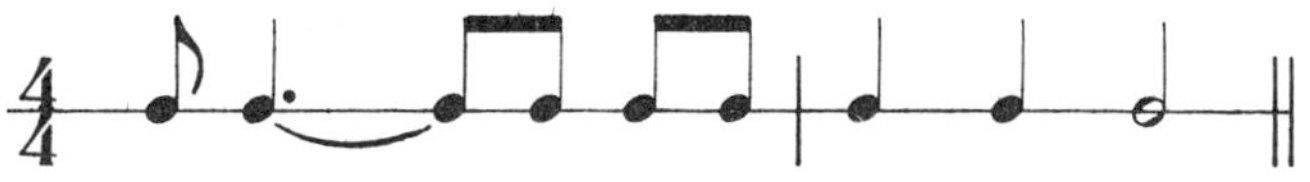

It's the opening bars of the famous march used in the movie *Bridge on the River Kwai.*

Colonel Bogey

K. J. ALFORD

uh oh —can't go on—
too complicated.

Really, I should leave it up to you to see if you know any other song where this rhythmic pattern is used.

Whis-tle, daugh-ter, whis - tle, and

And do you recognize this?

I'll write it differently, and maybe it will be easier to recognize:

Or like this:

(It's the old "shave and a haircut, two bits.")

In Lesson 4 we haven't introduced many new henscratches:

 a shouted or spoken word, or a handclap.

> placed over or under a note
gives it a specially strong accent

But for most people this lesson will be the most difficult. You've got to train your ear so that when you see 

you know what it's supposed to sound like.

The guessing game. Answers on page 94.

1.

2.

This is the way *I* know this song.
See page 74 for the way you may know it.

3.

4.

5.

6.

7.

8.

9.

10.

11. If you're from northeast England, you'll know this one:

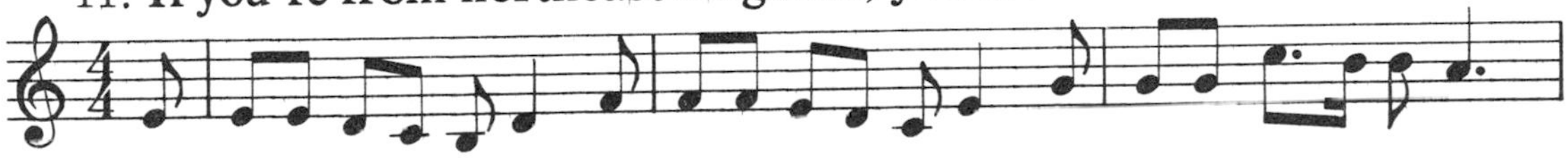

12. This ridiculous song I must print complete.

Answers

1. "The MTA Song"
2. "Mambo Walk" ("Jamaican Rhumba")
3. "Tom Dooley"
   Words and music collected, adapted, and arranged by Frank Warner, John A. Lomax, and Alan Lomax from the singing of Frank Proffitt
4. "London Bridge Is Falling Down"
5. "No Beer Today, No Beer Today, We Don't Sell Beer On Sunday"
6. "Mary Ann"
   Collected and adapted by Marius Barbeau and Alan Lomax
7. "Four Night's Drunk"
8. "Wabash Cannonball"
9. "Tzena Tzena"
   Words by Mitchell Parrish, music by Issacher Myron and Julius Grossman.
10. "La Paloma"
11. "Wa' Geordie's Lost His Penker"
12. "Oh, Miss Bailey, Unfortunate Miss Bailey"

It just occurs to me: Some people, including me, have learned to read music by learning to write it down. Try doing these tests backwards. Try writing down the first lines of some of the melodies you know. In G or C. Then check and see if you've written it down the same way I have.

Now on to Lesson 5 and a new rhythm.

Notes

Lesson 5

Triple Rhythm: 3/4 Time

So far all our melodies have been in 4/4 time, or 2/4 time. Let's try a new time signature:

$\frac{3}{4}$ *three quarter time or three-four time* (three quarter notes in each measure.)

It's the same as that old-fashioned dance called a waltz. The German bands would play it

"*OOM*-pah-pah, *OOM*-pah-pah"

Try the following songs now, tapping out three beats per measure with your fingers as you sing.

Remember: ♩ ♩ ♩ = 𝅗𝅥. = 𝅗𝅥 ♩ = ♩ 𝅗𝅥

Goodnight, Irene

Words and Music by
HUDDIE LEDBETTER
and JOHN A. LOMAX

I - rene, good - night, I -
rene, good - night. Good - night, I - rene, good -
night, I - rene, I'll see you in my dreams.

Last Night I Had The Strangest Dream

Words and Music by
ED McCURDY

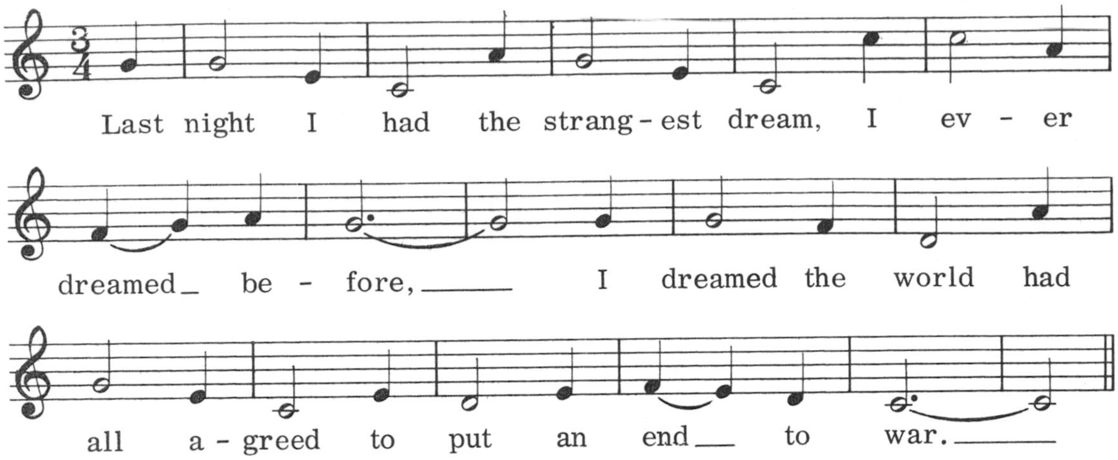
Last night I had the strang - est dream, I ev - er
dreamed_ be - fore, ___ I dreamed the world had
all a - greed to put an end ___ to war. ___

The 1890's produced a rash of pop songs in three-four time. From a distance they sound much alike. Here's several.

Bicycle Built For Two

Words and Music by HARRY DACRE

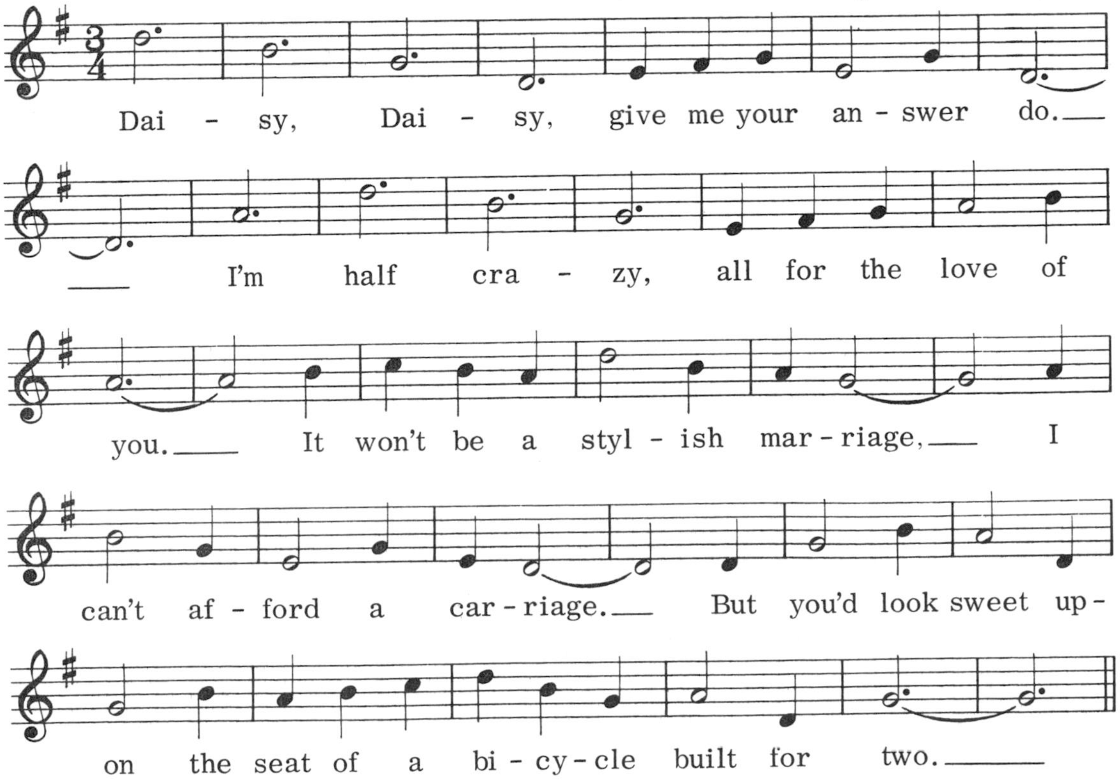
Dai - sy, Dai - sy, give me your an - swer do. ___
___ I'm half cra - zy, all for the love of
you. ___ It won't be a styl - ish mar - riage, ___ I
can't af - ford a car - riage. ___ But you'd look sweet up -
on the seat of a bi - cy - cle built for two. ___

School Days
(When We Were a Couple of Kids)

Words by WILL D. COBB
Music by GUS EDWARDS

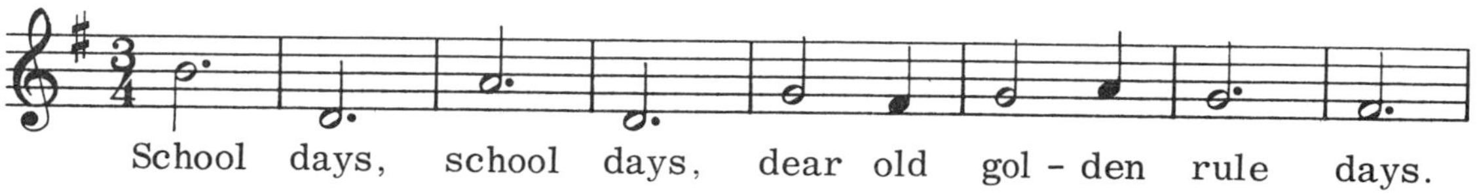
School days, school days, dear old gol - den rule days.

This one served as a campaign song for Alfred E. Smith in 1928 (he lost to Herbert Hoover).

East Side, West Side

Words and Music by
JAMES W. BLAKE and
CHARLES B. LAWLER

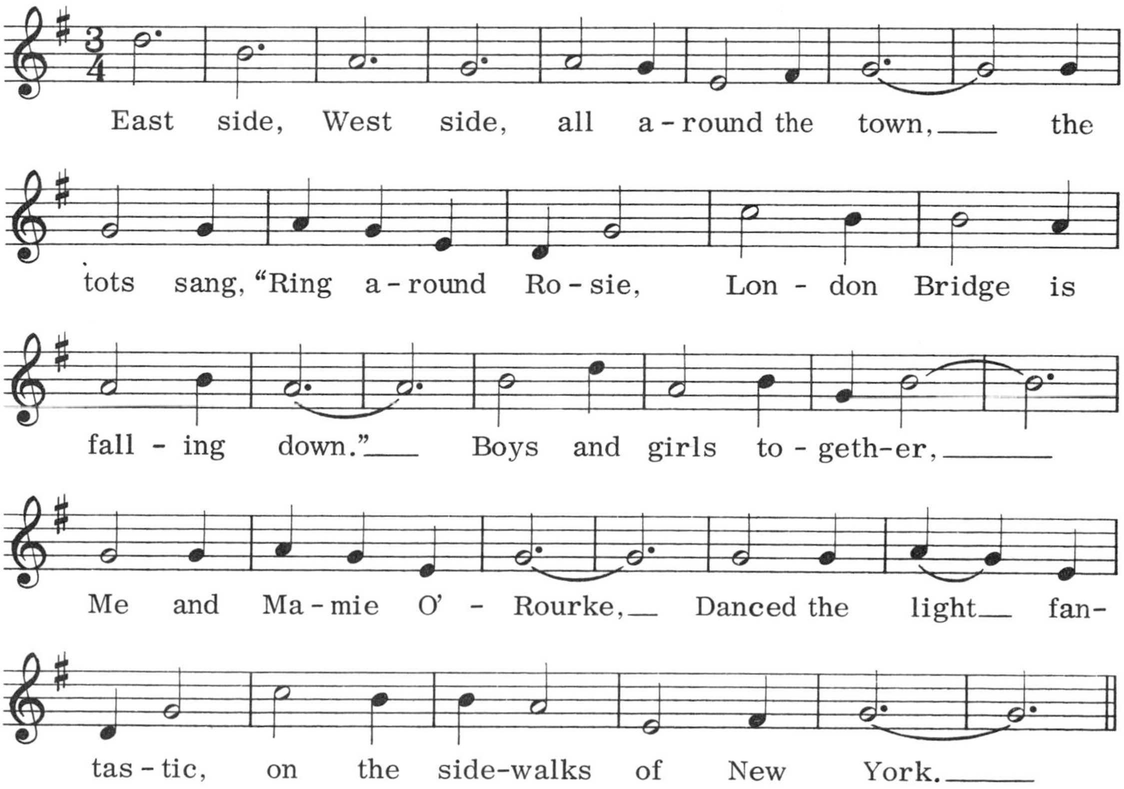
East side, West side, all a - round the town, the
tots sang, "Ring a - round Ro - sie, Lon - don Bridge is
fall - ing down." Boys and girls to - geth-er,
Me and Ma - mie O' - Rourke, Danced the light fan-
tas - tic, on the side-walks of New York.

But this one, with its Elizabethan verses and medieval melody, is ten times as ancient. There's a moral here, somewhere.

On Top Of Old Smoky

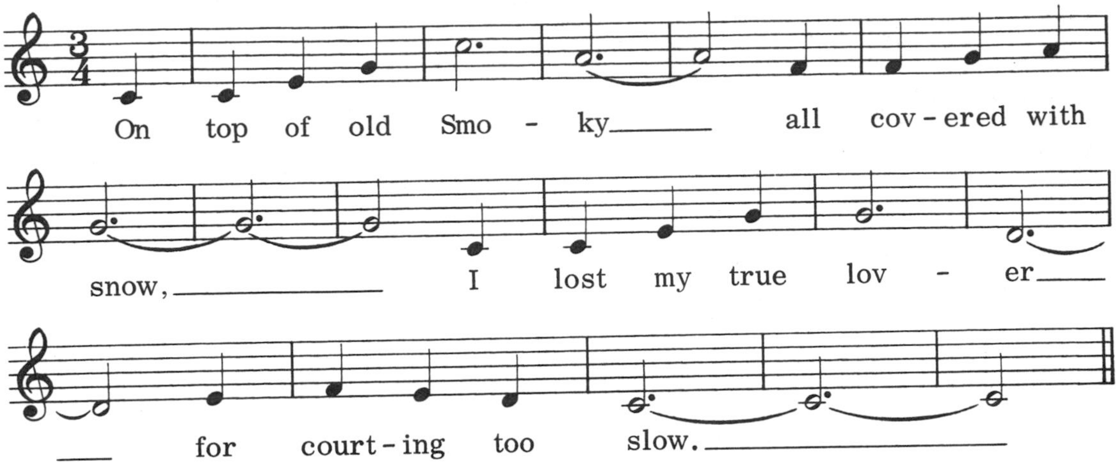
On top of old Smo - ky all cov - ered with
snow, I lost my true lov - er
for court - ing too slow.

An old soldier's song from the Boer War, which Joseph Marais introduced to America in 1940.

Oh Brandy Leave Me Alone

Words and Music by
JOSEPH MARAIS

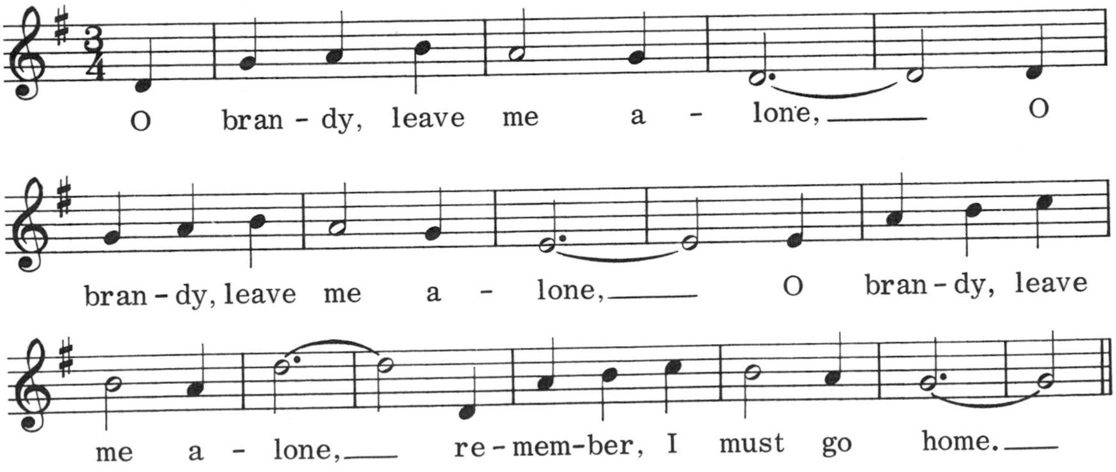
O bran - dy, leave me a - lone, O
bran - dy, leave me a - lone, O bran - dy, leave
me a - lone, re - mem - ber, I must go home.

Now in the next songs, remember:  (one *beat*).

Keep the beats going, even through the long tied notes:

I Never Will Marry

New words and new music arrangement by
Mrs. TEXAS GLADDEN
(based on a traditional song)

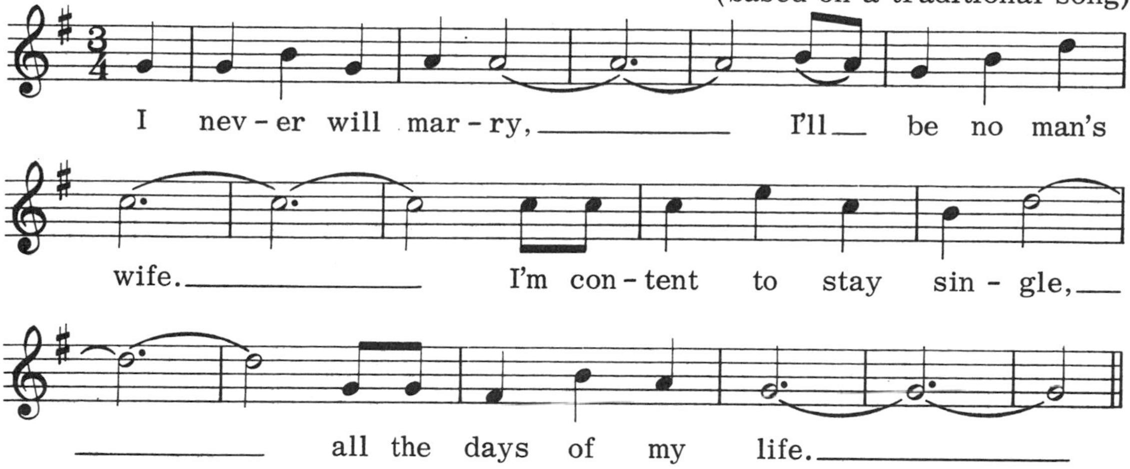
I nev-er will mar-ry, ___ I'll ___ be no man's
wife. ___ I'm con-tent to stay sin-gle, ___
___ all the days of my life. ___

Here's four fragments. Keep the beat regular: 1, 2, 3.

Little Boxes

Words and Music by
MALVINA REYNOLDS

Lit-tle box-es on the hill-side, lit-tle box-es made of
tick-y tack-y, lit-tle box-es, lit-tle box-es, lit-tle
box-es all the same...

The Ash Grove

The ash grove so_ peace-ful...

Home On The Range

O give me a home where the buf - fa - lo roam, where the...

Halleluya I'm A Bum

Hal-le - lu - ya I'm a bum, Hal - le - lu - ya bum a - gain...

(The rest of this song in Lesson 6)

More eighth-notes:

We Wish You A Merry Christmas

We wish you a Mer-ry Christ-mas, we wish you a Mer-ry
Christ-mas, we wish you a Mer-ry Christ-mas, and a Hap - py New Year!

Now here's a new rhythm to put in a 3/4 measure: ♩. ♪ ♩

It's what you find in the following four songs.

America

(Tune: God Save The King)

My coun-try 'tis of thee, sweet land of lib - er-ty, of thee I...

Blow The Man Down

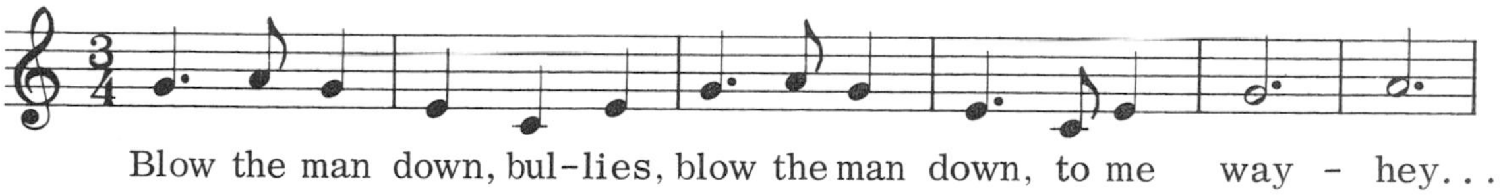
Blow the man down, bul-lies, blow the man down, to me way - hey...

Hymn Of Thanksgiving

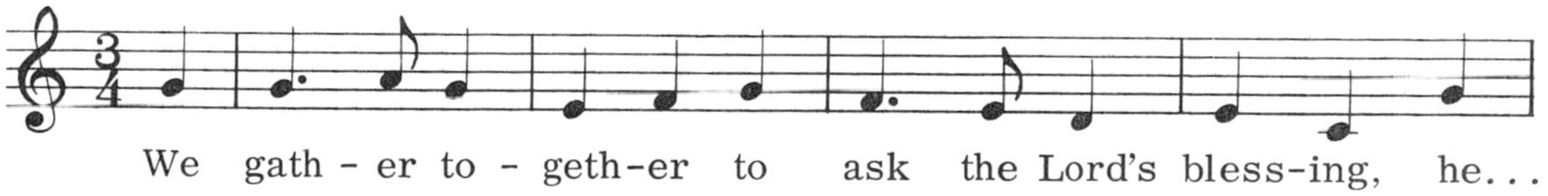
We gath - er to - geth-er to ask the Lord's bless-ing, he...

Silent Night

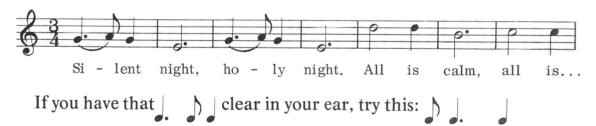

Si - lent night, ho - ly night. All is calm, all is...

If you have that ♩. ♪ ♩ clear in your ear, try this: ♪ ♩. ♩

Where Has My Little Dog Gone?

Where, O where has my lit-tle dog gone? O where O

where can he be?_____ With his

And this: 

Ach, Du Lieber Augustin

Ach, du lieb-er Au-gus-tin, Au-gus-tin, Au-gus-tin! Ach, du lieb-er...

And now you should be able to read this:

I Ride An Old Paint

I ride an Old Paint, I lead an Old Dan, I'm
going to Mon - ta - na to throw the Houl - i - han they
feed 'em in the Cou - lees; They wa - ter in the draw. Their
Chorus:
tails are all mat-ted; their backs are all raw. Ride a -
round, lit - tle do - gies; ride a - round them slow.
For the "Fier - y" and "Snuf - fy" are rar - ing to go.

And this:

The Cowboy Lament

Collected, adapted and arranged by
JOHN A. LOMAX AND ALAN LOMAX

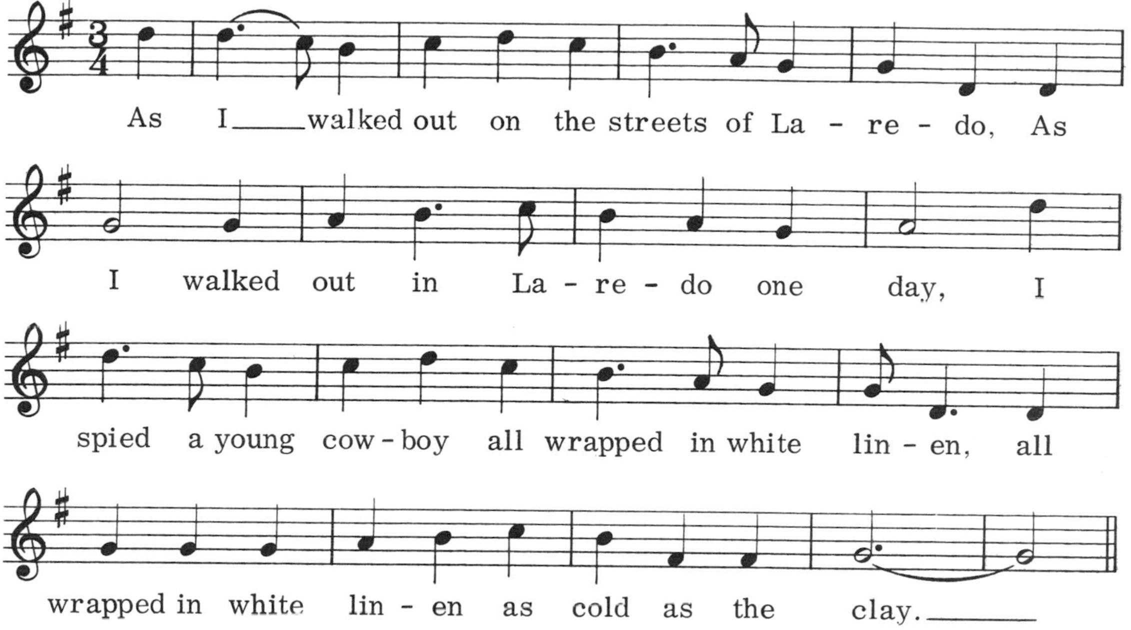
As I ___ walked out on the streets of La - re - do, As
I walked out in La - re - do one day, I
spied a young cow - boy all wrapped in white lin - en, all
wrapped in white lin - en as cold as the clay. ___

If you've handled the last couple pages OK, the next three songs shouldn't throw you.

Widdecombe Fair

Collected by CECIL SHARP

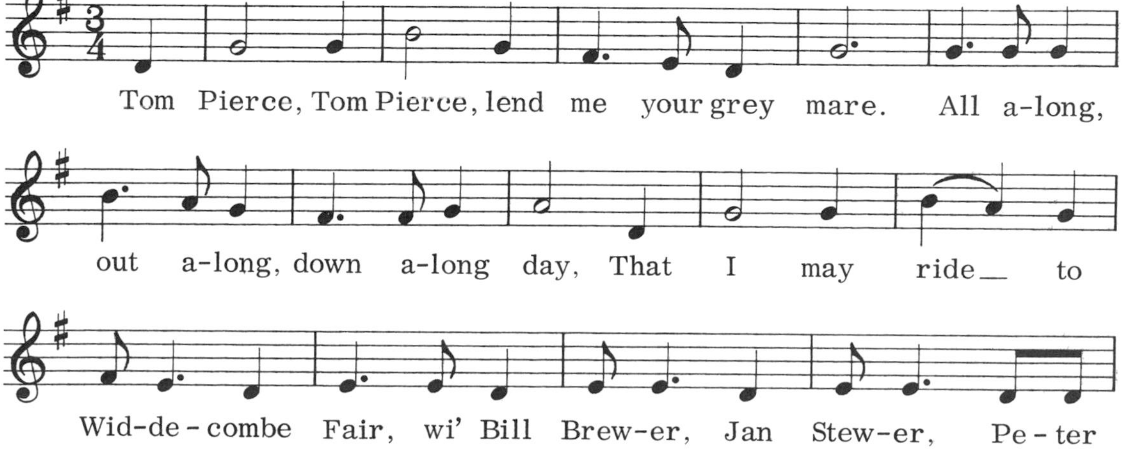
Tom Pierce, Tom Pierce, lend me your grey mare. All a-long,
out a-long, down a-long day, That I may ride _ to
Wid-de - combe Fair, wi' Bill Brew-er, Jan Stew-er, Pe - ter

Gur-ney, Pe-ter Da-vey, old Un - cle Tom Cob - ley and
all, old Un - cle Tom Cob - ley and all.

Dona Nobis Pacem

One of the world's loveliest rounds. It means "Give us peace" in Latin. Pronounce the *C* as in Italian—"pachem."

3
4
Do - na no - bis pa - cem, pa - cem; Do - na
no - bis pa - cem. Do - na no - bis
pa - cem, Do - na no - bis pa - cem, Do - na
no - bis pa-cem, Do - na no - bis pa - cem.

(The Ring On My Finger Is)
Johnny Give Me

By SPENCER HOWELL
and ROGER ABRAHAMS

3
4
The ring on my fin-ger is John-ny give me. The ring on my

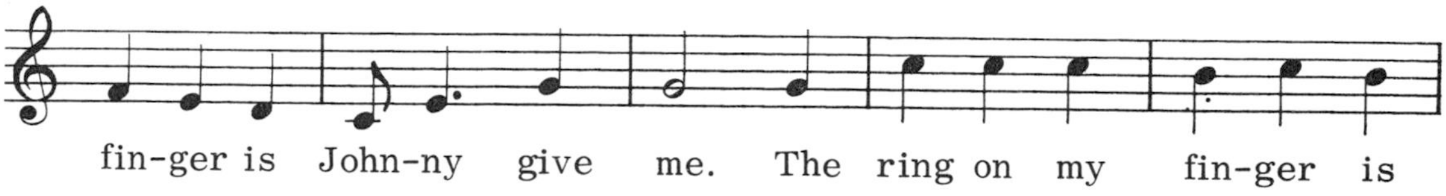
fin-ger is John-ny give me. The ring on my fin-ger is

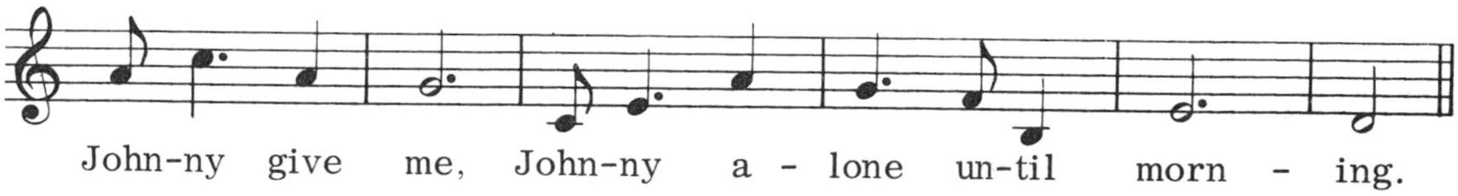
John-ny give me, John-ny a - lone un-til morn - ing.

2. The dress that I wear, it is Johnny give me (3 times)
   Johnny alone until morning.
3. The shoes that I wear, etc.
4. The hat that I wear, etc.
5. Johnny says that he loves me, but I do not believe, etc.
6. The ring on my finger is Johnny give me, etc.

You should be able to handle most North American songs in 3/4 time now:

So Long, It's Been Good To Know Yuh
(Dusty Old Dust)

Words and Music by
WOODY GUTHRIE

So long, it's been good to know you. So long, it's

been good to know you

Roll On Columbia

Words by WOODY GUTHRIE
Music based on "Goodnight, Irene"

Roll on, Col - um - bia, roll on; Roll

on, ___ Col - um - bia, roll on; Your pow - er is turn-ing our
dark-ness to dawn, So roll on, Col-um - bia, roll on. ___

And the great refrain which Burl Ives tacked on to "Sweet Besty from Pike":

Sweet Betsy From Pike

Chorus:
Hoo-dle dang fol - dee - di - do. Hoo-dle dang fol - dee day.

But songs from Latin America are a different matter. They go in for a great deal of syncopation down there. Work on this till you get it; it's worth it. "La-la" your way through if you don't know Spanish.

Cielito Lindo

from Mexico

De la sier - ra, mo - re - na cie - li - to
lin - do vie - nen ba - jan - do ___ un par de oj -
i - tos ne-gros, cie - li - to lin - do de ___ con - tra -
ban - do, ___ Ay, ay, ay, ay ___ can -

tay no llo - res
Por - que, can - tan - do, se a -
leg-ran cie - li - to lin-do, los cor - a - zo - nes.

2. El amor es un bicho, cielito lindo, que cuando pica
No se encuentra remedio, cielito lindo, en la botica
(Love is a bug, dear, that when it bites, there is no
remedy in the drug store . . .)

Before I close this chapter, I'll mention that occasionally you'll run into 3/2 time. It's just a slow 3/4.

Santa Lucia

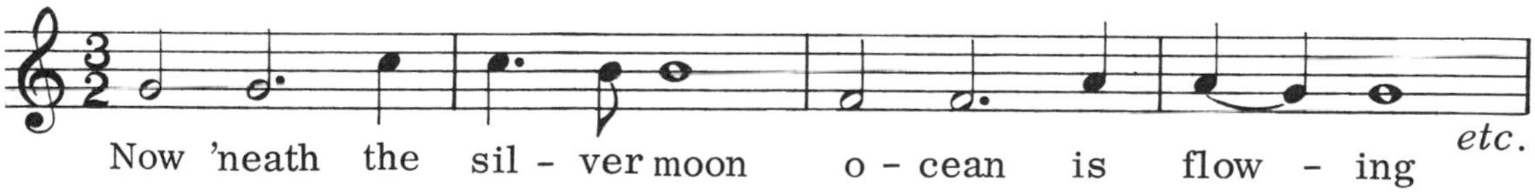
Now 'neath the sil - ver moon o - cean is flow - ing
etc.

But it's hard for the average person to read 3/2. I once put some English words to the noble Russian melody "Stenka Razin":

River of My People

Words by PETE SEEGER
Music: Traditional

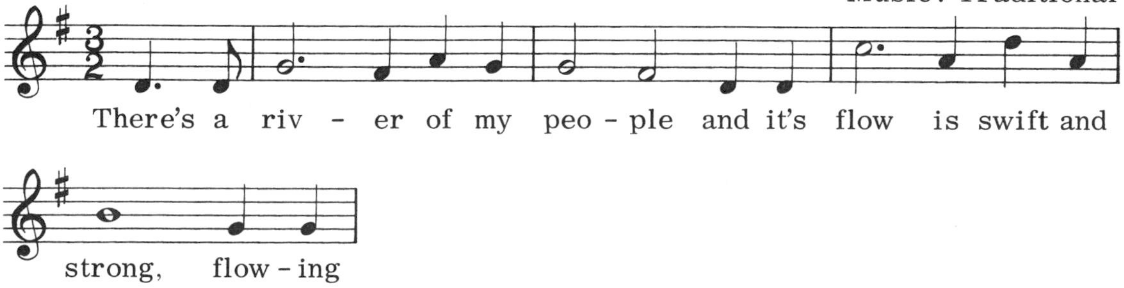
There's a riv - er of my peo - ple and it's flow is swift and
strong, flow - ing

Thinking to write it more easily and accurately, I tried:

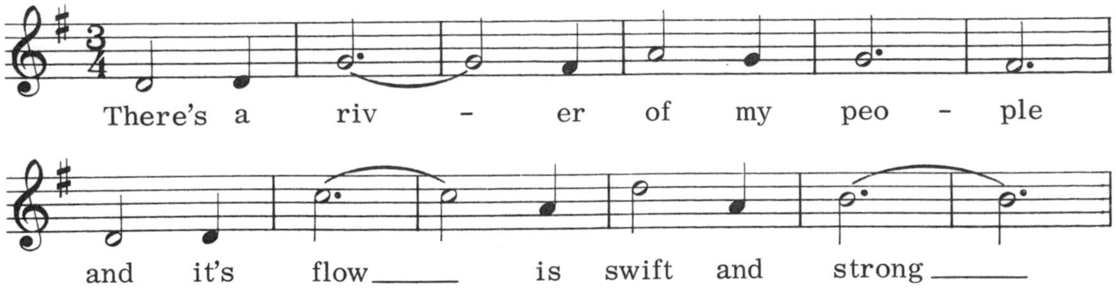
There's a riv - er of my peo - ple
and it's flow ___ is swift and strong ___

In the end I wrote it out like this, with the word *slowly* at the upper left, where tempo directions are usually given.

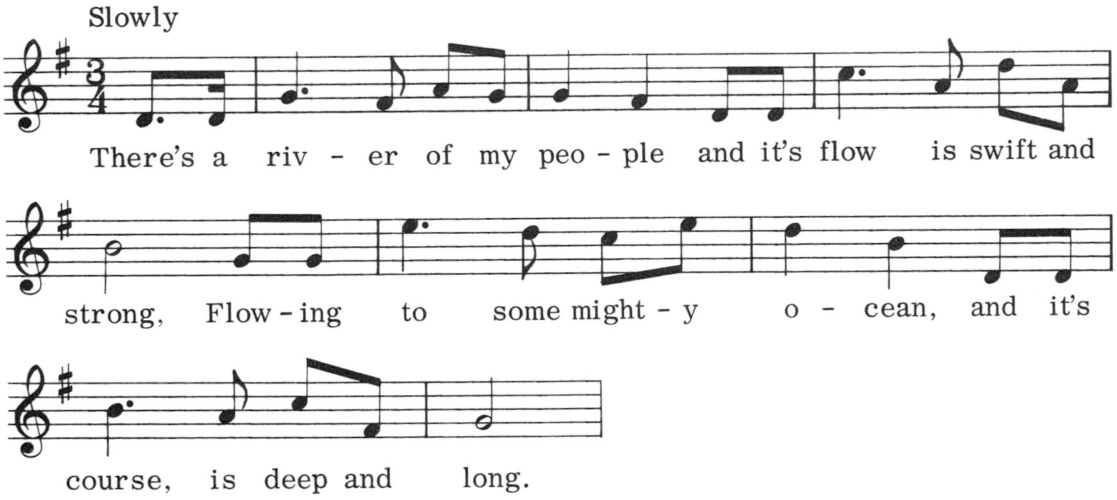
Slowly
There's a riv - er of my peo - ple and it's flow is swift and
strong, Flow - ing to some might - y o - cean, and it's
course, is deep and long.

If the song has a fast tempo, you could write *fast* in the upper left-hand corner, or you could write it in 3/8 time:

Los Cuatro Generales

Spanish Civil War, 1937

Los cua-tro ge - ne - ra - les ___ los cua-tro ge - ne -
ra - les ___ los cua-tro ge - ne - ra - les, ma - mi - ta

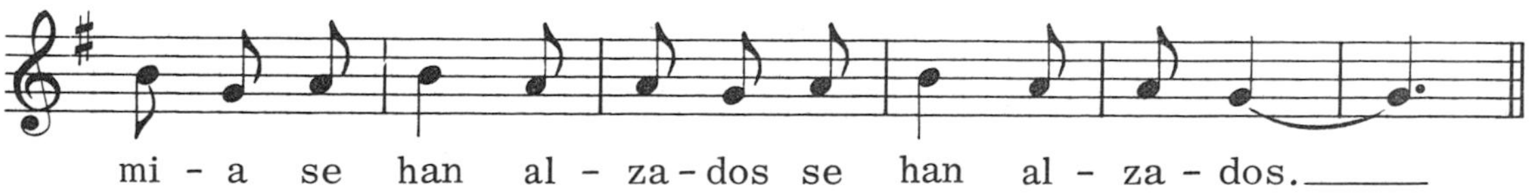
mi - a se han al - za - dos se han al - za - dos.

A Hole In The Bucket

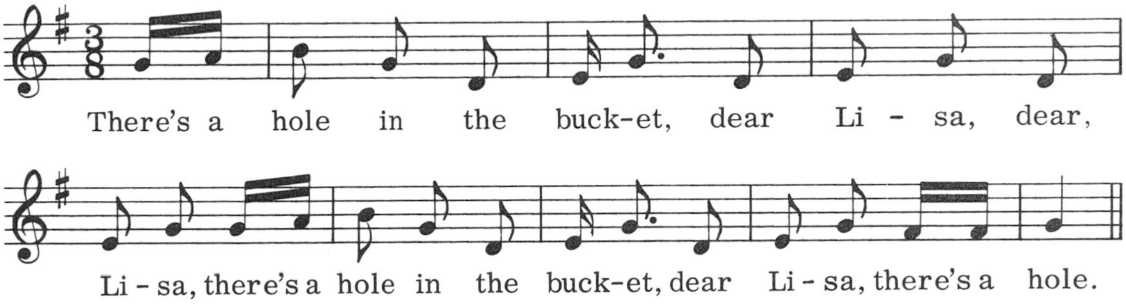
There's a hole in the buck-et, dear Li - sa, dear,
Li - sa, there's a hole in the buck-et, dear Li - sa, there's a hole.

Really, this would be more commonly written in 3/4 time.

Here's your test for Lesson 5. Write out "Bucket" in 3/4 time. I'll start it for you:

There's a hole in the

Waltz around the world now. Answers on page 114.

1.
2.
3.

4.

5.

6.

7.

8.

9.

10.

11.

12. (worse and worse)

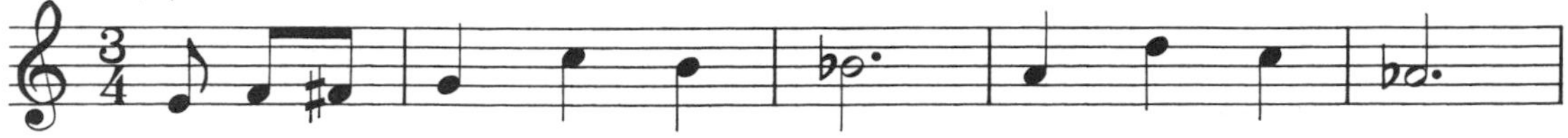

13.

14.

15.

16.

17.

18.

19.

20.

21.

22. Such a great chorus—I must give it all:

Most of these melodies are European or neo-European. My apologies to Asia and Africa, where much of the world's greatest music may be found. But now, by God, if you ain't got the hang of 3/4 time in some small way, it ain't my fault. End Lesson 5.

Answers:

1. "After the Ball" (USA)
2. "Sweet Betsy from Pike" (tune is Old English)
3. "La Cucaracha" (Mexico)
4. "The Skye Boat Song" (Scotland)
5. "The Squid Jigging Ground" (another Newfoundlander) by Arthur Scammell
6. "Abiyoyo" (South Africa) Music: African traditional
7. "La Golondrina" (Spain)
8. "La Donna E Mobile" (Italy)
9. "My Wild Irish Rose" (from the land of Bathos)
10. "The Rose of Tralee" (Ireland)
11. "When Irish Eyes Are Smiling" (from the land of Bathos)
12. "Girl of My Dreams" (from the land of Bathos)
13. "The Man on the Flying Trapeze" (Circus World)
14. "The Band Played On" (USA)
15. "Now Is the Hour" (New Zealand) by Maewa Kaihan, Clement Scott, Dorothy Stewart
16. "Oh, Tannenbaum" (Germany)
17. "O Holy Night"
18. "He Told Her He Loved Her but O How He Lied"
19. "Suzanne Was a Girl Who Had Plenty of Class"
20. "Lord Thomas and Fair Eleanor"
21. "Italian Christmas Carol"
22. "She's-a-big lass and a bonny lass
    And she likes her beer
    And they call her Coshi Butterfield
    And I wish she were here!"
    (from Newcastle-on-Tyne)

Notes

Lesson 6

Triple Rhythm: 6/8 Time

When a triple rhythm goes fast, it's more commonly written as *six-eight time.* Each measure has two accented beats.

Two groups of three eighth-notes.

	♩ ♪ ♩ ♪
or	*One,* two, three, *four,* five, six
or	♩. ♩ ♪
or	♩. ♩.

Watch it, 𝅗𝅥. equals two beats now, not three.

Since there are two main accents per measure, it really is a "*one,* two" rhythm, with each foot-tapping beat now equal to a *dotted* quarter note: ♩.

The Bear Went Over The Mountain

The bear went o-ver the moun-tain, The bear went o-ver the moun-tain, The
oth - er side of the moun-tain, The oth - er side of the moun-tain, The

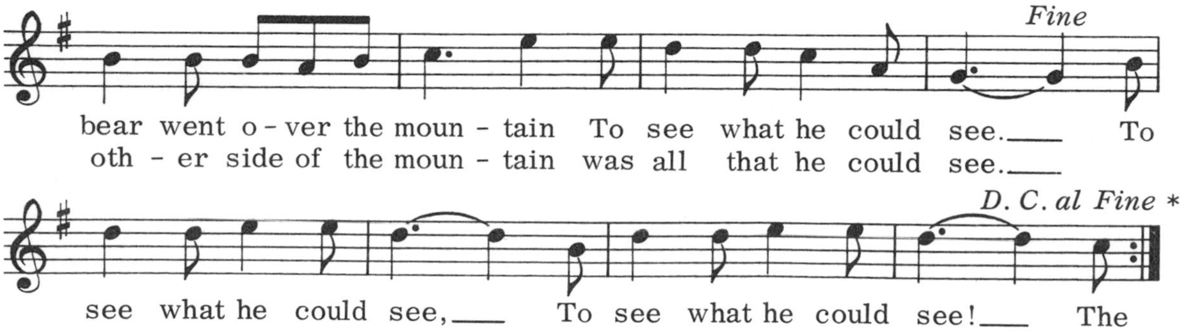
Fine
bear went o - ver the moun - tain To see what he could see.___ To
oth - er side of the moun - tain was all that he could see.___
D. C. al Fine *
see what he could see,___ To see what he could see!___ The

The Irish were great for 6/8 time. "Irish jigs" they call 'em. Here's other words to this tune:

We got a pig in the parlor (3 times)
And he is Irish, too.

(Those words may seem just humorous now, but one hundred years ago, it was the same old story: another race-insulting set of words. Irish were all accused of being dirty and ignorant.)

Here, I'll let you puzzle your way thru the famous "Irish Washerwoman."

(Do you know how to whistle?)

The Irish Washerwoman

*I trust you are all straight on this business of repeats. See page 63. But who is Al Fine? *Fine* (FEEnay) is Italian for "end." *D.C. Al Fine* means, go back to the beginning and stop where it says *Fine*. Got it? *D.C.* means *Da Capo*—Italian for "head" or "beginning." If you weren't supposed to go all the way back to the beginning of this song, you might see *D. S. Al Fine*. *D. S.* stands for the Italian *Da Signe* ("from the sign") and you'd see a fancy 𝄋 over the note.

And another great Irish dance tune you probably never heard of, but now's a good time to learn. It's from the Irish of Newfoundland.

I'se The B'y That Built The Boat

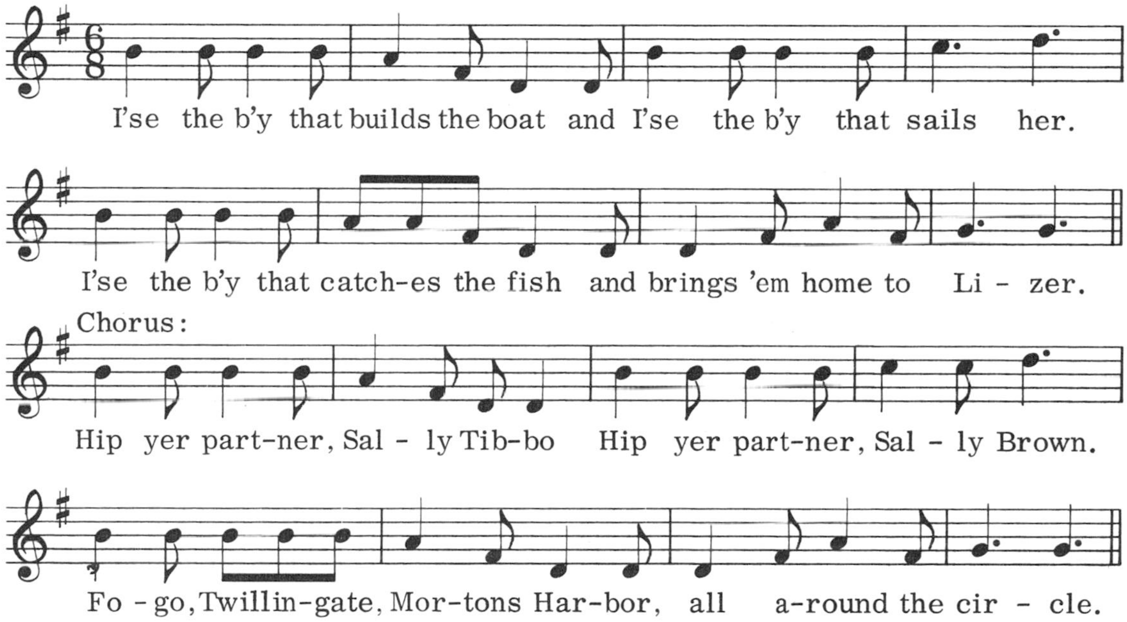
I'se the b'y that builds the boat and I'se the b'y that sails her.
I'se the b'y that catch-es the fish and brings 'em home to Li - zer.
Chorus:
Hip yer part-ner, Sal - ly Tib-bo Hip yer part-ner, Sal - ly Brown.
Fo - go, Twillin-gate, Mor-tons Har-bor, all a-round the cir - cle.

Sods and rinds to cover your flake,
Cake and tea for supper,
Codfish in the spring o' the year,
Fried in maggoty butter.

I don't want your maggoty fish,
That's no good for winter.
I could buy as good as that
Down in Bonavista.

(Here's an extra verse. I can't remember where it comes from.)

Susan White she's out of sight,
Her petticoat wants a border.
Old Sam Oliver in the dark
He kissed her in the corner.

(The towns are all little Newfoundland fishing ports. How come some of the lonesomest places in the world have some of the best songs? People have to sing to stay alive, mebbe.)

The Scots like 6/8 time, too.

Comin' Through The Rye

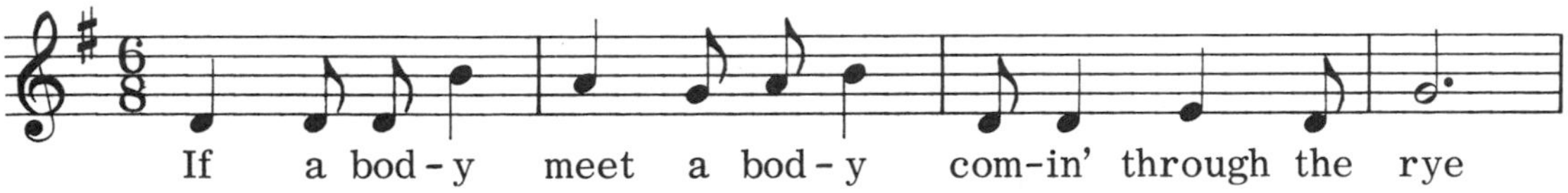
If a bod-y meet a bod-y com-in' through the rye

Well, here's two 6/8 tunes you never heard of:

Three Blind Mice

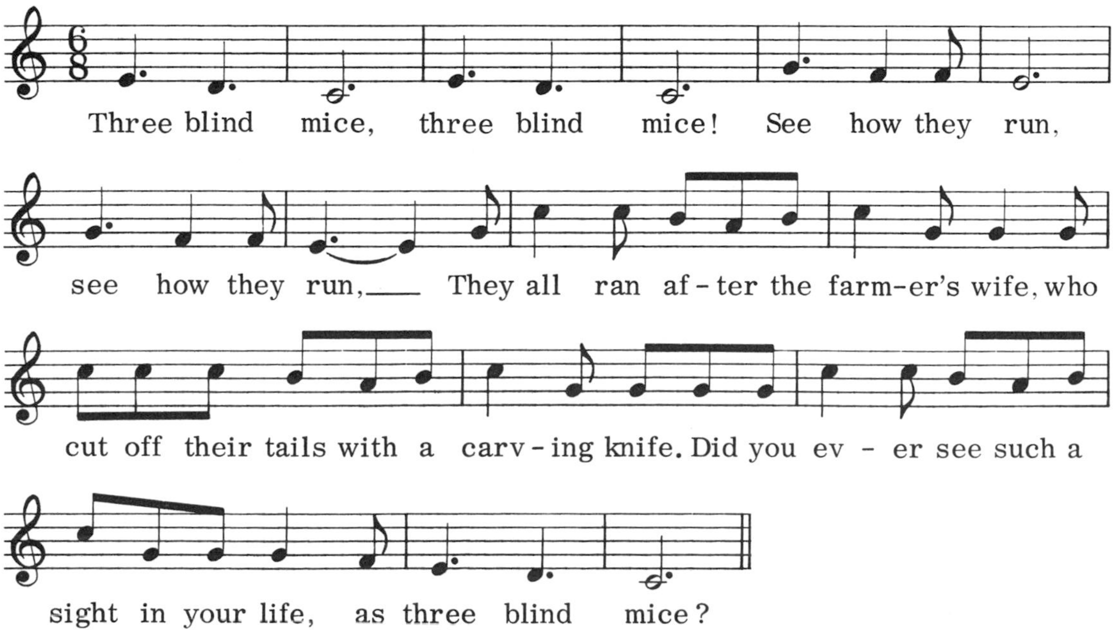
Three blind mice, three blind mice! See how they run,
see how they run, They all ran af-ter the farm-er's wife, who
cut off their tails with a carv-ing knife. Did you ev - er see such a
sight in your life, as three blind mice?

Row, Row, Row Your Boat

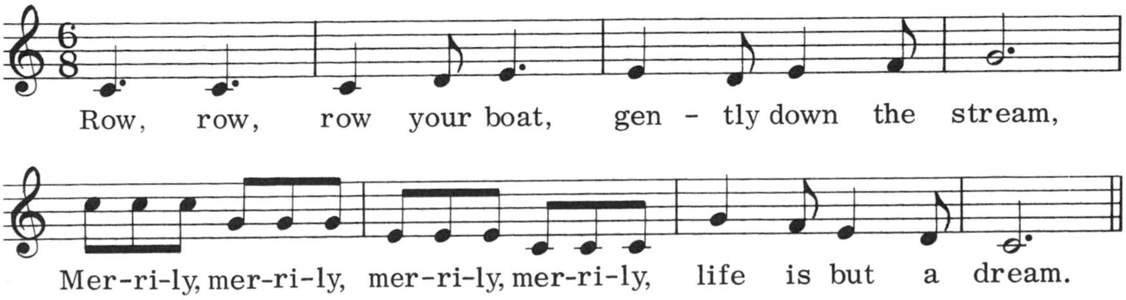
Row, row, row your boat, gen - tly down the stream,
Mer-ri-ly, mer-ri-ly, mer-ri-ly, mer-ri-ly, life is but a dream.

Don't be surprised if occasionally you find a song in a slow 6/8 time:

The Frozen Logger

Words and Music by
JAMES STEVENS

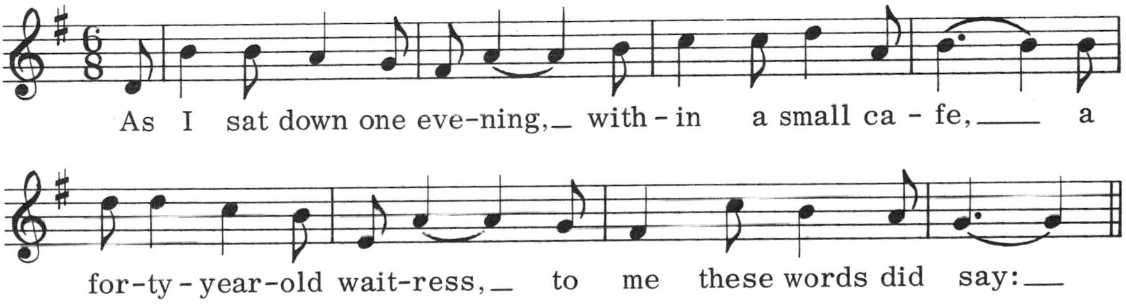
As I sat down one eve-ning,_ with - in a small ca - fe,__ a
for-ty - year-old wait-ress,_ to me these words did say:__

I see you are a logger and not a common bum
For nobody but a logger stirs his coffee
with his thumb.

My lover was a logger, there's none
like him today,
If you'd pour whiskey on it,
he would eat a bale of hay.

He never shaved the whiskers from
off his horny hide,
He'd drive 'em in with a hammer
and bite 'em off inside.

My lover came to see me upon one freezing day,
He held me in a fond embrace which broke
three vertebrae.

He kissed me when we parted, so hard
he broke my jaw,
I could not speak to tell him he'd
forgot his mackinaw.

I saw my lover leaving, a-sauntering
through the snow,
Going gravely homeward at forty-eight below.

The weather tried to freeze him,
it tried its level best,
At a hundred degrees below zero,
he buttoned up his vest.

It froze clean through to China,
it froze to the stars above,
At a thousand degrees below zero,
it froze my logger love.

They tried in vain to thaw him,
and if you'll believe me, Sir,
They made him into axeblades to chop
the Douglas fir.

And so I lost my lover, and to this cafe I come
And here I wait till someone stirs his coffee
with his thumb.

This same song could be written in 3/4 time and often is.

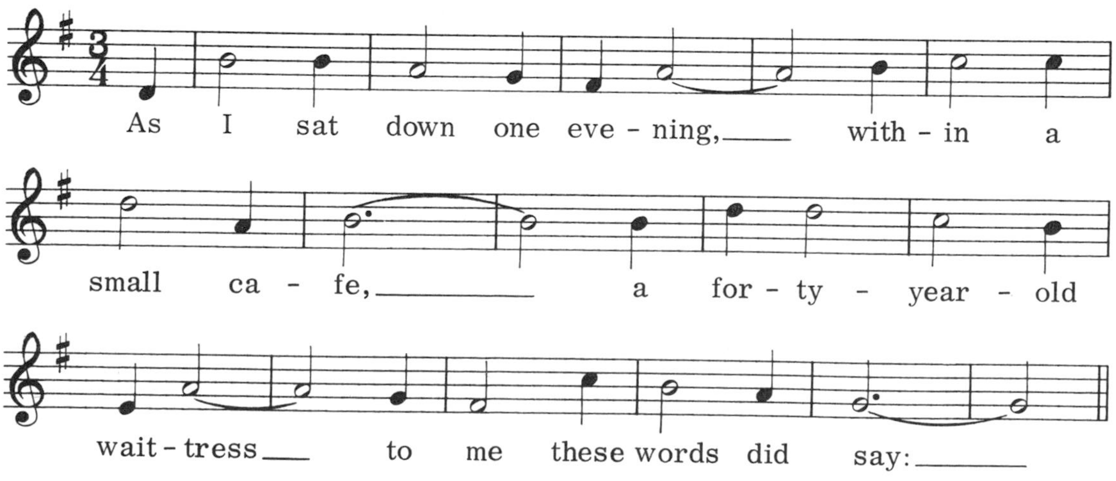
As I sat down one eve - ning,___ with - in a
small ca - fe,___ a for - ty - year - old
wait - tress___ to me these words did say:___

Once in a blue moon a slow 6/8 is written as 6/4

Very rarely (in the USA) you come across a song in 9/8 time—that is three groups of three:  three beats per measure.

Clementine

Oh, my dar - ling, Oh, my dar - ling, Oh, my dar - ling Clem-en-
tine, You are lost and gone for-ev - er, dread-ful sor-ry, Clem-en-tine.

Because it's unusual, people are often confused by 9/8 time, but here's another example:

Down in the Valley

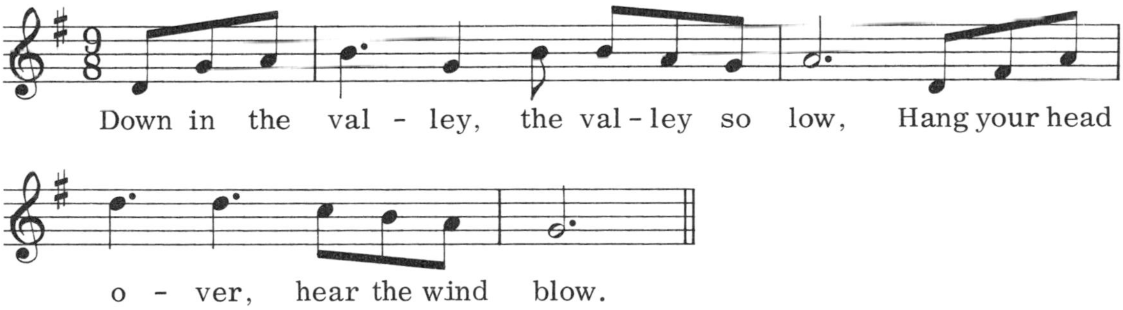
Down in the val - ley, the val - ley so low, Hang your head
o - ver, hear the wind blow.

Test yourself: Try rewriting this in 3/4 time.

Down in the val -

A lot of rhythm and blues, rock and roll, and other pop music of the 1960's had an underlying triple rhythm within a standard 4/4 time. Gospel songs, too. That's why the freedom song "We Shall Overcome" is accompanied with this pulse:

12
8

12/8 time (four beats per measure) is rarely used.

The melody of this song is always printed:

We Shall Overcome

New words and music arrangement by
ZILPHIA HORTON, FRANK HAMILTON,
GUY CARAWAN & PETE SEEGER

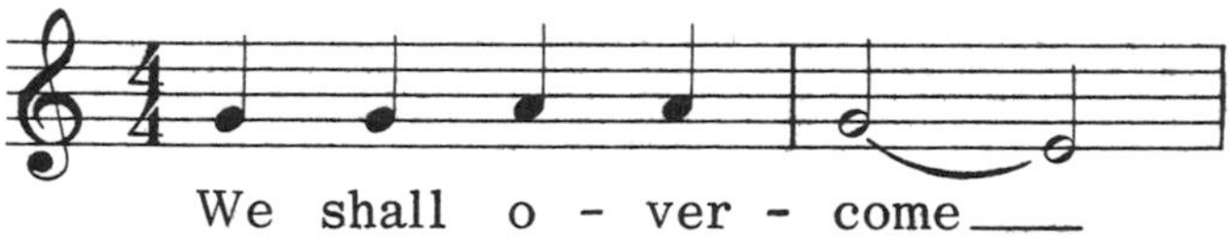
We shall o - ver - come

If you'll stop to analyze it, there are two basically different march rhythms. Both are 4/4 time, but in one of them the eighth notes are equal in strength:

Oh, the mon-key wrapped his tail a - round the flag - pole

In the other, there may still be a pair of eighth notes written down, but the first note in each pair is emphasized much more than the second. You would be misled in reading it thus:

Mine eyes hath seen the glo - ry of the com - ing of the

Let's analyze it further.

Here's the first line of America's great revolutionary song, written three ways. The first most accurately reflects the way it is usually sung; the second is easiest to read but most inaccurate; the third is the way it's usually given in songbooks.

John Brown's Body

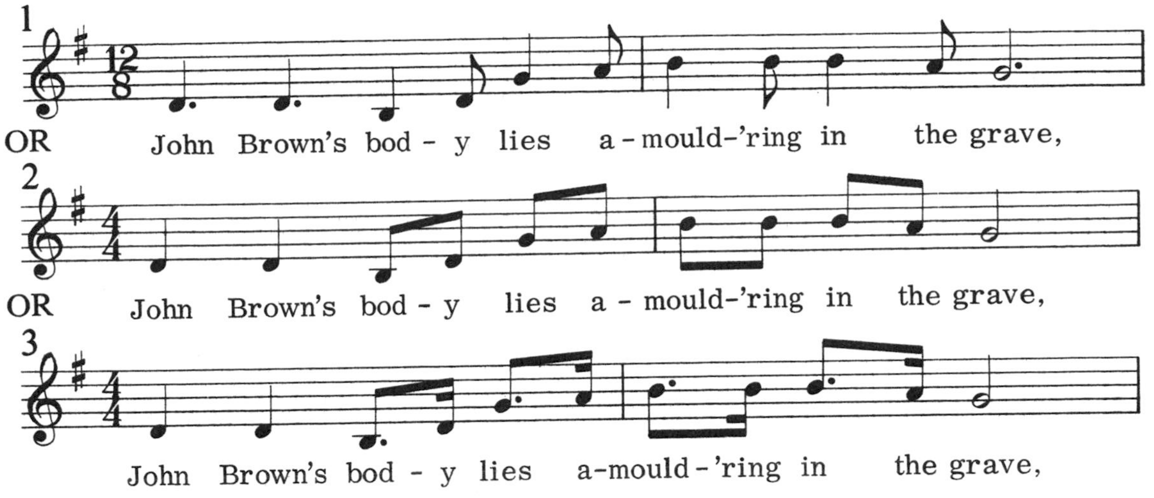
1
OR
John Brown's bod - y lies a - mould-'ring in the grave,
2
OR
John Brown's bod - y lies a - mould-'ring in the grave,
3
John Brown's bod - y lies a-mould-'ring in the grave,

To solve the problem of how to divide a quarter note into three equal parts, one sometimes uses *triplets*. See the next song. The number *3* written above the staff indicates that *three eighth-notes add up only to the time allotted for two.*

(same melody—a British army parody)

3
3
3
3
One staff of - fi - cer jumped right o-ver the oth-er staff of-fi-cer's back

Here's another use of triplets, within 3/4 time.

Halleluya I'm A Bum

Hal-le - lu - ya, I'm a bum, Hal-le - lu - ya, bum a - gain! Hal-le-
3
lu - ya, give us a hand - out to re - vive us a - gain!

Triplets can be used to make three-quarter notes equal one half note. Here's the opening of a famous show tune:

3
3

(Recognize it? Cole Porter's "Begin the Beguine.")

Do you know this old drinking song?

The Dutch Companee

Glo - ri-ous, glo - ri-ous, one keg of beer for the four of us...

At the end you have to write it out with triplets:

3
Drunk last night, drunk the night be-fore. Gon-na get drunk to -

3
3
3
night, if I nev-er get drunk an - y-more...

Note this triplet: 
3
plus
=

Incidentally, the same little bracket over some notes can be used for other rhythmic variation. A West African tune I know squeezes in five equal notes where four ordinarily go. So above the measure is the number 5: 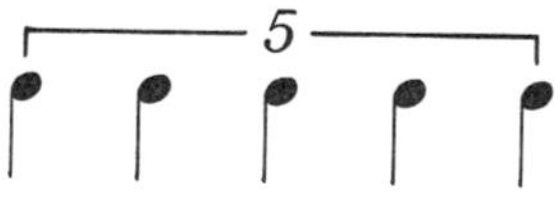
5

And in playing 6/8 time you may occasionally see two equal notes squeezed in where three are supposed to go. This could be written

 But it also could be written 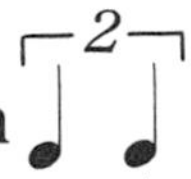 Both ways are correct. The two equal notes in either case equal 

All of this is to try and help your ear to hear a rhythm when your eye reads it. It's not easy. If there's any single tune you come to that you can't decipher, try the following procedure:

1. Take one measure at a time.
2. Slow it down, down, *down* till you can count out the rhythm slowly and evenly.
3. Count up or down till you are sure of the pitch of the note.
4. *Then* speed up to tempo.

The  below is just  speeded up.

Garry Owen

Irish Fiddle Tune

FROM NOW ON: Check time signature first (songs are still in either key of C or G). Answers on page 130.

1.

2.

3.

4.

3
3

5.

6.

7.

8.

9.

10.

11.

12.

13.

14.

15. This is too good to abbreviate:

16.

17.

Answers

1. "I'm Popeye the Sailor Man"
   Words and music by Sammy Lerner
2. "The Monkey Wrapped His Tail Around the Flag Pole" (Sousa)
3. "Summer Is A-Coming In" (Old English round)
4. "Here Comes the Bride" (Richard Wagner)
5. "A-Hunting We Will Go"
6. "Loch Lomond" (Scottish)
7. "Auprès de Ma Blonde" (Canadian)
8. "The Campbells Are Coming" (Scottish)
9. "Ring Around the Rosie"
10. "Alouette" (Canadian)
11. "Here We Go 'Round the Mulberry Bush"
12. "Tramp, Tramp, Tramp"
13. "Humoresuqe" (Anton Dvorak) ("Passengers will please refrain from flushing toilets while the train . . .")
14. "The Ball of Bellamuir" (Scottish)
15. "Jesu, Joy of Man's Desiring" (organ part by J. S. Bach)
16. "Haul on the Bowline, the Bowline HAUL!"
17. "My Bonnie Lies Over the Ocean"

Notes

Lesson 7

Rests—All of 'em

As I mentioned way back on page 25, there are times when the voice stops singing, but the rhythm continues. To fill in the gaps, rests are used. They come in all sizes:

a whole rest = 𝅝 (or a whole measure in any meter.)

a half rest = 𝅗𝅥

a quarter rest = ♩

an eighth rest = ♪

a sixteenth rest = 𝅘𝅥𝅯

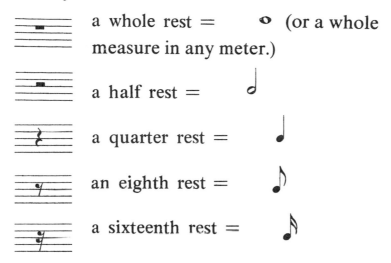

And any of them can be increased by fifty percent by a dot, thus 𝄽. = ♩ plus ♪ = 𝄽 plus 𝄾

(And if you want to get fancy, 𝄽.. = 𝄽 + 𝄾 + 𝄿)

Rests are essential in writing down some songs:

Pop Goes The Weasel

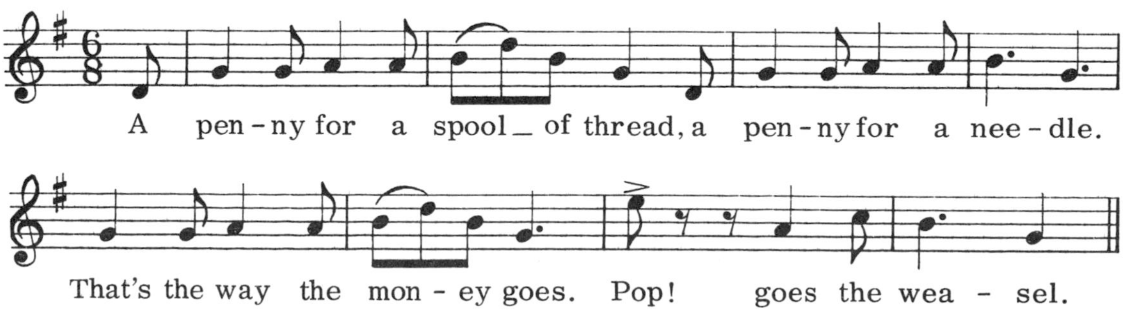
A pen - ny for a spool _ of thread, a pen - ny for a nee - dle.
That's the way the mon - ey goes. Pop! goes the wea - sel.

(I'm told this tune was originally French. This version must owe more to the London streeet singers of a few centuries ago. A weasel was a cobbler's tool.)

I wonder if any reader knows this 1830 hit song? Rests are used in the last line.

My Grandfather's Clock

By SAMUEL WOODWARD

My grand - fa-ther's clock was too large for the shelf, so it
stood nine-ty years in the hall.___ It was tall - er by
half than the old man him - self, Though it weighed not a
pen - ny-weight more.___ It was bought on the
morn of the day that he was born; It was al - ways his
pleas - ure and pride.___ But it stopped short,
nev-er to run a - gain when the old man died.___

Here's another song which has to be printed with rests:

Freiheit

by Paul Dessau

Die Hei - mat ist weit Doch wir sind be - reit Wir
kämpf - en und sieg - en für dich Frei - heit!

"The homeland is far, but we are ready. We fight and win for you—freedom!" It was the song of the bravest of the brave—German anti-fascists, who escaped from concentration camps but volunteered for the International Brigade in Spain, 1937, to try to keep fascism from taking over that country.

A number of songs I've given you already should have had rests, to help sing them right:

The Dutch Companee

Drunk last night, drunk the night be-fore, Gonna get drunk to-

Volga Boatmen

Ay - yukh - neh!

But no songbook bothers printing "Jingle Bells" this way:

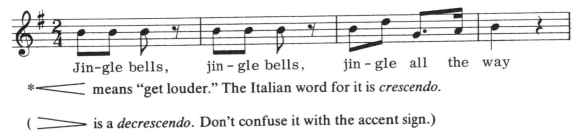

Jin-gle bells, jin - gle bells, jin - gle all the way

*< means "get louder." The Italian word for it is *crescendo.*

(> is a *decrescendo*. Don't confuse it with the accent sign.)

Colonel Bogey

(March from *River Kwai*)

K. J. ALFORD

A dot above or below a note means *staccato.* The note is sung crisply as if it were a short note with a short rest after it. See page 138.

And this:

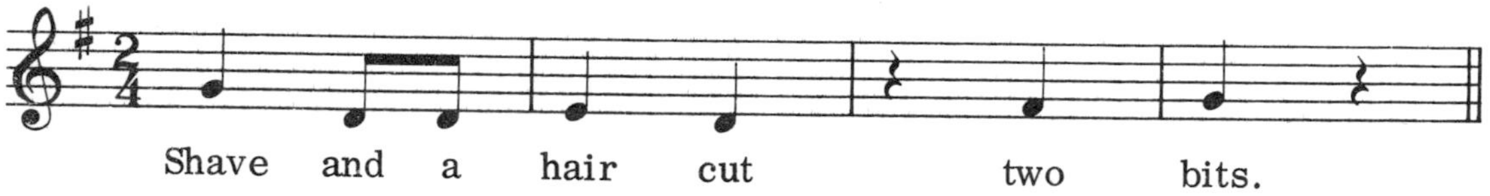
Shave and a hair cut two bits.

The Israeli tune the Weavers sang in 1950 had an important rest in the second measure:

Tzena, Tzena

Words by Mitchell Parrish,
Music by Issachar Myron and Julius Grossman

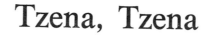

Tze-na, Tze-na, Tze-na, Tze-na, Tze-na, Tze-na, Tze-na,

The British army song quoted earlier needs rests to show the clipped, brisk feeling:

I've Got Sixpence

I've got six-pence, jol-ly, jol-ly six-pence. I've got six-pence to
last me all my life. I've got tup-pence to spend, and
tup-pence to lend, and tup-pence to send home to my
wife. (Poor wife) No cares have I to grieve_ me, no
pret-ty lit-tle girls to de-ceive_ me. I'm as hap-py as a...

(Happy? Oh, oh, oh what a lovely war . . .)

When a note is to be held out, and the rhythm stops, a *fermata* 𝄐 ("eyebrow") is sometimes put over it. Hymnbooks often use a comma sign to show you where to breathe, but they still use the 𝄐 for the last note.

Old Hundred

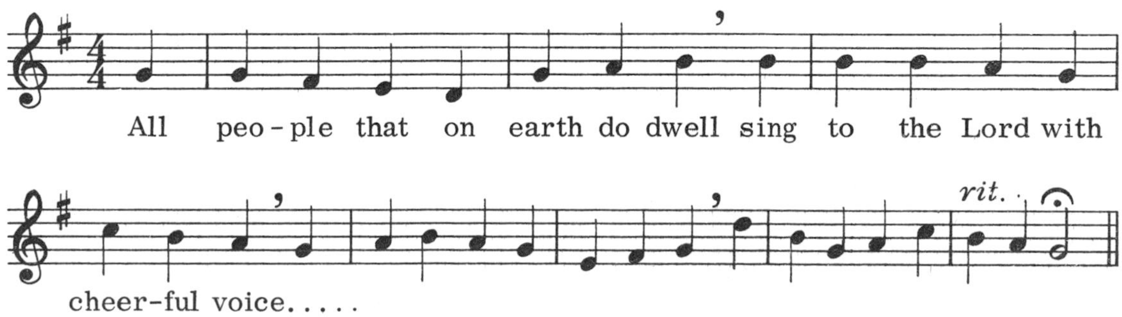
All peo-ple that on earth do dwell sing to the Lord with
cheer-ful voice.....
rit.

rit. stands for ritardando, the Italian way of spelling "slow down."

ADVICE TO SINGERS: Put in your own rests where you need 'em.

A reminder: Dots *under* or *over* a note indicate that it is to be sung or played *staccato*—that is, in a brief, sharp clipped-off way.

You all know this spooky phrase (what *is* the name of the melody? I suppose it's from some old opera.)

Those last four notes could have been written this way:

but it would have looked awful messy.

This short chapter is over. A quick review test.

Write in equivalent rests for all the below notes:

And a quick review of the following signs. If you don't know what they mean, look up the page mentioned.

And to see if you have really learned your rhythms, test your sense of rhythm now.

Here are a few tunes to test what you covered in this lesson. Answers on next page.

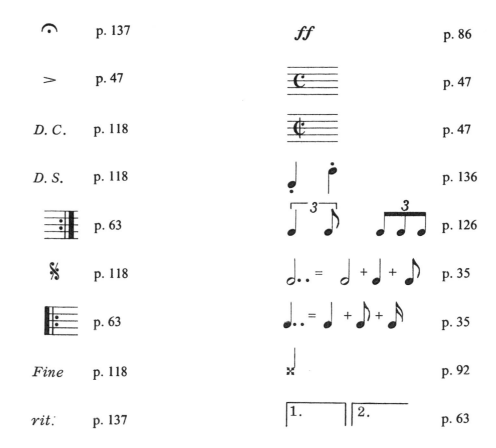

Problem now: Keep rhythm straight. Take rests into account.

1.

3

2.

3. And this version you may know:

4.

5.

6.

Clap!

7. Some hymns:

8.

9. But this is no hymn.

10.

11.

12.

Answer:

1. "Where Have All the Flowers Gone?"
   by Pete Seeger
2. "Londonderry Air"
3. "Tom Dooley"
   Words and music collected, adapted, and arranged by Frank Warner, John A. Lomax, and Alan Lomax.
4. Opening of Beethoven's Fifth Symphony.
5. "We Saw the Sea"
   by Irving Berlin
6. "Bright Shines the Moon" (Russian dance)
7. "Holy, Holy, Holy"
8. "Old Hundred"
9. "The E-ri-ee Was A-Rising"
10. "Oh, Watch the Stars"
    from *Exploring Music*, Book 1, Teacher's Edition, by Eunice Boardman and Beth Landis.
11. "A Mighty Fortress Is Our God"
12. "O God Our Help in Ages Past"

But you're not through with rhythm yet. I got a new kind of test for you. Turn the page.

See if you can identify the melodies below just from the rhythm. If you are stumped, look up the page mentioned. All songs have been given in previous lessons.

1. (p. 86)

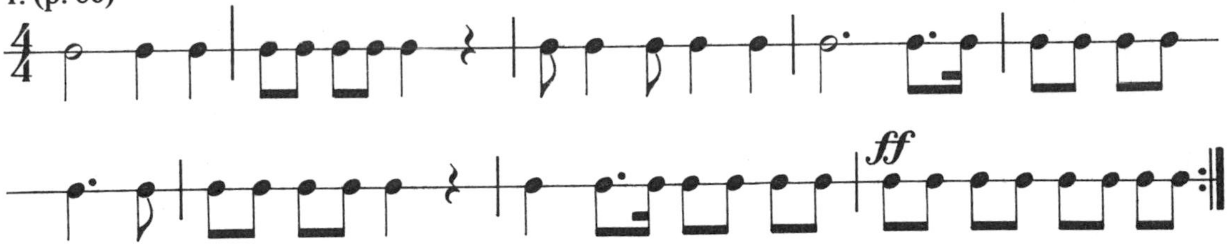
4/4
ff

2. (p. 83)

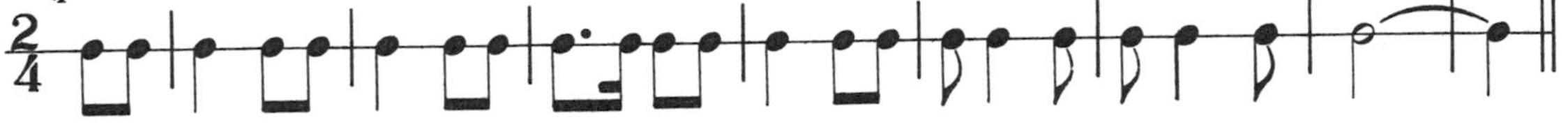
2/4

3. (p. 57)

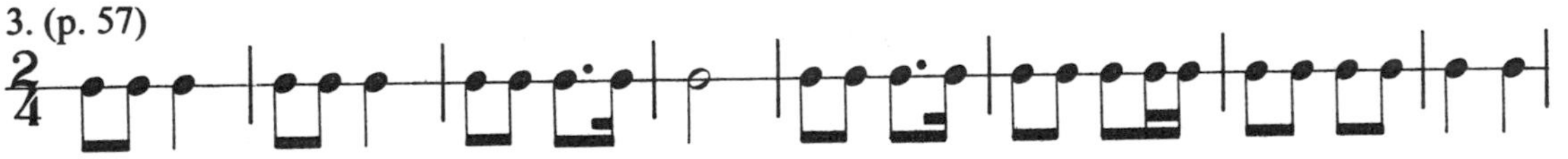
2/4

4. (p. 125)

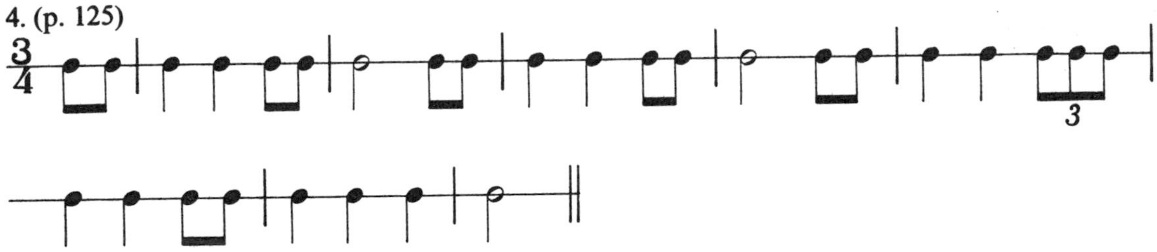
3/4
3

5. (p. 88)

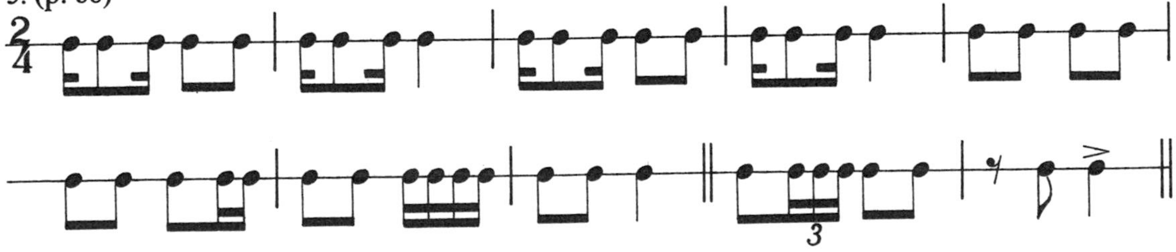
2/4
3

6. (p. 123)

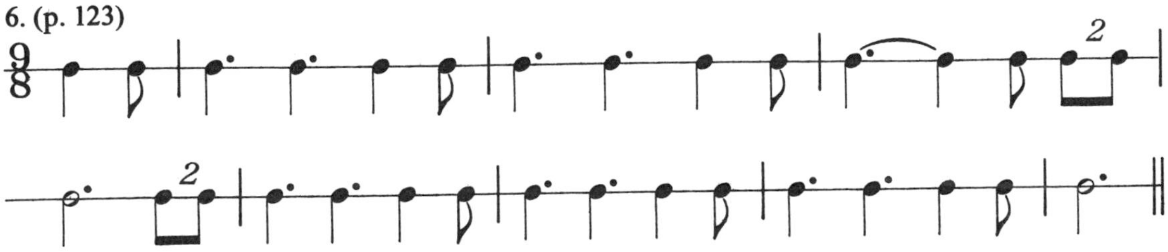
9/8
2
2

7. (p. 121)

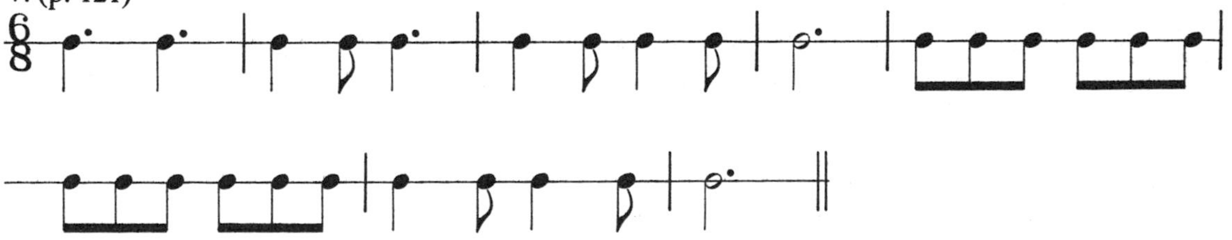

8. (p. 117)

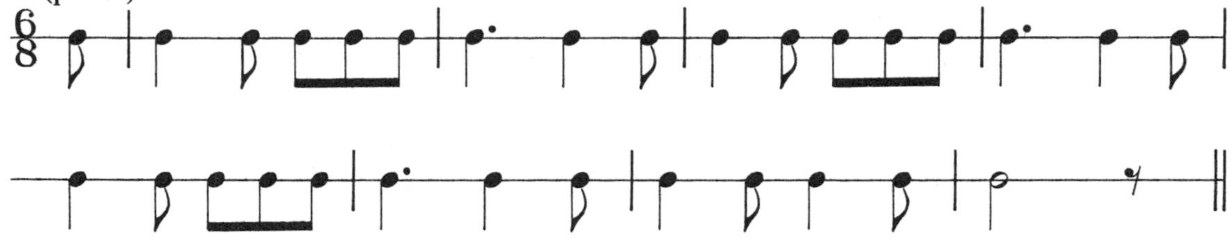

9. (p. 107)

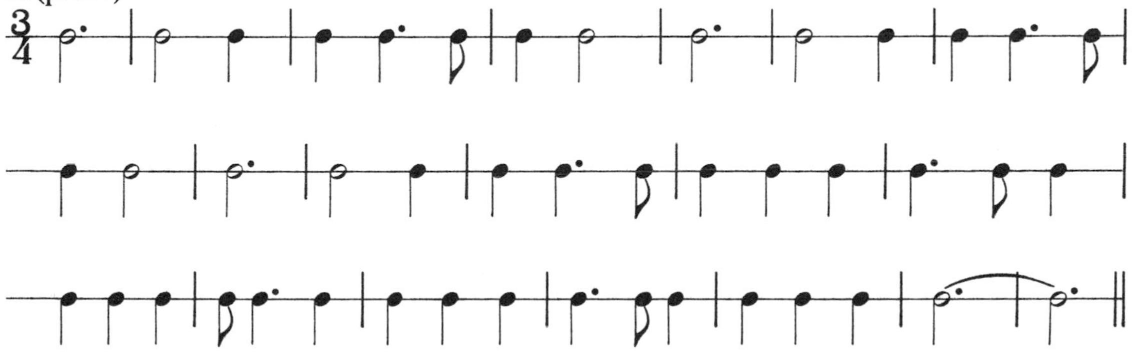

10. (p. 104)

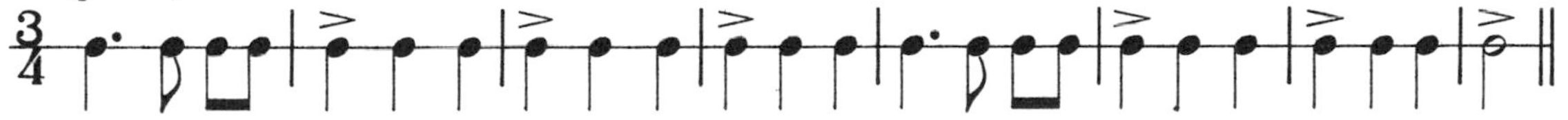

11. (p. 103)

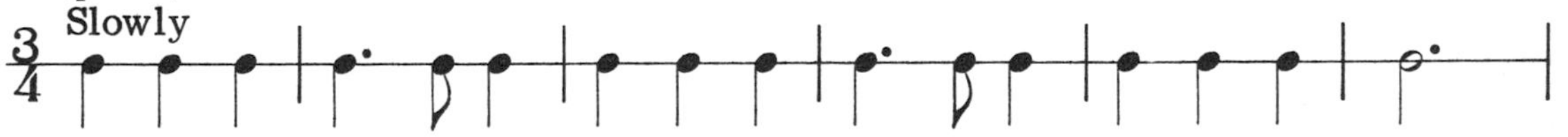
Slowly

12. (p. 136)

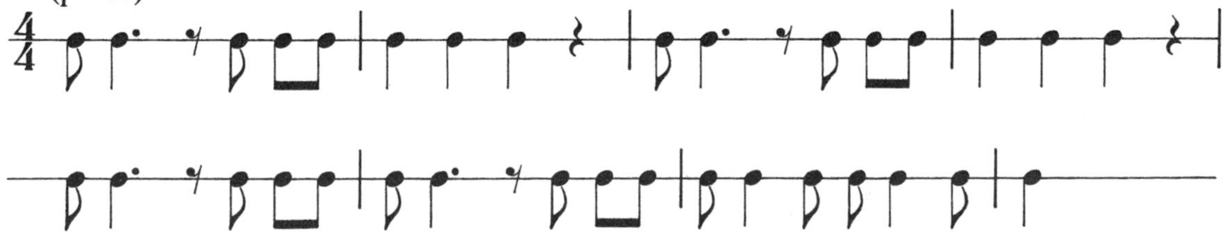

13. (p. 73)

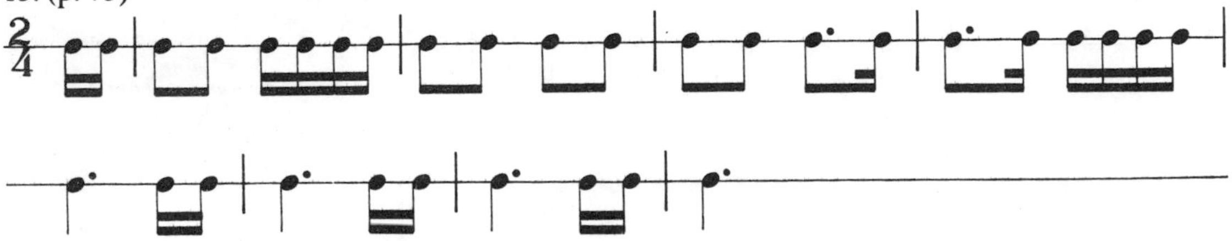

14. (p.41)

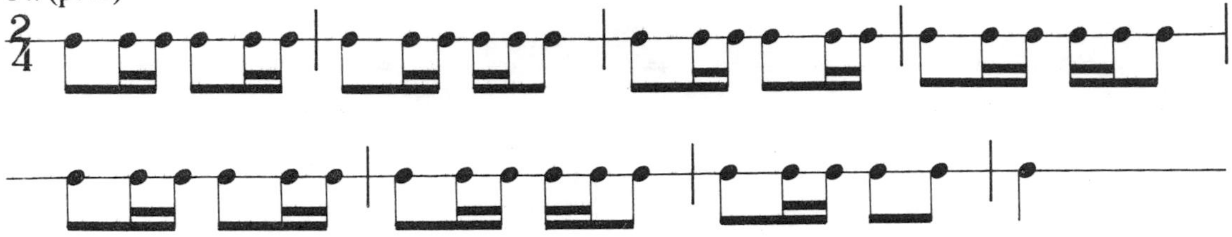

15. (p. 133)

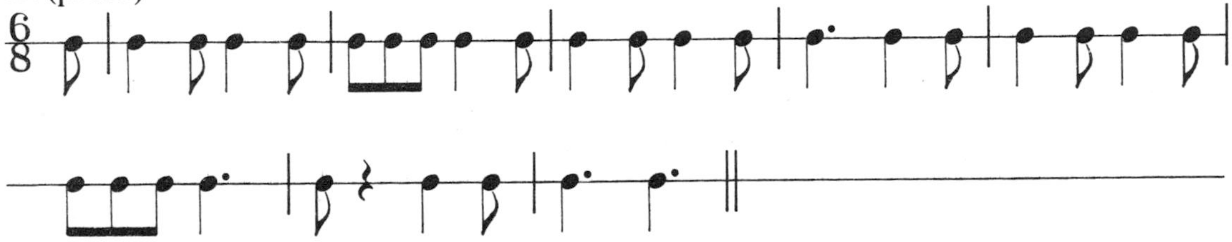

MORAL: KNOW YOUR RHYTHMS. WE START A WHOLE NEW SECTION NOW.

Notes

Lesson 8

Sharps, Flats, Naturals

Sing a scale "Do, re, mi, fa, sol, la, ti, do."

You probably never noticed that the notes of a scale are not all an equal distance apart.

Look at a piano. There are no black notes between E and F, or between B and C. There's something irregular here.

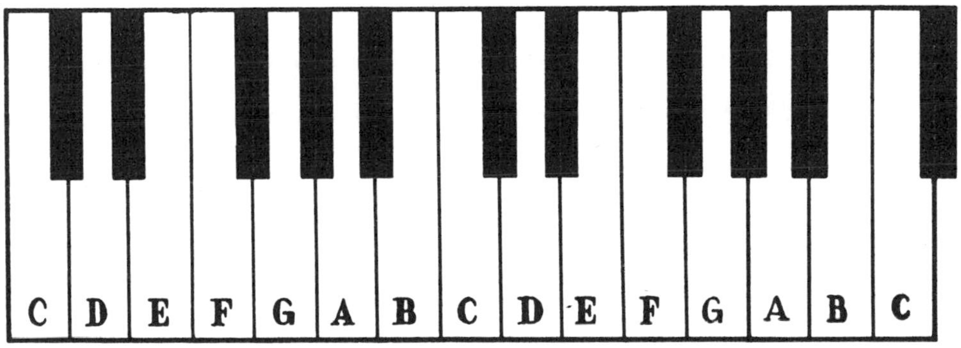
C D E F G A B C D E F G A B C

Play a scale on a guitar or any fretted instrument. You skip a fret between each note except between the third and fourth notes, and the seventh and eighth notes of the scale.

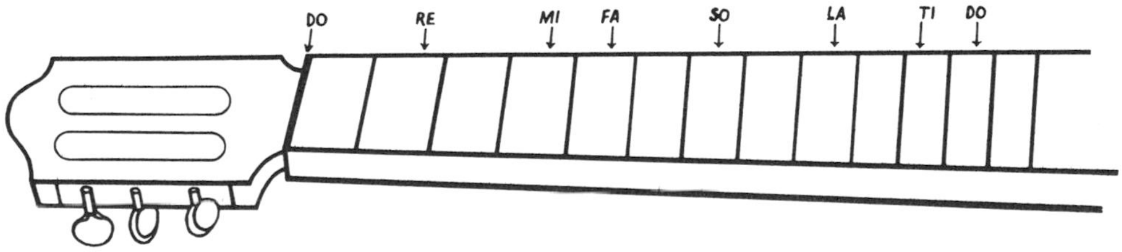
DO RE MI FA SO LA TI DO

Between "mi" and "fa" of any major scale there is only a *half step,* and likewise between "ti" and the top "do." Between the other notes of the scale is a whole tone.

Sing it.

On a five-line music staff, if you want to sing "one of the black notes" you put a *sharp* sign ♯ or a *flat* sign ♭ in front of the note. These sharps and flats are called *accidentals.* Don't ask me why. This whole system of music writing seems an accident to me.

♯ Raises the pitch a half step.

♭ Lowers it a half step.

And checking with a piano keyboard again, you'll see that

C♯  is the same as D♭ 

(At least this is true of pianos, guitars, etc. A concert violinist would disagree, and say that there is a hair's difference in pitch between C♯ and D♭.)

The easiest way to understand it all is to try a few tunes with sharps or flats in them.

ONWARD!

The tune "White Christmas" uses a half step on the syllable *Chris.* Check the notes with a ♯ sign in front of them, on some of the following melodies:

Kevin Barry

Author unknown, Dublin, 1920

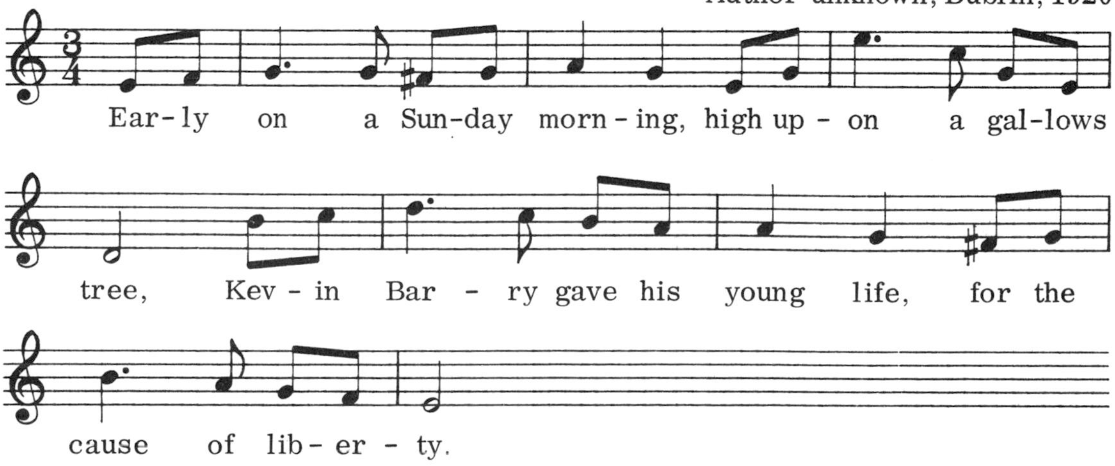
Ear-ly on a Sun-day morn-ing, high up-on a gal-lows
tree, Kev-in Bar-ry gave his young life, for the
cause of lib-er-ty.

Some Enchanted Evening

By RICHARD RODGERS
and OSCAR HAMMERSTEIN II

Beautiful Dreamer

by STEPHEN FOSTER

Beau - ti - ful dream - er, wake un - to me.

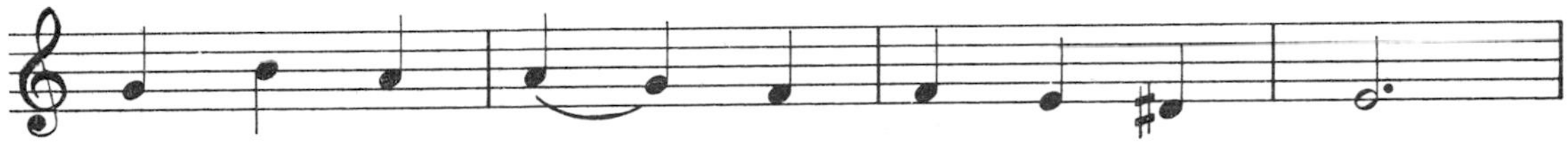

Moonlight Bay

Words by EDWARD MADDEN
Music by PERCY WENRICH

We were sail-ing a - long down moon-light bay,

THE RULE IS: The ♯ sign or ♭ sign applies only to the measure it is used in. The rest of the song uses notes as directed by the key signature at the beginning. See arrows.

Tarara Boomdeay

Ta-ra - ra boom-de-ay, Ta-ra-ra boom-de-ay

etc.

In the third measure, all three notes are sung sharp. In the fourth measure, the G is sung *natural.*

In A Shanty In Old Shanty Town

by LITTLE JACK LITTLE, JOE YOUNG and JOHN SIRAS

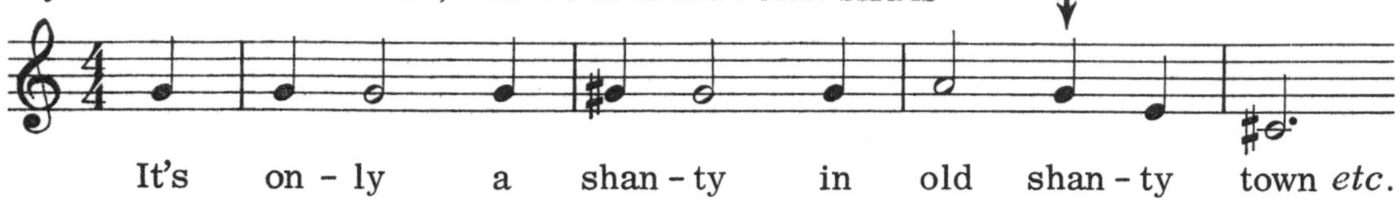
It's on - ly a shan - ty in old shan - ty town *etc.*

For easier reading, though, a natural sign ♮ is sometimes put in the following measure.

Wedding March

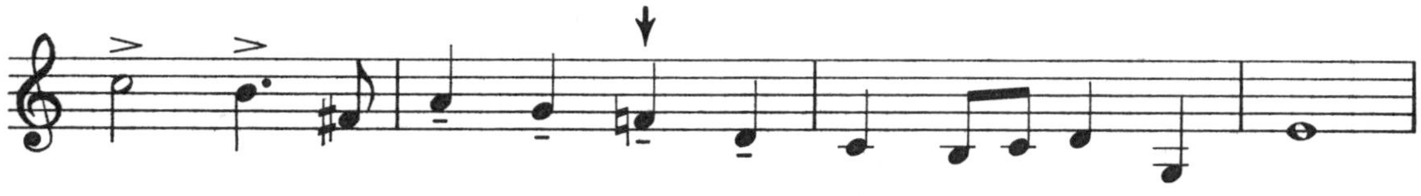

I won't bother arrowing notes from now on.

Get Up And Go

Words collected and adapted and set to original music by Pete Seeger

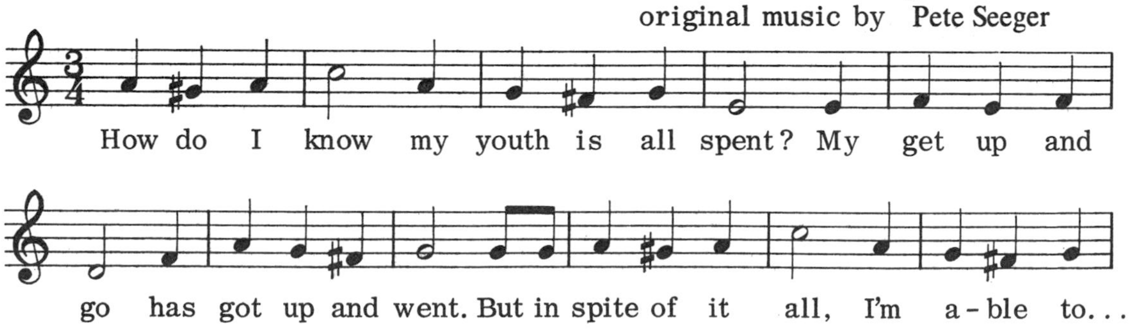
How do I know my youth is all spent? My get up and
go has got up and went. But in spite of it all, I'm a - ble to. . .

Anybody remember this old Calypso song?

Sly Mongoose

By LIONEL BELASCO

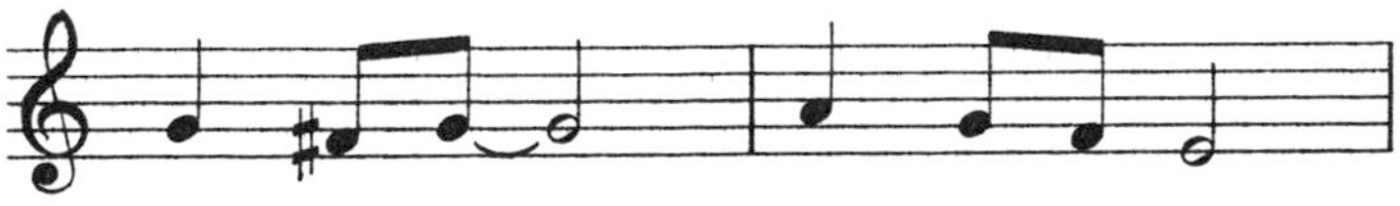

But if you revert to the "natural" pitch of a note within the same measure, you *have* to put the natural sign before it. If it's in another measure, it still helps. Remember the song, "Down by the Old Mill Stream?"

by TELL TAYLOR

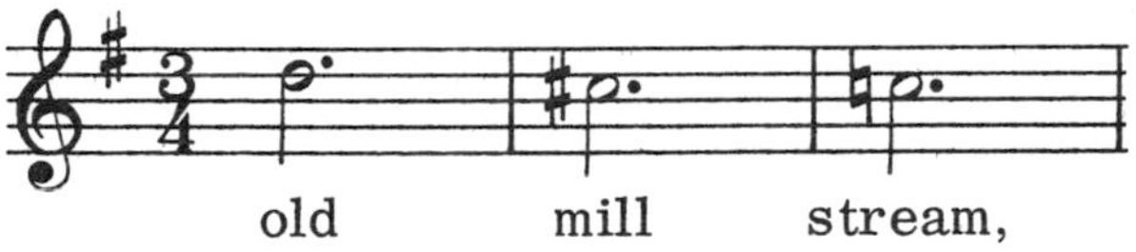
old
mill
stream,

Ci-ri-ci-ri-bin

"Chi-ri-chi-ri-bin,"

Because this can get to look a little messy, they usually try to avoid it by using another line, and the alternate accidental sign. See two ways, below, of writing the same line.

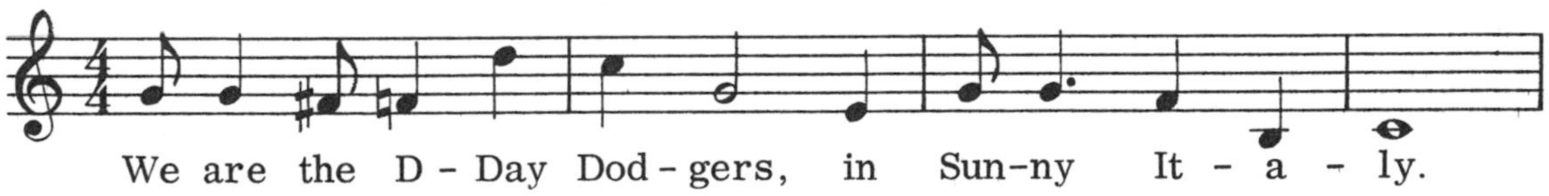
We are the D - Day Dod - gers, in Sun-ny It - a - ly.

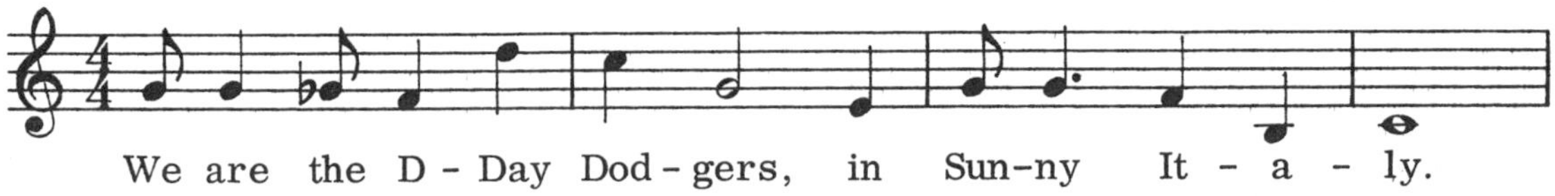
We are the D - Day Dod - gers, in Sun-ny It - a - ly.

There's an interesting history to this song. The melody was once:

Lilli Marlene

Music by NORBET SCHULTZE
German words by HANS LEIP
English words by TOMMIE CONNOR

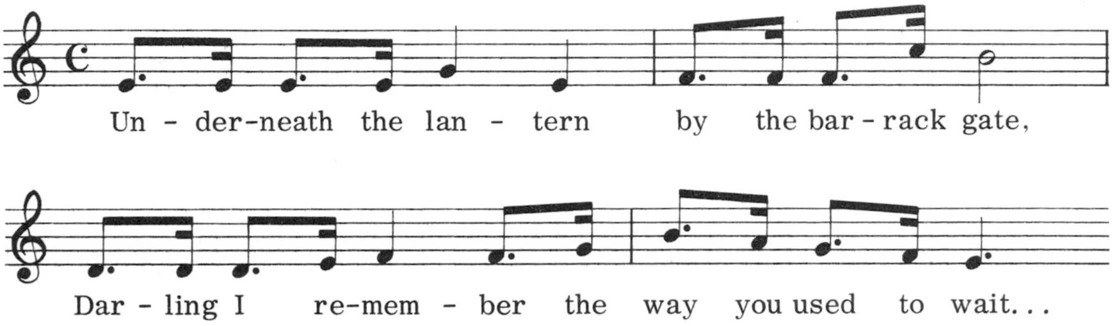
Un - der-neath the lan - tern by the bar - rack gate,
Dar - ling I re-mem - ber the way you used to wait...

Now compare this:

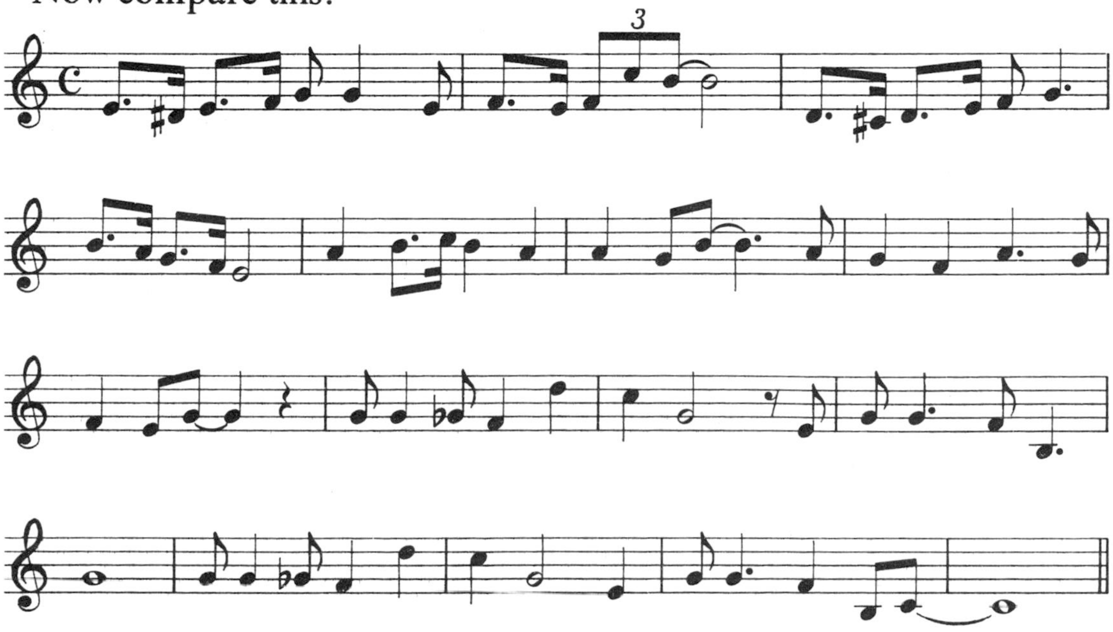
3

This is, of course, nothing but a folk variant of "Lilli Marlene," the famous song written and well copyrighted in Germany, 1940. The English soldiers in Italy, 1944, captured it and made it serve for one of the greatest soldier songs.

Here's all the words. It seems that Lady Astor had made a speech in Parliament, "Now our boys are needed on the Normandy beach-head. What are those D-Day Dodgers doing, loafing down in Italy?"

We're the D-Day Dodgers, 'way off in Italy,
Always on the vino, always on the spree.
Eighth Army scroungers and our tanks,
We live in Rome, among the Yanks.
We are the D-Day Dodgers, in Sunny Italy.
We are the D-Day Dodgers, in Sunny Italy.

We landed at Salerno, a holiday with pay;
The Jerries brought the bands out to greet
us on the way
Showed us the sights and gave us tea,
We all sang songs, the beer was free
To welcome the D-Day Dodgers to Sunny Italy
To welcome the D-Day Dodgers to Sunny Italy.

On the way to Florence, we had a lovely time.
We ran a bus to Rimini, right through the
Gothic Line.
Anzio and Sangro were just names.
We only went there to look for dames.
The artful D-Day Dodgers, in Sunny Italy
The artful D-Day Dodgers, in Sunny Italy

Dear Lady Astor, you think you know a lot
Standing on a platform and talking Tommyrot
You're England's sweetheart and her pride.
We think your mouth's too bleeding wide
    That's from your D-Day Dodgers, in Sunny Italy
    That's from your D-Day Dodgers, in Sunny Italy

Look around the mountains in the mud and rain.
You'll find the scattered crosses,
  there's some which have no name.
Heartbreak and toil and pain all gone—
The boys beneath them slumber on.
    Those are the D-Day Dodgers, who'll stay in Italy
    Those are the D-Day Dodgers, who'll stay in Italy

Words composed by Hamish Henderson, Scots poet and foremost folklorist. If you ever get paid $ for singing the song, send some $ to him, 27 George Square, Edinburgh, Scotland. He needs 'em for collecting Scottish folklore and food and beer along the way.

I said way back in Lesson 1 that you'd learn why a sharp sign is put near the 𝄞 when you write a song in the key of G. Maybe now you know. Look at that piano keyboard again. Play a G scale:

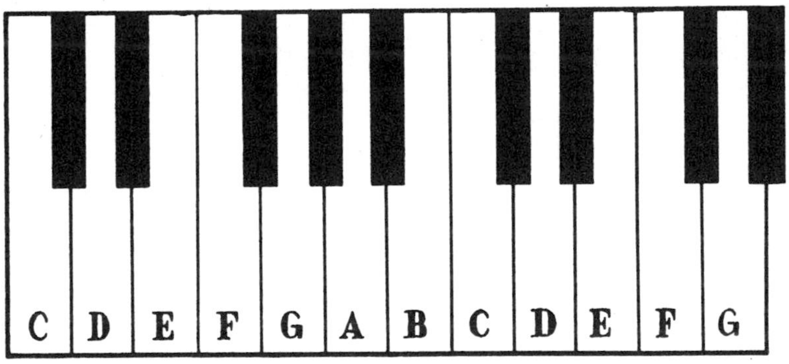
C
D
E
F
G
A
B
C
D
E
F
G

Between "ti" and "do" there's supposed to be only a half step, so you sharpen all F's throughout the song. At the left of each staff is that 

And now if you want to lower "ti" a half tone in the key of G, you put a "natural" sign ♮ in front of the note. In subsequent measures the pitch reverts to the F♯ the song normally had throughout. See arrows.

There'll Come A Time

By MALVINA REYNOLDS

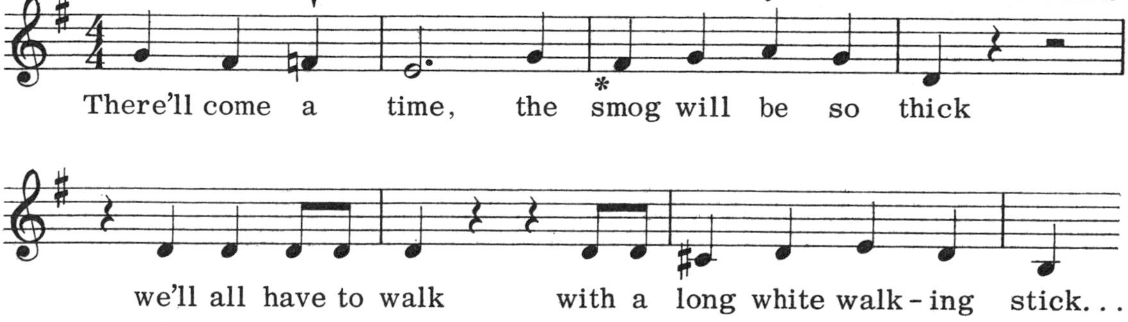
There'll come a time, the smog will be so thick
we'll all have to walk with a long white walk-ing stick...

Little Buttercup

by SIR ARTHUR A. SULLIVAN

If the same two songs were written in the key of C, a B ♭ would be written, where F ♮ was used when singing in G. See arrows.

There'll Come A Time

by MALVINA REYNOLDS

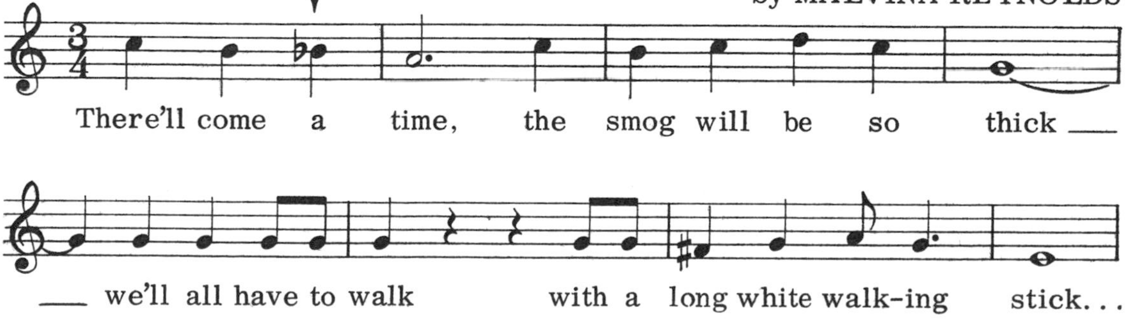
There'll come a time, the smog will be so thick
we'll all have to walk with a long white walk-ing stick...

*This note is F♯ as directed by the key signature.

If you want to know all of this song and more good ones too, send $ to the author, Malvina Reynolds, 2027 Parker Street, Berkeley 4, California. She's one of the best songwriters in the U.S. but a lot of her songs are too hot for the airwaves. Truly, one of America's most remarkable and wonderful people.

Little Buttercup

by SIR ARTHUR A. SULLIVAN

Be thankful you're not studying the music of some Eastern country where the songs go in for quarter-tone intervals, not just half tones. India, Arabia. Great music. Hell to write down.

Get your ear used to distinguishing between a flatted seventh note of the scale, and the usual kind. See arrows below:

Oh, What A Beautiful Morning

By RICHARD RODGERS
and OSCAR HAMMERSTEIN II

(B natural)

Some songs use a flatted seventh throughout. If you want to get fancy about it, this scale is called the *Mixolydian Mode.* That is, a major scale with a flatted seventh.

Old Joe Clarke

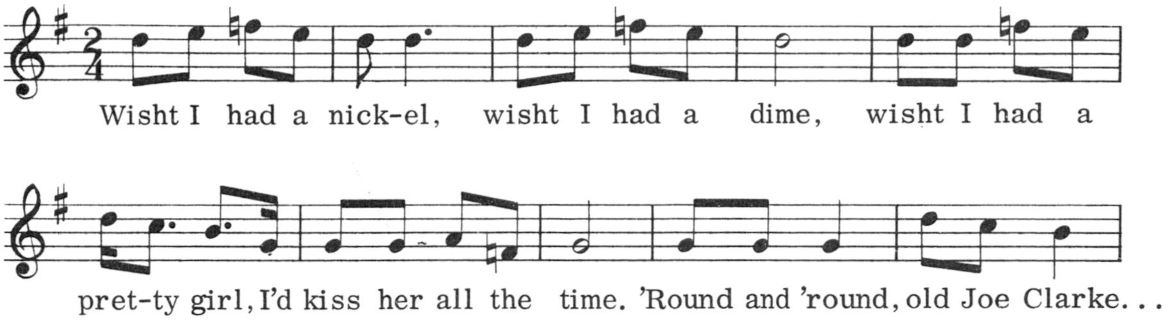
Wisht I had a nick-el, wisht I had a dime, wisht I had a
pret-ty girl, I'd kiss her all the time. 'Round and 'round, old Joe Clarke...

Wasn't That A Time

By LEE HAYS
and WALTER LOWENFELS

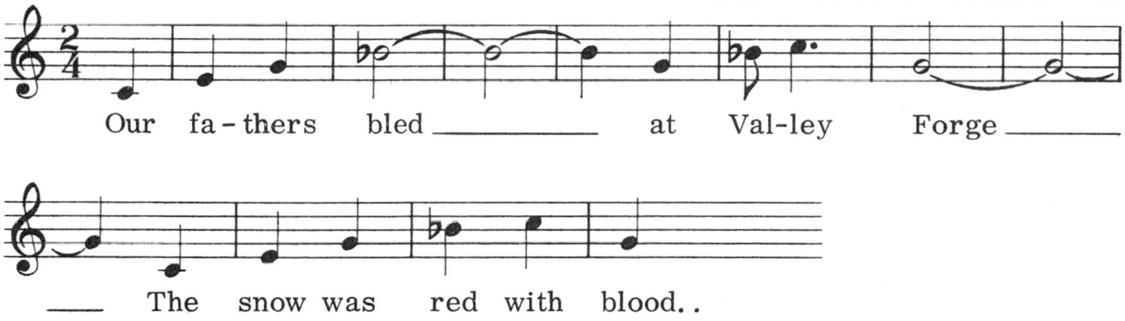
Our fa-thers bled ___ at Val-ley Forge ___
___ The snow was red with blood..

Back Water Blues

Words and Music by
BESSIE SMITH

Well it rained five days ___ and the wind be-gin ___ to blow ___ *etc.*

More quizzes! B♯!
(Answers on next page)

1.

2.

3.

4.

5.

6.

7.

Watch it now: Barbershop harmony. Above is the melody, below the harmony.

8.

Answers

1. "Won't You Come Home Bill Bailey"
2. "(The Wreck of the) *John B.*"
   Words and music adapted by Lee Hays from a collection by Carl Sandburg
3. "The Old Gray Mare She Ain't What She Used to Be"
4. "Stars and Stripes Forever" (Sousa)
5. "We Shall Not Be Moved"
6. "Oh, Mary Don't You Weep"
7. "Gee But I Want to Go Home"

   (5–7:) First cousin melodies (You'll see if you sing 'em through.)
8. "Sweet Adeline"
9. "Glowworm"
10. "Where Is Little Maggie?"
11. Melody by James H. Waters for the ballad, "The Great Silkie" and also used for the poem "I Come and Stand at Every Door" by Nazim Hikmet.
12. "Sailing, Sailing, Over the Bounding Main"

To close off this lesson check with yourself that your ear can distinguish all these different notes we've been talking about.

If you have a musical instrument around the house which can play two notes at once, (piano, accordion, guitar, xylophone, etc.), try to devise some tests for your ear. Perhaps a friend can help.

The idea is to play two notes at once, and tell what the interval between them is.

It's easy to tell a unison—two notes of the same pitch.

And it's easy to tell when notes are one octave apart:

But can your ear tell you whether two notes are a whole note apart—or a half tone apart?

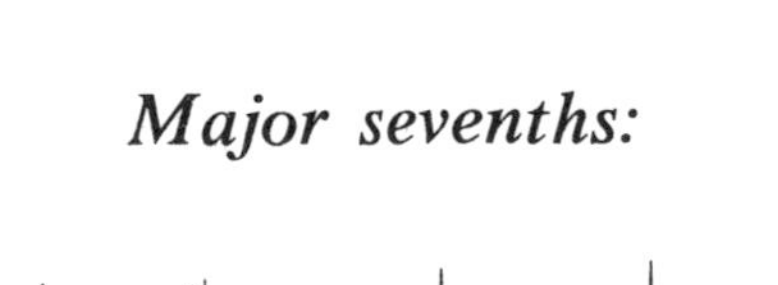

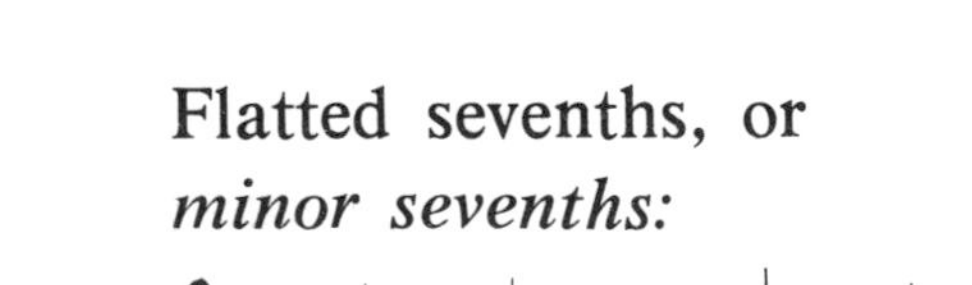

Using the last few songs to help you, can you tell the difference between the two kinds of *sevenths?*

Major sevenths:

Flatted sevenths, or *minor sevenths:*

If you're not sure, go over page 140 again.

Make sure your ear can tell which is a *Major third:*

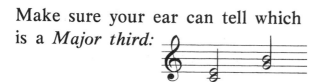

—and which is a flatted third, or *minor third*

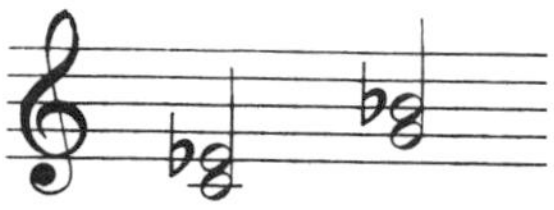

Then play a whole bunch of thirds all over the place, high and low, and have your ear tell you if they are major thirds or minor thirds.

Then see if you can do the same thing with major sixths and minor sixths.

If you are in doubt whether an interval is a minor sixth or not, start singing the opening two notes of the following two songs. If it fits the first, it's a major sixth. If it fits the second, it's a minor sixth.

My wild I - rish rose___

When Is - rael was in E - gypt land

Major sixths:

minor sixths:

While you're about it, make sure you can tell the difference between a fourth and a fifth. It's not as easy as you think. In reading a strange song off a piece of paper, you want to be able to tell which is which.

(Your eye has it. Does your ear? Measure it on a guitar string. Sound two notes at once. Keep testing yourself till you're used to it.)

Hope you're not confused by all this. We ain't seen nothing yet. In the next lesson we take up songs in minor.

Minor scales always have the third note of the scale a half tone lower than in a major scale and may or may not have a lowered sixth, or lowered seventh.

Notes

Lesson 9

Songs in Minor

You'll find, if you check a piano keyboard, that you can play a minor scale all on the white notes, if you start on A.

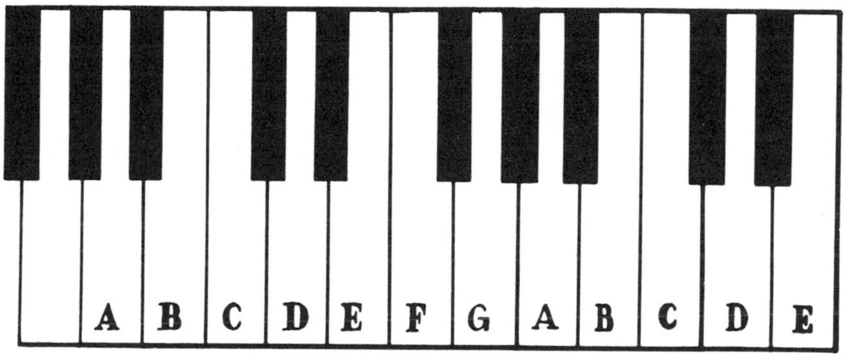
A B C D E F G A B C D E

And you can play an E minor scale by using only one black note, an F♯. On a guitar, this kind of minor scale would look like this:

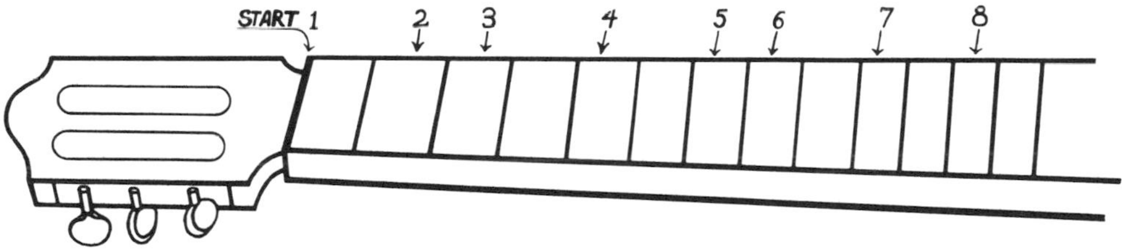
START 1
2
3
4
5
6
7
8

So without using any new key signature, you can now read some songs in A minor and E minor.

That spooky theme I mentioned on page 138 was actually in E minor.

And perhaps you noticed it already—the "Volga Boatmen" is minor.

Ay___ ukh - nyem! Ay___ ukh - nyem!
(I don't know the Russian words here but it don't matter.)

Who knows this next one?

Hey Ho, Nobody's At Home

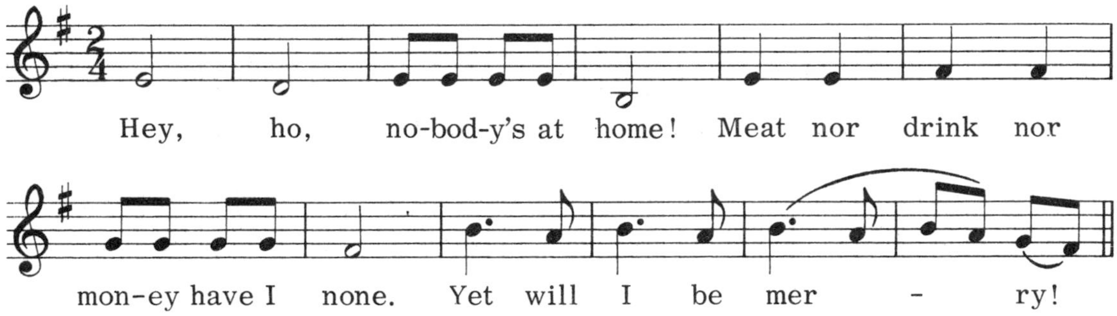
Hey, ho, no-bod-y's at home! Meat nor drink nor
mon-ey have I none. Yet will I be mer - ry!

And who doesn't know the next one?

When Johnny Comes Marching Home

by PATRICK GILMORE

When John-ny comes march-ing home a-gain, hur - rah,___ hur-
rah!___ We'll give him a heart - y wel - come then, hur -

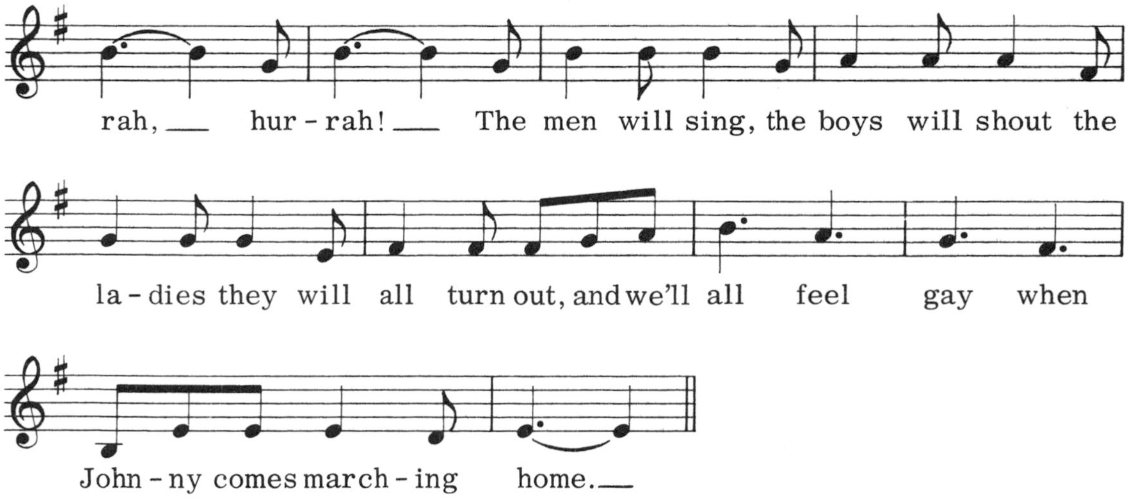
rah, hur-rah! The men will sing, the boys will shout the
la-dies they will all turn out, and we'll all feel gay when
John-ny comes march-ing home.

(But maybe you didn't know that only the words were composed in 1870. The tune is ancient Irish. Some know it as "Johnny Fill Up the Bowl," others as "Johnny I Hardly Knew Ya.")

And this:

God Rest Ye Merry, Gentlemen

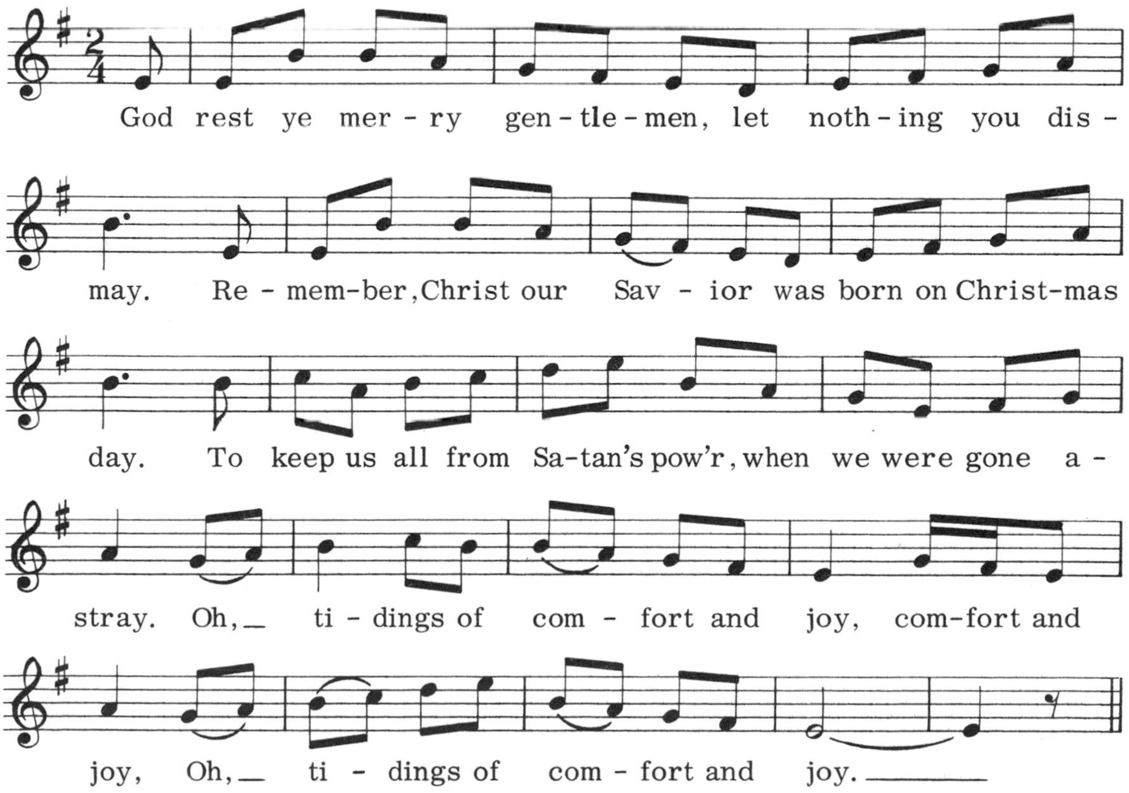
God rest ye mer-ry gen-tle-men, let noth-ing you dis-
may. Re-mem-ber, Christ our Sav-ior was born on Christ-mas
day. To keep us all from Sa-tan's pow'r, when we were gone a-
stray. Oh, ti-dings of com-fort and joy, com-fort and
joy, Oh, ti-dings of com-fort and joy.

Next a useful tune, if you ever find yourself with a small baby in your arms. The words were composed by some black mother, whose own child lay unattended in the slave cabins, while she had to work in the big house.

All The Pretty Little Horses

Collected, adapted, and arranged by
JOHN A. LOMAX and ALAN LOMAX

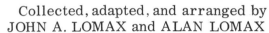

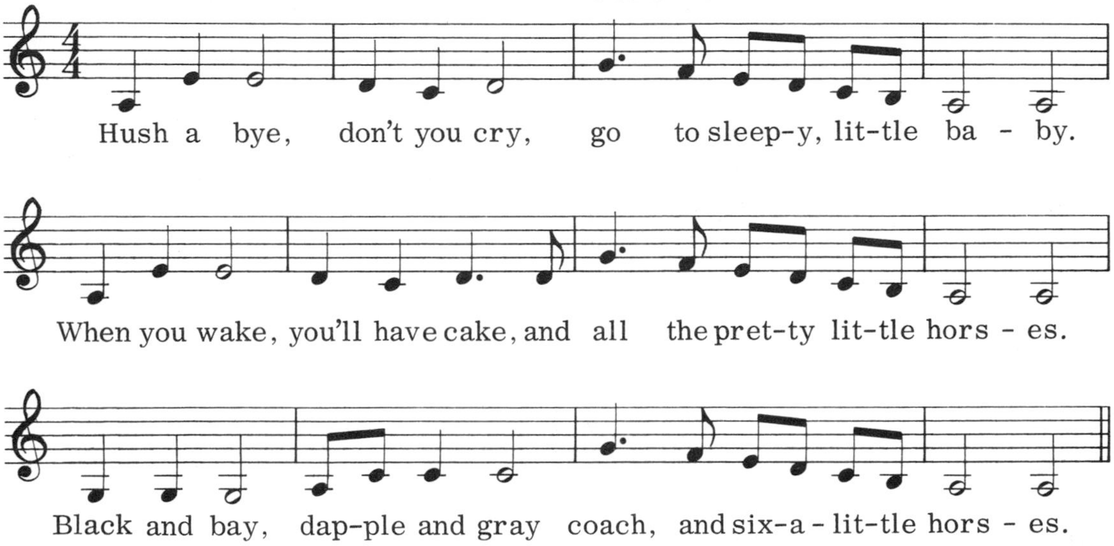
Hush a bye, don't you cry, go to sleep-y, lit-tle ba - by.
When you wake, you'll have cake, and all the pret-ty lit-tle hors - es.
Black and bay, dap-ple and gray coach, and six-a - lit-tle hors - es.

Way down yonder, down in the meadow
There's a poor little lambie,
The bees and the butterflies pecking on its eyes
And the poor little thing cries "mammy."

NOTE: In all these new tunes I trust you check, as always, the time signature, rhythm, and the key—and where "do, re, mi" is.

Every European country has its minor tunes. Ireland's got some of the best:

Fillimeeooreay

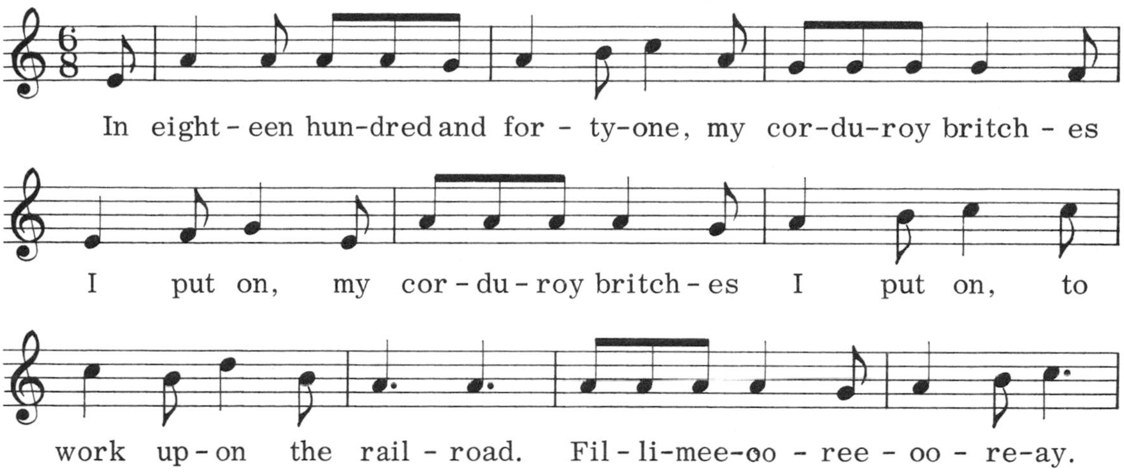
In eight - een hun-dred and for - ty-one, my cor-du-roy britch - es
I put on, my cor - du - roy britch - es I put on, to
work up - on the rail - road. Fil - li-mee-oo - ree - oo - re-ay.

And an Irish fiddle tune I learned thirty years ago, but missed the name when we were introduced, and I've been ashamed to ask since:

*Repeat four times.

Russia has some great minor melodies. (This one has Yiddish verses—actually collected in New York, by Ruth Rubin.)

Tumbalalaika

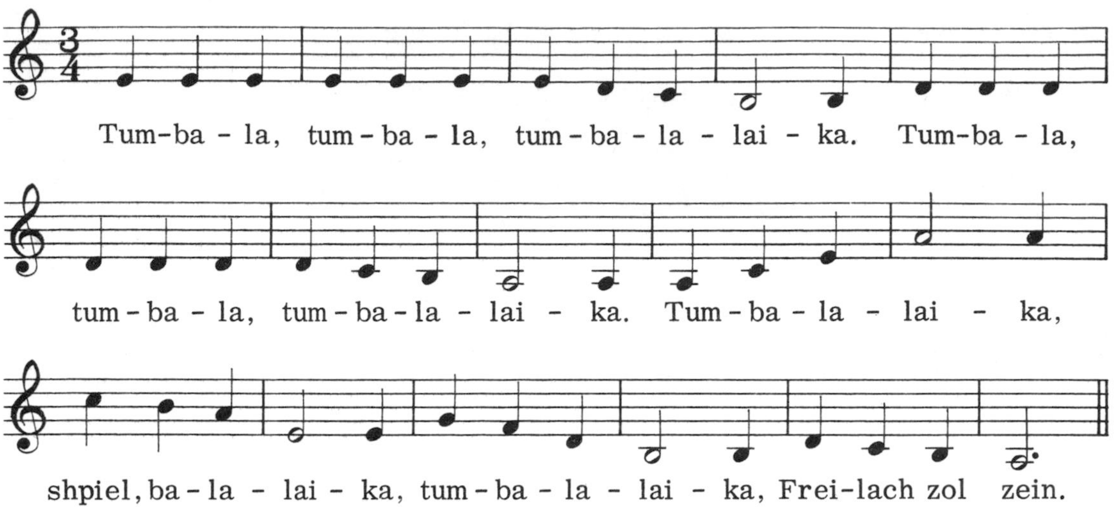
Tum-ba - la, tum - ba - la, tum - ba - la - lai - ka. Tum-ba - la,
tum - ba - la, tum - ba - la - lai - ka. Tum - ba - la - lai - ka,
shpiel, ba - la - lai - ka, tum - ba - la - lai - ka, Frei-lach zol zein.

This Eastern European minor melody is now the national anthem of Israel.

Hatikva

I have to admit, the first words I heard to this were street verses from New York's Lower East Side:

When I was a little girl I didn't know what to do,
Sat on a door step lacing up my shoe.
Now I am a big girl I don't know what to do,
I have so many children, I don't know what to do.
  One cries, mama, gimme a piece of bread,
  One cries, mama, tuck me into bed,
  Six or seven others, all to be clothed and fed,
  Papa comes home with a broken head.

One of the confusing things now is that there are several kinds of minor scales. The tunes you've just read have mostly used the *natural* minor, or *Aeolian Mode*. If you sing a minor scale, but raise the sixth (in a major scale), you have a different kind of minor scale.

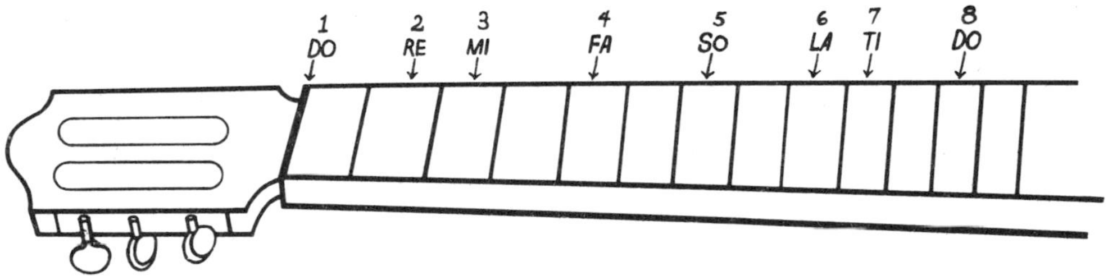
1 DO
2 RE
3 MI
4 FA
5 SO
6 LA
7 TI
8 DO

In case anyone ever tells you a song is in the *Dorian Mode,* this is what it is. The version of "Greensleeves" most people know starts off in the Dorian mode:

A - las, my love, you do me wrong, To

A number of classic old British ballads were sung to tunes in the Dorian mode.

When a song is in a Dorian minor, nevertheless the key signature usually stays the same. The sixth note of the scale has to be sharpened each time you come to it.

Henry Martin

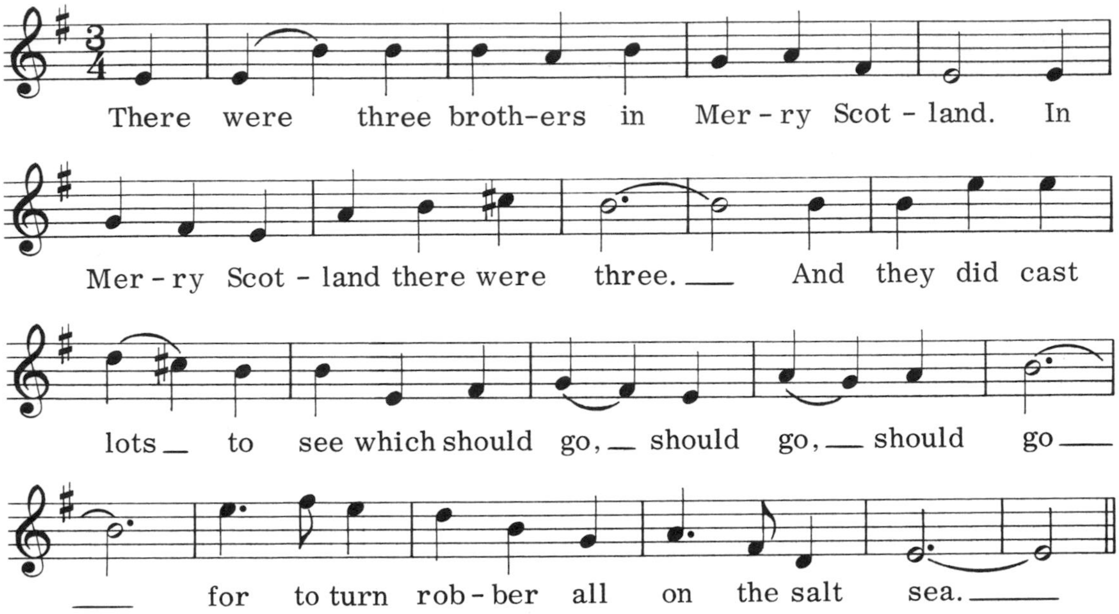
There were three broth-ers in Mer-ry Scot-land. In
Mer-ry Scot-land there were three. And they did cast
lots to see which should go, should go, should go
for to turn rob-ber all on the salt sea.

And one of America's most startling hymns uses this kind of minor. It was composed in the mid-nineteenth century by a preacher who thought he was about to die. He didn't, at that time, though, and lived to see his hymn become quite popular.

O Lovely Appearance of Death

Oh love-ly ap-pear-ance of death, no
sight up-on earth is so fair, Not all the gay
*

*Yes, you can place a *hold* over a rest as well as over a note.

pag-eants that breathe can with a dead_ bod-y com-pare.
In___ sol-emn de-light I sur-vey the
corpse when the_ spir-it is fled.__ In___ love with the
beau-ti-ful clay, and long-ing to_ lie in it's stead.

Now, if you raise the seventh note of a minor scale, but keep the lowered sixth (and of course lowered third), you get what's called the *harmonic minor.*

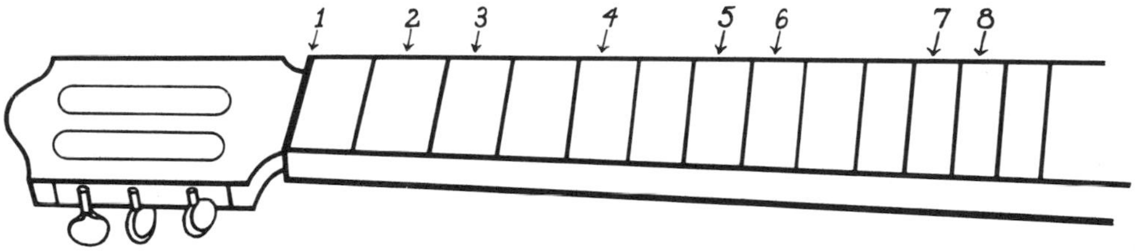
1
2
3
4
5
6
7
8

Some Eastern European melodies use this kind of minor scale. Here's one of the world's most beautiful lullabies.

Rozhinkes Mit Mandeln

(Raisins with Almonds)

by ABRAHAM GOLDFADEN

Un-ter yi-de-les vi-ge-le.___ Shteyt a

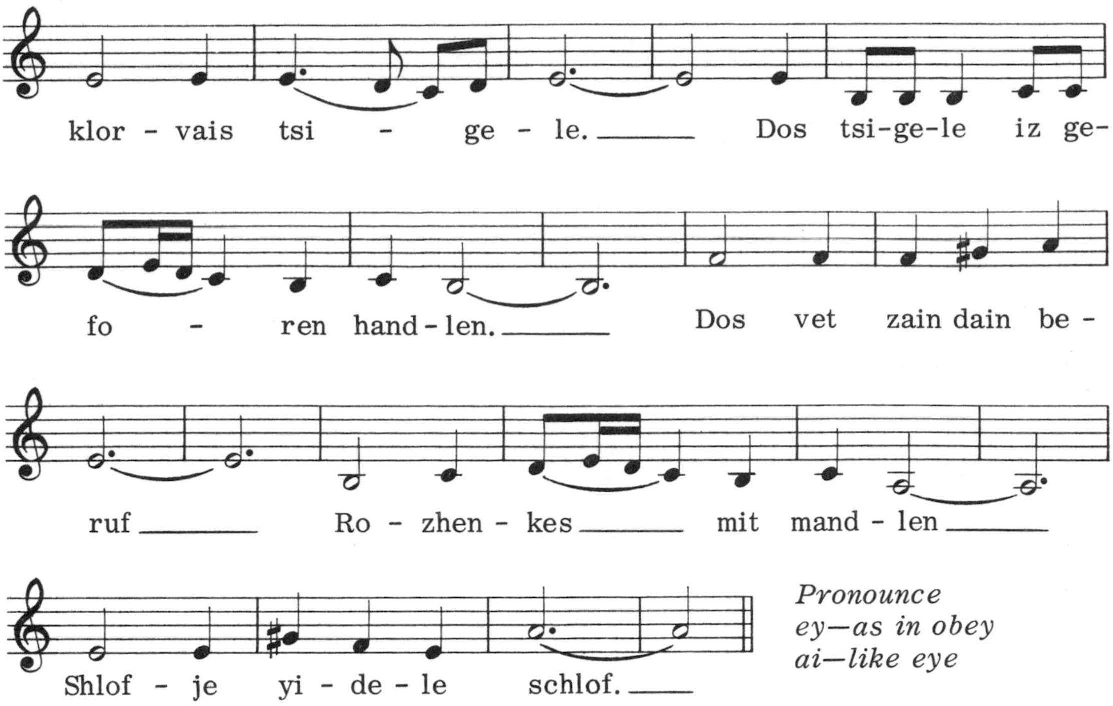
klor - vais tsi - ge - le. Dos tsi-ge-le iz ge-
fo - ren hand - len. Dos vet zain dain be -
ruf Ro - zhen - kes mit mand - len
Shlof - je yi - de - le schlof.

Pronounce
ey—as in obey
ai—like eye

Translation: Behind little Judah's cradle
Stands a pure white kid,
The kid went off to trade,
That will be your calling,
Raisins and almonds,
Sleep, little Judah, sleep.

In the third from last measure you can hear that harmonic minor. The next few songs use it too, though it's not so obvious.

Yes My Darling Daughter

By JACK LAWRENCE

Members of Local 65, Warehouse Union, in New York, in the early 1940's, used to sing this one—union lyrics to an old tune, of course.

He's A Fool

Once I was walk-ing down Thir-ty-fifth Street, I ran
in-to a guy who looked dead on his feet. He wore no green
but-ton, nor smile on his face, kept push-ing a truck 'round and
get-ting no place. He's a fool, he's a fool,
he's a fool for not join-ing the un-ion.

He worked every night till eight-thirty
Then he asked if he could leave
The boss gave a look that was dirty
Or else he just laughed up his sleeve,
his sleeve, yeah!

(repeat chorus)

He cried like a baby, a union he craved.
He wanted a minimum from which he could save.
He joined "Sixty Five," boy, did the boss rave,
"That's what I get for being so good to my slave."

He's no fool, he's no fool,
For he upped and he joined with the union. (twice)

So don't trust your boss, he's just good
on the surface.
Join "Sixty-Five" for a life with a purpose.
You will have happiness, gayness galore.
So brothers and sisters, give out with a roar.

Be no fool, be no fool,
Come on and join with our union. (twice)

by anonymous members of Local 65, N.Y.C. 1940

Zandunga

Ai, Zan-dun-ga que! Zan-dun-ga pla-ta,
ma-dre de Dios! Zan-dun-ga tu a-mor me
ma-ta. Cie-lo de mi co-ra-zon.

(Hey, isn't that a great melody? One of the world's greatest. From Mexico.)

Three songs in A minor which use flatted sixths and sevenths at some times, at other times not.

Charlie Is My Darling

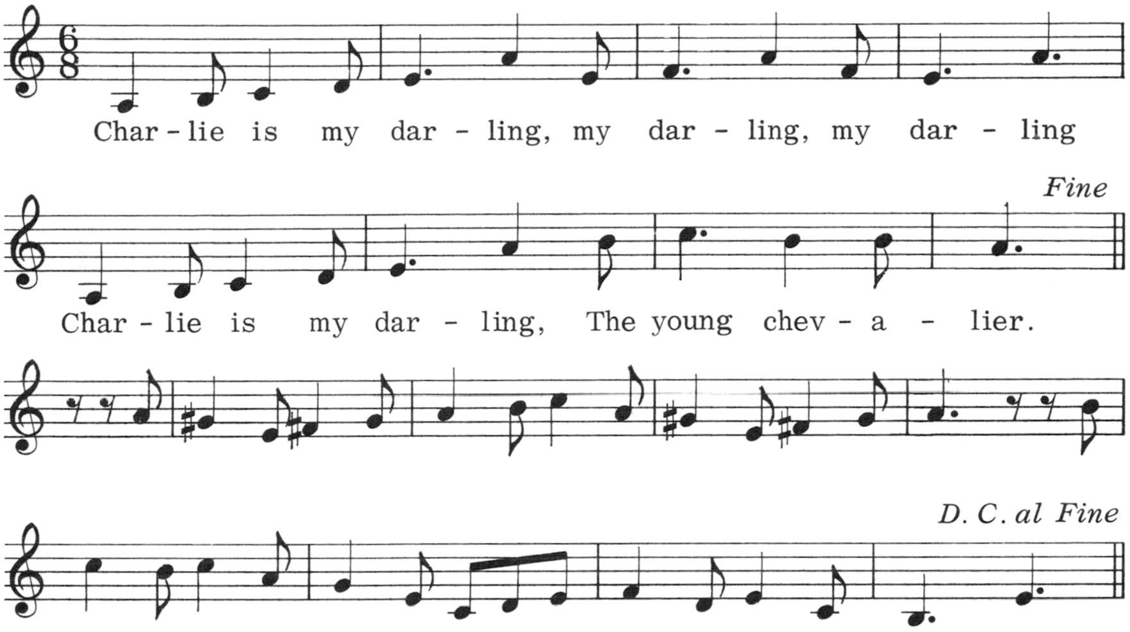
Char - lie is my dar - ling, my dar - ling, my dar - ling
Fine
Char - lie is my dar - ling, The young chev - a - lier.
D. C. al Fine

Moscow Nights

by V. SOLOVIEV-SEDOY
and M. MATUSOVSKY

Viva La Quince Brigada

Adapted and arranged by
BART VAN DER SCHELLING

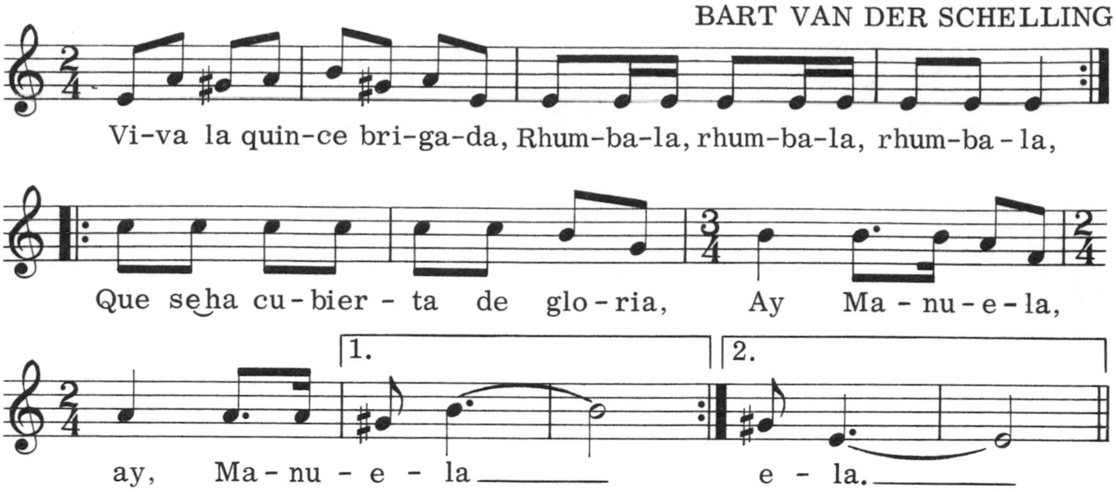
Vi-va la quin-ce bri-ga-da, Rhum-ba-la, rhum-ba-la, rhum-ba-la,
Que se ha cu-bier-ta de glo-ria, Ay Ma-nu-e-la,
1. 2.
ay, Ma-nu-e-la e-la.

In actual practice, as you see, a lot of minor songs use *both* lowered *and* raised sixth and seventh notes of the scale, at various times in the melody. Take good old "Greensleeves":

Greensleeves

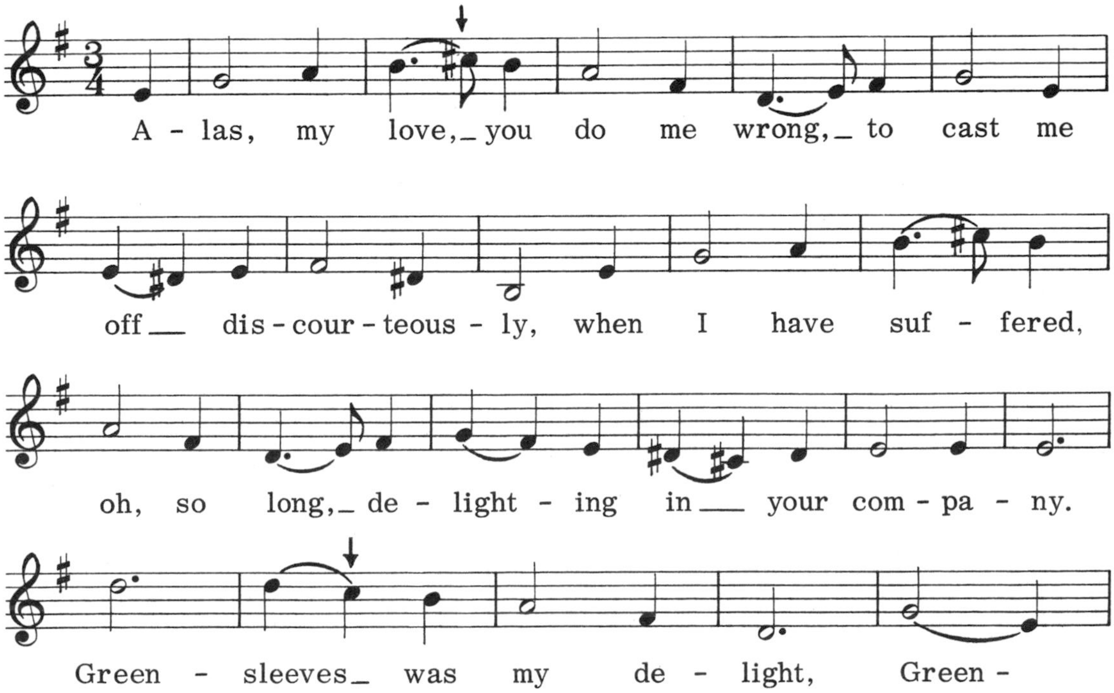
A-las, my love, you do me wrong, to cast me
off dis-cour-teous-ly, when I have suf-fered,
oh, so long, de-light-ing in your com-pa-ny.
Green-sleeves was my de-light, Green-

sleeves _ was all my joy. Green - sleeves was my
heart of gold, _ and who but my La - dy Green - sleeves.

So far, you've tried songs in A minor or E minor. If a song was written in C minor, you'd find three flats (the "key signature") next to the G-clef sign at the left end of each staff. Try writing the melody of "Greensleeves" below in C minor. I'll start it off for you.

3
4
*
A - las, my love, _ you do me wrong, to cast me
off dis - cour - teous - ly, when I have suf - fered,
oh, so long, de - light - ing in your com - pa - ny.
Green - sleeves was my de - light, Green -
sleeves was all my joy. Green - sleeves was my
heart of gold, and who but my La - dy Green - sleeves.

*This note as written now, is an A♭. You decide if you want to make it A♮ or not.

(Hardest job in the world, isn't it?—making up your own mind.)

Here's another in C minor—this time the seventh note of the scale is not flatted. The *harmonic* minor scale.

Thou Poor Bird

Thou poor bird, mournst this tree where
thou_ didst_ war-ble in thy wan-d'rings free

This one, with its flatted seventh and sixth, doesn't even need a flatted third to be sung as a *natural minor.* It's actually a *pentatonic* (five-note) scale.

Which Side Are You On?

Words by FLORENCE REECE
Music: Traditional

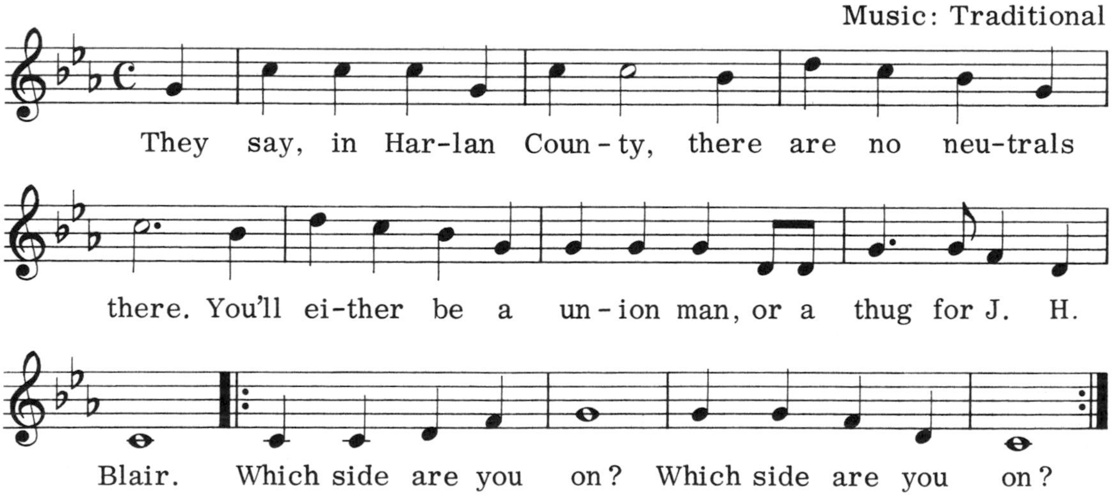
They say, in Har-lan Coun-ty, there are no neu-trals
there. You'll ei-ther be a un-ion man, or a thug for J. H.
Blair. Which side are you on? Which side are you on?

(Irrelevant aside: A friend of mine once worked on an advertising campaign for a brassière firm. Their slogan was: "Don't B♯, Don't B♭, B♮!")

An old hymn with a different pentatonic minor scale:

Wayfaring Stranger

I'm just a poor ___ way - far - ing stran - ger, ___
___ a - trav'l - ling through ___ this world of woe. ___
___ But there's no sick - ness, toil nor dan - ger ___
___ in that bright land ___ to which I go. ___ I'm go - ing
there ___ to meet my fa - ther. ___ I'm go - ing there ___
___ no more to roam. ___ I'm just a - go - ing o - ver
Jor - dan. ___ I'm just a - go - ing o - ver home. ___

More typically, this song has at one time a flatted seventh and another time a raised seventh:

House Of The Rising Sun

Adaptation of words and music by LEE HAYS
RONNIE GILBERT and FRED HELLERMAN

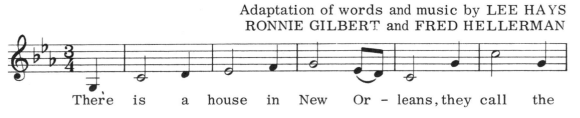

There is a house in New Or - leans, they call the

Ris - ing Sun._____ It's been the ru - in of
man-y poor girl, and me, O God,_ I'm one._____

Now you've become acquainted with songs in C minor, try a song in G minor. The key signature has two flats.

The F♮ already represents a flatted lowered seventh in the G minor scale.
When you need an F♯, just write it in:

Johnny Has Gone For A Soldier

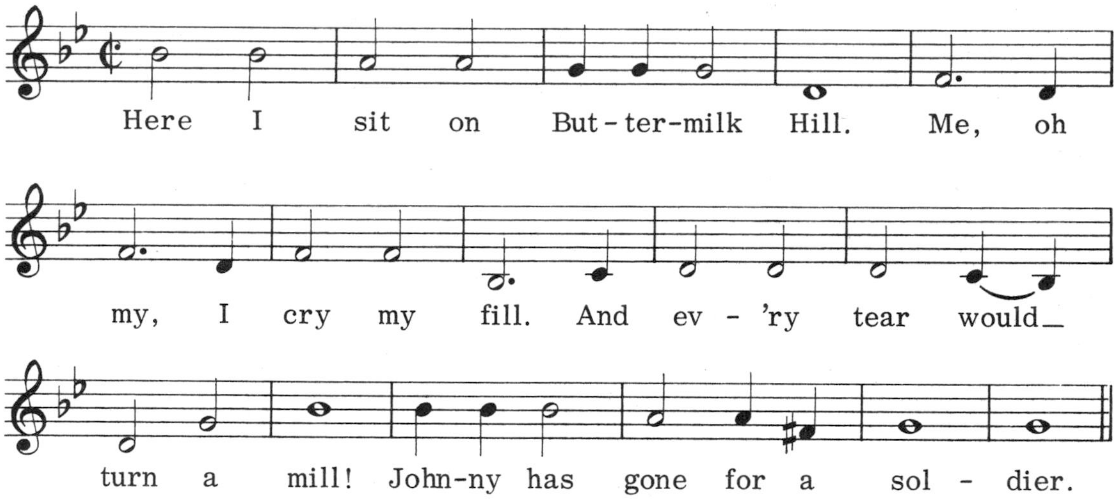
Here I sit on But - ter-milk Hill. Me, oh
my, I cry my fill. And ev - 'ry tear would_
turn a mill! John-ny has gone for a sol - dier.

Bei Mir Bist Du Schön

JACOBS-SECUNDA-CAHN-CHAPLIN

You've had two tough long chapters. Hope you've not got indigestion from too much at once. To summarize:

1. Get your ear to recognize a half step as different from a whole step.

We were sail-ing a - long
down Moon-light
Bay

Get to recognize a lowered, flatted, or natural seventh (page 156).

2. Get your ear to recognize the difference between the ordinary major scale, and a minor scale, with the third a half tone lower.

3. Get your ear to recognize when the sixth of the scale is lowered also, and when not. And the seventh.

4. When looking at a strange song in a book, sometimes you can tell it's in minor by looking at the guitar chords, but if it hasn't got these you can deduce it from the key signature. If the last note of the song is on E, and the left hand of the staff looks like this  (one sharp) you can guess it's probably E minor.

Likewise:

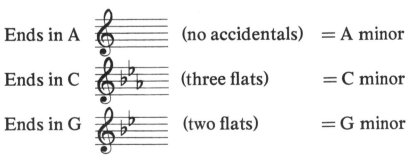

Ends in A  (no accidentals) = A minor

Ends in C  (three flats) = C minor

Ends in G  (two flats) = G minor

Of course,. there are exceptions to this rule—so—

Here's a postscript

When it comes to blues, notes are often sung in such a way that it's impossible to write them down exactly. The voice is in motion when the words come out. The accompaniment will be in major, but the ear seems to hear a minor third sung. For example, the opening note of "St. Louis Blues" (the word "I") has this kind of slur.

Often a little extra note called a "grace note" is used to indicate where the voice slurs from or slurs to.

Far - ther a - long

Grace notes carry no time value. They are just tacked on where needed.

The third of the scale is a favorite to slur. Take this southern square dance tune. It might be written—and would probably be sung—like this: (But no one would have the patience to read it.)

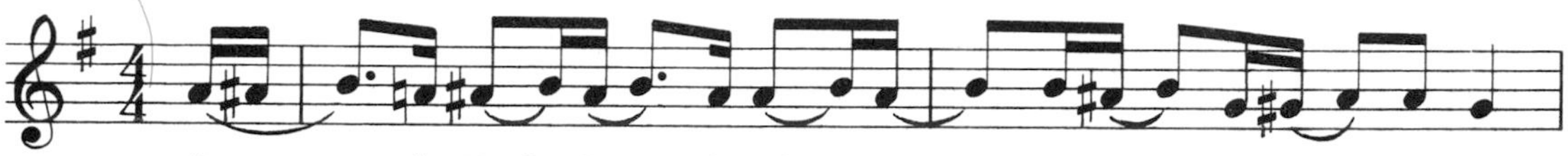
I - da Red,_I - da Blue,_I ___ got stuck_on I - da too.

Besides the third note of the scale, the seventh is also a favorite for slurring. In singing "Old Joe Clark" over the years, I came to feel that the pitch of the note as written was something the voice skidded up to, as on skis, but rarely started or stayed on.

Think of the notes in a songbook as the bare skeleton of a melody. The voice has to change them to bring them to life. But this is why you have to know the idiom of the song. Otherwise you're like someone trying to learn a foreign language out of a book.

In reading a song, you must know the idiom a song is in, before you can tell how it's supposed to sound.

A batch of minor tunes now for you to identify. They are in four different keys:

A minor

G minor

E minor

C minor

(Answers page 187.)

1.

2.

3.

4.

5.

6. One from Brazil:

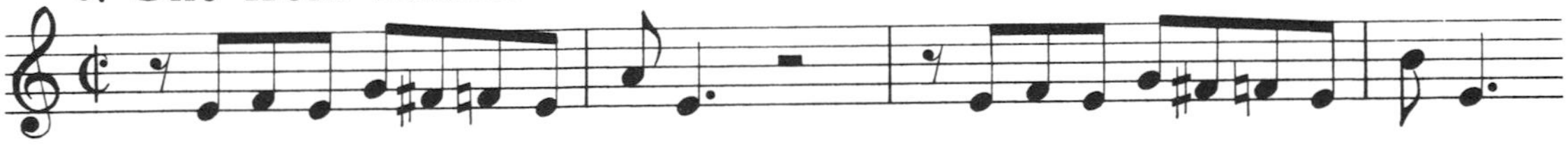

7. Some from Russia:

8.

9.

10. Some from the Irish:

11.

12. (Chorus only)

13.

14.

15.

And three by John Jacob Niles, one of America's greatest melody writers:

16.

17.

18.

Answers

1. "What Shall We Do with the Drunken Sailor?"
2. "Black Girl"
   Words and music by Huddie Ledbetter
3. "Peat Bog Soldiers"
   Words by Johann Esser and Wolfgang Langhoff,
   music by Rudi Goguel
4. "Go Down Moses"
5. Theme from *Carmen* (Bizet)
6. "Carioca"
   Music by Vincent Youmans, words by Gus Kahn and Edward Eliscu
7. "Two Guitars"
8. "Ochi Tchorniya" ("Dark Eyes")
9. "Khorobushka" ("The Peddler")
10. "Blue Mt. Lake" (Adirondack ballad)
11. "My Name is Mick McGuire"
12. "And Drill Ye Tarriers, Drill; Drill Ye Tarriers, Drill!"
13. Sicilian "Tarantella" (one of many)
14. "Hava Nagila"
15. "I Wonder As I Wander," by John Jacob Niles,
    from "Songs of the Hill Folk"
16. "Lulloo Lullay," by John Jacob Niles,
    from "Ten Christmas Carols from the Southern Appalachian Mountains"
17. "Black Is the Color," by John Jacob Niles,
    from "More Songs of the Hill Folk"
18. When I was a kid, we knew this as "Oy Oy Musseltov."
    Darned if I know what kind of minor scale you'd call
    this. A Serbian minor? Tchaikovsky uses it in "March Slav."
    Play this on your guitar.

If you want to get the complete words and music to some song which you've seen on these pages, I suggest you haunt your local music store or library. Church libraries have hymns; the SPEBQUSA* has barbershop harmony books. Oak Publications and *Sing Out!* magazine (both at 33 West 60th Street, New York, New York) have all kindsa folk songs, and *Broadside* magazine (215 West 98th Street, New York, New York), the protesty ones. The publishers listed as copyright owners are mostly in New York City too; you can write to them for sheet music.

(Society for the Preservation and Encouragement of Barbershop Quartet Singing in America, Inc. (6315 3rd Avenue, Kenosha, Wisconsin).

Notes

Lesson 10

Songs in All Keys

I told you in the very beginning of this book that you could sing a song in any key, high or low. If you play a chromatic scale (all consecutive notes, black and white, on a piano), you have twelve tones.

C C♯ D D♯ E F F♯ G G♯ A A♯ B C

Same notes; five of them named differently:

C B B♭ A A♭ G G♭ F E E♭ D D♭ C

Since you can start a scale on any one of those notes, you can play a song in any of twelve keys of our well-tempered clavichord—piano to you. (If you want to sing in the cracks between the keys, I guess you can do that too, but I don't know a convenient way of writing it down.)

Most guitar players like to play in C and four "sharp" keys—G, D, A, and E. And in A minor, E minor (one sharp), and D minor (one flat). So a lot of songbooks nowadays print songs in these keys. You already know the key signatures for C major and A minor, and G major and E minor (one ♯ on the top line, F.)

Because one major key and one minor key both share the same key signature, one is said to be a *relative* of the other. Thus C is the *relative major* of A minor. D minor is the *relative minor* of F major. And so on. Note that all of them are a major third apart.

Key signature for D (and B minor) is two sharps: 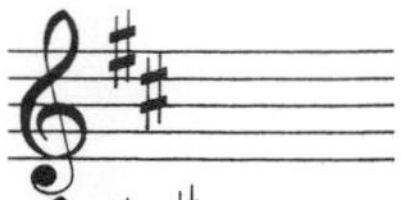

Key signature for A (and F♯ minor) is three sharps: 

Key signature for E (and C♯ minor) is four sharps: 

Now, supposing you leaf through a songbook and want to read a song. The key signature is four sharps.  Your eye flicks to the last note. An E—so you know the song isn't in C♯ minor (unlikely anyway). If the guitar symbols above that last note say *E,* you know you're right.

So just make that bottom line of the staff your "do" and sing up, "do re mi," etc. or down, "do ti la sol," till you get to the note of the song you start on. Here we go. (This "movable do" system can be used for *any* key.)

Do, re, mi

Red River Valley

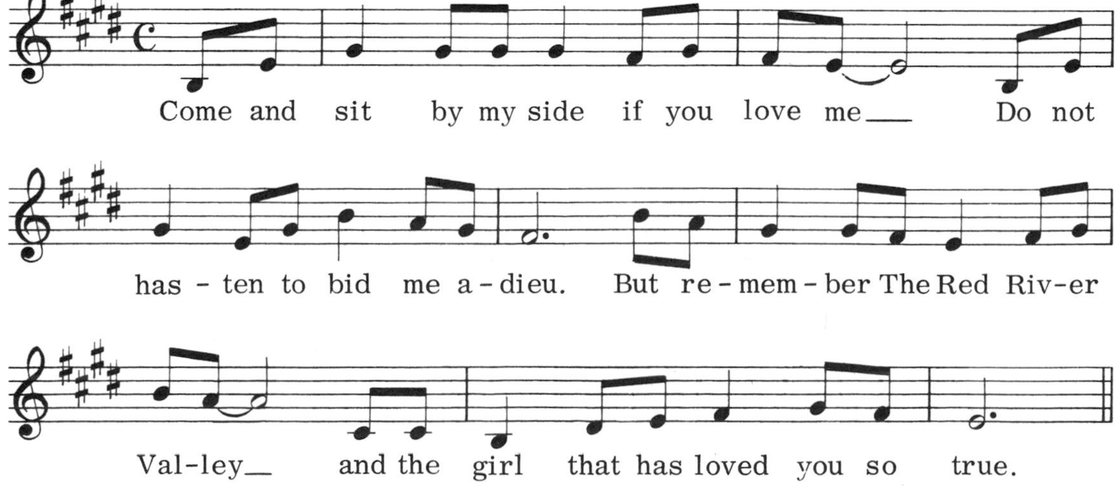
Come and sit by my side if you love me___ Do not
has - ten to bid me a - dieu. But re - mem - ber The Red Riv-er
Val-ley__ and the girl that has loved you so true.

Orchestral instruments tend to prefer the "flat" keys, so a lot of popular sheet music will be printed in F, E♭, B♭, as well as in C.

Key signature for F (and D minor or Dm) is one flat: 

Key signature for Bb (and Gm) is two flats: 

Key signature for E♭ (and Cm) is three flats: 

Key signature for A♭ (and Fm) is four flats: 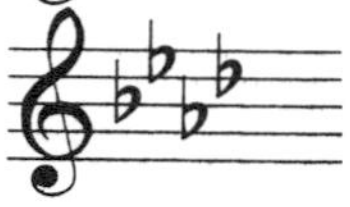

Now suppose you are leafing through a songbook and come to a song with three flats as its key signature. Suppose it has no guitar chord indications to guide you. The last note is on the bottom line. So you guess it's E♭ major, not C minor. Again, make that bottom line of the staff your "do" and sing scales up and down. Here we go again.

Do, re, mi do, ti, la, sol

Red River Valley

Come and sit by my side if you love me___ Do not
has - ten to bid me a - dieu. But re-mem - ber The Red Riv-er
Val - ley___ and the girl that has loved you so true.

The notes look the same, but if played on a piano would all sound a half tone lower than the version on the previous page.

These two pages are purely for reference. As you use them, you'll gradually memorize them. The keys at the bottom are rarely used (and there are others I haven't listed).

In each key I've written a familiar musical phrase which starts and ends on "do."

Key of C major:
Key of A minor:
G major:
E minor:
D major:
B minor:
A major:
F♯ minor:
E major:
C♯ minor:
B major:
G♯ minor:
F♯ major:
D♯ minor:

Most guitar players never worry about more than three or four keys, because they can buy or make the device that is called a *capo.* It clamps over all strings, and then the guitarist need only play a D minor and it rings out, for all the world to hear, a D♯ minor—six sharps! (or any other key, depending where you clamp it.)

Here's a schoolboy trick to remember what key it is. Look for the second flat from the right. That line or space gives the name of the major key. (With sharps, it's the line or space just above the sharp on the right.)

Key of D

F major:
D minor:
B♭ major:
G minor:
E♭ major:
C minor:
A♭ major:
F minor:
D♭ major:
B♭ minor:
G♭ major:
E♭ minor:

*C♭ = B♮ Right?

Some people love to play the piano in G♭—that's on all the black keys. I'm told Irving Berlin can only play in G♭, and all his songs were plunked out in this key—but he had a special piano built. He cranks the keyboard left or right and he can play G♭ and it will come out C, or F, or anything else he wants. A piano capo!

A few familiar songs in some unfamiliar keys, to see if you are on your toes:

Shalom Chaverim

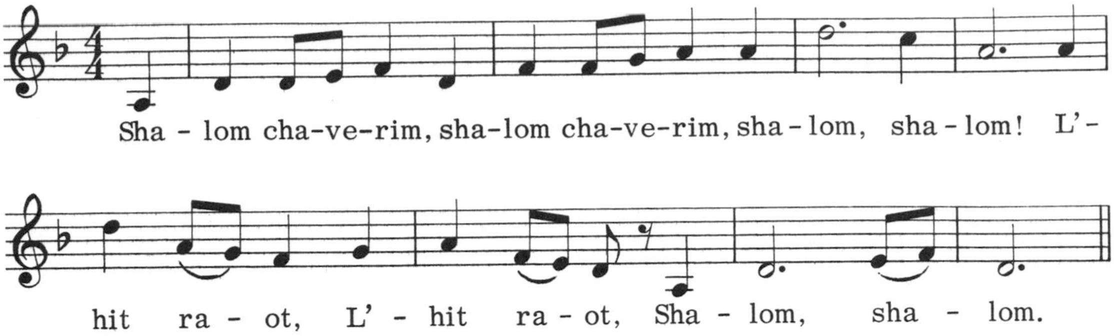
Sha - lom cha-ve-rim, sha-lom cha-ve-rim, sha - lom, sha - lom! L'-
hit ra - ot, L' - hit ra - ot, Sha - lom, sha - lom.

Johnny Has Gone For A Soldier

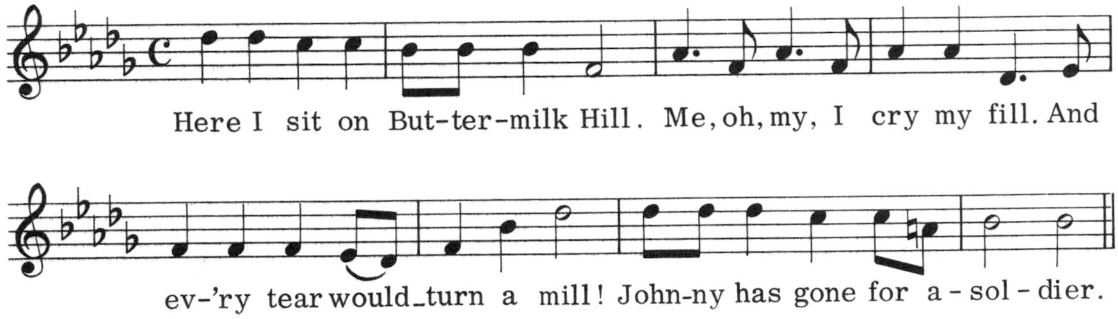
Here I sit on But-ter-milk Hill. Me, oh, my, I cry my fill. And
ev-'ry tear would_turn a mill! John-ny has gone for a - sol - dier.

For whistle players of all sorts:

Sicilian Tarantella

to beginning

And a few unfamiliar ones

Chanukah O Chanukah

Cha-nu-kah O cha-nu-kah a yom - tel a shein - er a
lus - ti - ker, a frei-lich - er nit o nach a zei - ner
Al - le nacht in drei - dl___ spiel - en___ mir,
hei - se fet - te lat - ke___ es - sen___ mir. Ge-schwin-der ,
tsint kin - der die Cha - nu-kah licht - e - lech

on
Lum mir al-le zing-en,
Lum mir al-le
D. S.
spring-en
Lum mir al-le tanz-en in
kann.

Translation: Chanukah, O Chanukah, a joyous happy holiday.
All night we spin tops, eat hot pancakes.
Quickly, children, light the Chanukah candles
Let's all sing, let's all dance.

A great traditional Japanese melody (now there's a country really likes tunes in minor.) It starts on the second note of a B minor scale. Ends on the fifth note!

Koroda Bushi

(You'd not believe, unless you heard, how complicated that melody can sound, when elaborated on by a good Japanese musician.)

It's not too uncommon for a song to start in one key and then switch to a new key signature halfway through. "St. Louis Blues" does this; so does "Come Back to Sorrento." The fiddle tune "Flopped-Eared Mule" is half in D, half in A. The Erie Canal song, "I got a mule and her name is Sal," starts in E minor, but changes to G major for the refrain. This is called *modulating,* a common device in pop music arrangements as well as symphonies. Often when modulation occurs, a new key signature is not printed.

Hall Of The Mountain King

E. GRIEG

*8va
etc.

I told you earlier that you could always tell what key a song was in by the final note, or by looking at the guitar chords. That's not one hundred percent true. Here's a song that starts off in an Em chord, but is really in the key of G:

Blue Skies

By IRVING BERLIN

*"8va" means "sing this an octave higher than written." It's used to avoid using so many ledger lines above the staff. Funny, but since men's voices are an octave below women's, they already sing melodies an octave lower than written. Ledger lines aren't all that valuable that you have to save them, of course. But space *is,* in this ever-more crowded world.

And here's some more songs which *don't* end on "do."

Mack The Knife

WEILL-BRECHT-BLITZSTEIN

That one ended on the sixth note of the scale—sing it through. You'll see.

"The First Noel" ends on the third of the scale. "The Riddle Song" (p. 58) ends on the fifth. The National Anthem of India ends on the fourth. Here's one that ends on the second note.

I Know Where I'm Going

I know where I'm going, and I know who's go-ing with me.
I know who I love._ But the Dev-il knows who I'll mar-ry.

So far I haven't found a song which ends on the seventh note of the scale, but I probably haven't looked hard enough.
Speaking of crazy endings, though, do you like rounds? Here's one of my favorites. Sixteenth-century English, I think:

Oaken Leaves

Oaken leaves in the merry wood so wild,
When will you grow green-o?
Fairest maid, with thy slumb'ring child
Lullaby mayest thou sing-o.
Lulla, lullaby, lulla-lulla-lullaby,
Lullaby may'st thou sing, oh!

And as long as we're on the subject of irregularities and confusions, take note that some old folk tunes can change from major to relative minor by the subtlest difference. The next two songs use variants of the same melody. The third phrase in each is exactly the same. But one has a G major feeling, the other an E minor cast.

Young Man Who Wouldn't Hoe Corn

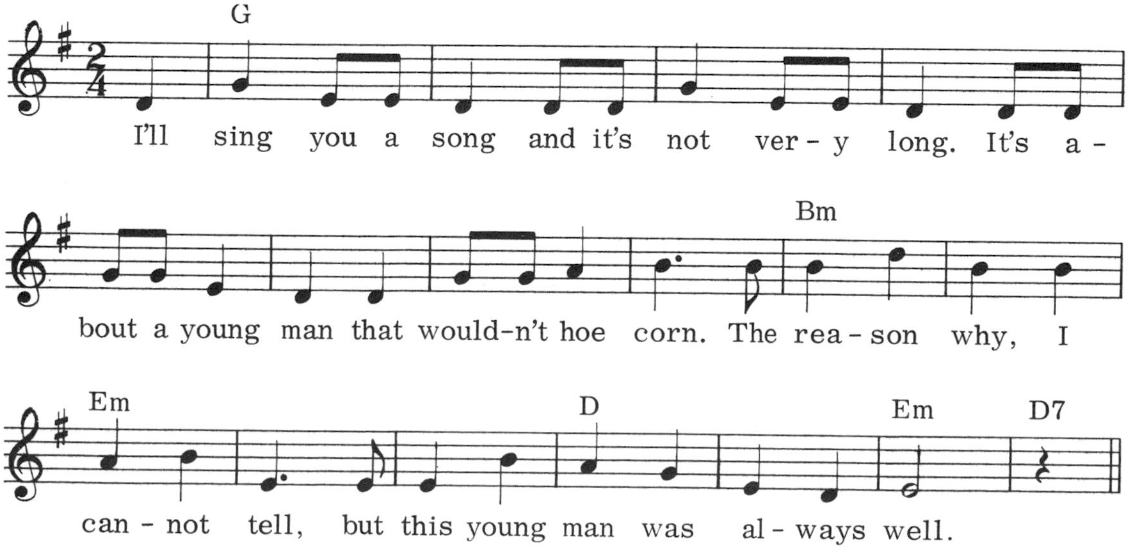
G
I'll sing you a song and it's not ver - y long. It's a -
Bm
bout a young man that would-n't hoe corn. The rea - son why, I
Em D Em D7
can - not tell, but this young man was al - ways well.

Leatherwing Bat

Collected, adapted and arranged by
JOHN A. LOMAX and ALAN LOMAX

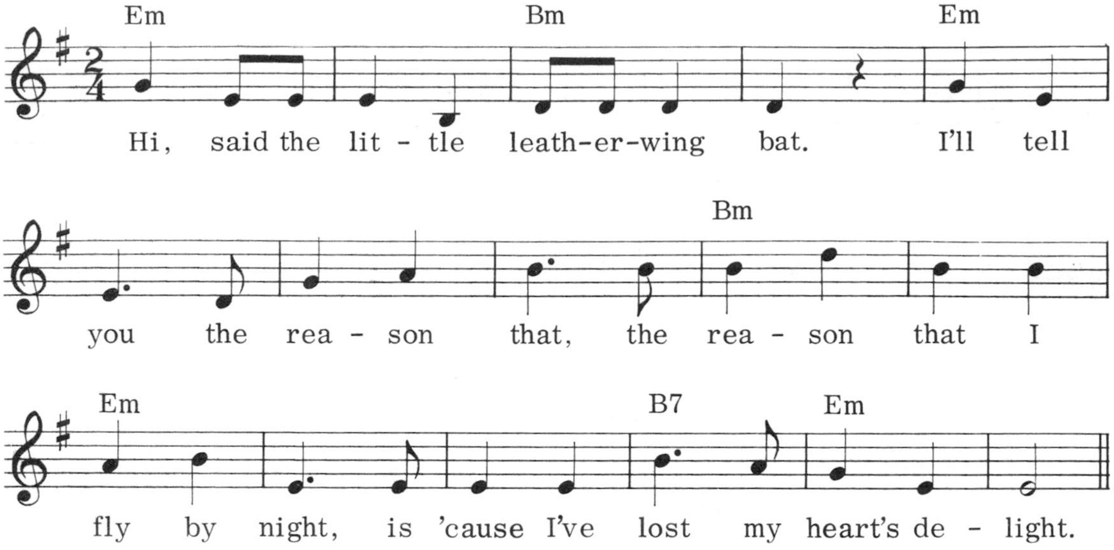
Em Bm Em
Hi, said the lit - tle leath-er-wing bat. I'll tell
Bm
you the rea - son that, the rea - son that I
Em B7 Em
fly by night, is 'cause I've lost my heart's de - light.

A similar case. The melody on the top staff is in C minor. The melody on the bottom staff (and a gamier song) is in E♭ major.

Sally My Dear

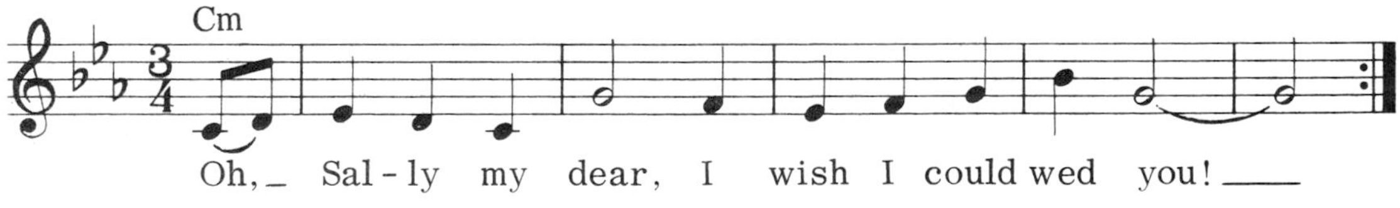
Cm
Oh, Sal - ly my dear, I wish I could wed you!

The Corporal Came A-Creeping

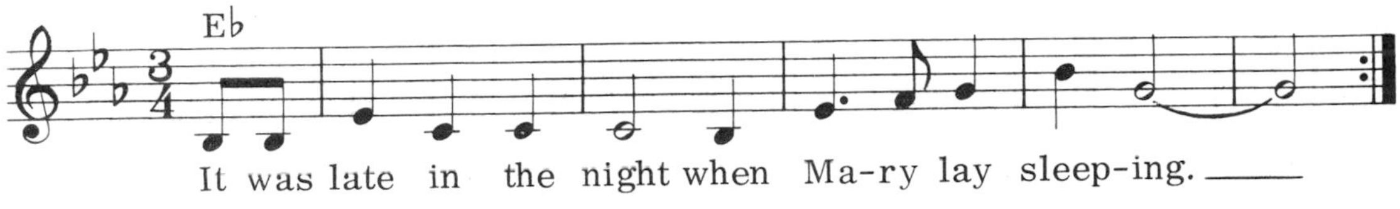
E♭
It was late in the night when Ma-ry lay sleep-ing.

I told you that you just have to get used to moving your "do, re, mi, fa" all over the staff. Below are all the key signatures you'll ever need, and more. Next to them is "do" for the major and minor scales that go with them. Here's your review test for this chapter. Label them all, as I have at the upper left and lower right.

C
Am
C♭
A♭m

A reminder: Like I said at the beginning of this book, you can sing a song in any key you feel comfortable in. No matter where that song is printed on the staff, you can just move that movable "do" wherever your own voice wants it. Don't worry about having "absolute pitch." Remember, horses have absolute pitch.

Your hardest test so far. Since the ending of the song is not given, you don't know if the song is in major or minor. You have to *start knowing only that your "movable do" is in one of two places.* The key signature gives you that much.

Here's where having a good ability to read rhythms will really help you out.

Have courage. I wish you luck.

1. First, a few songs of Woody Guthrie:

2.

3.

4.

5.

6.

7. A couple sailor songs:

8.

9.

10.

11.

12.

13.

14. Another which originated in France, but—

15.

16.

17.

18.

19. You may have heard the Clancy Brothers sing this:

20. Or may have heard Ewan MacColl sing these:

21.

3
3

22.

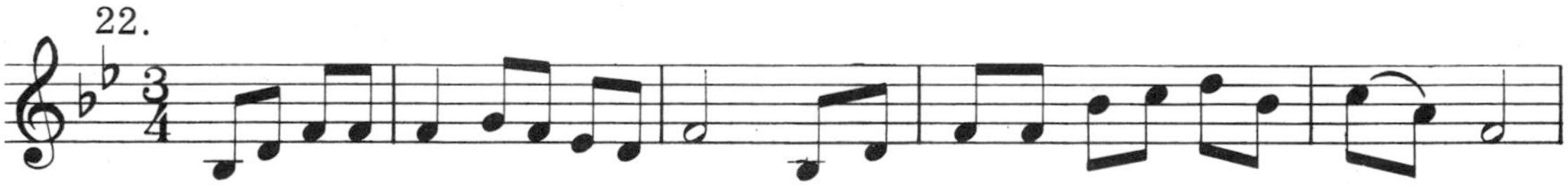

Answers

1. "Tom Joad"
   Words and music by Woody Guthrie
2. "Pastures of Plenty"
   Words and music by Woody Guthrie
3. "The Philadelphia Lawyer"
   Words and music by Woody Guthrie
4. "Why Oh Why"
   Words and music by Woody Guthrie
5. "Riding in My Car"
   Words and music by Woody Guthrie
6. "The 1913 Massacre"
   by Woody Guthrie
7. "Away, Rio!"
8. "Greenland Whale Fisheries"
9. "Rye Whiskey"
10. "Nancy Whiskey"
11. "Goober Peas"
12. "Wake Up, Wake Up, Darling Corey!"
13. "La Marseillaise"
14. "La Internationale" (Pierre Degeyter)
15. "Star-Spangled Banner" (Francis Scott Key)
16. "Toreadora, Don't spit on the Floora" (Bizet)
17. "Little Brown Church in the Vale"
18. "The Gift to Be Simple" (Shaker hymn)
19. "Roddy McCorley"
20. "Four Pence a Day"
21. "I'm a Four Loom Weaver as Anyone Knows"
22. "Shoals of Herring"
    by Ewan MacColl

Notes

Lesson 11

Irregularities and Ballad Style

This chapter is mainly concerned with IRREGULARITIES of one sort or another. You'll find it is typical for pedagogues to spend half the time giving you the rules, and the other half of the time pointing out the exceptions to the rules. So here we go.

Songs not only sometimes change key halfway through. They can change the rhythm. The verse might be in 3/4, the chorus in 4/4 time.

Some songs will throw extra beats in, and necessitate an occasional measure in 5/4 or 6/4 time.

Turn! Turn! Turn!

(To Everything There Is a Season)

Words: Book of Ecclesiastes

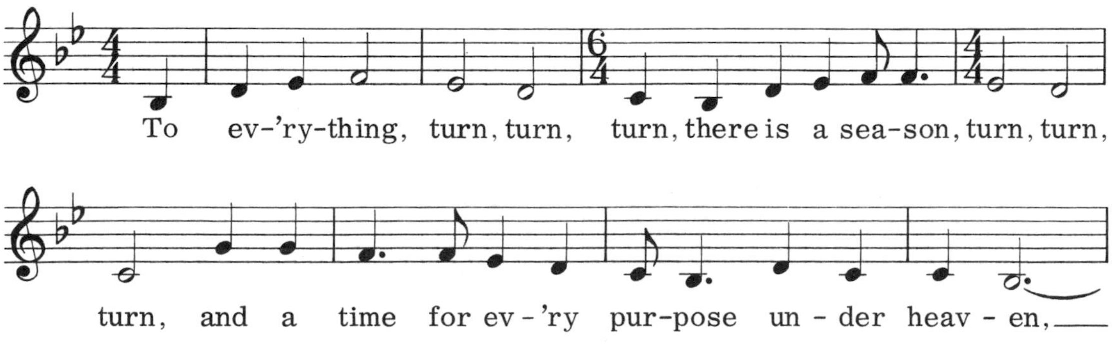
To ev-'ry-thing, turn, turn, turn, there is a sea-son, turn, turn,
turn, and a time for ev-'ry pur-pose un-der heav-en,

After the irregular measures are over, a new time signature gets you back to normal.
Sometimes you'll find whole songs in 5/4 time, or other exotic rhythms. In the Balkans they love to dance to such rhythms as 9/8 or 11/8. Here's a famous Greek song in 7/8 time.

Yerakina

If you'll count out the rhythm as one long beat and two short beats, it's not so hard: 

Sometimes the meter of a song seems to alternate between 3/4 and 4/4, so the songbook prints both, and leaves the reader to keep track.

Johnny Riley

Freely
As I walked out one_Sun-day morn - ing.___ To breathe the
sweet and_pleas-ant air. Who should I spy, but a fair young
maid - en. She___ seemed to me like a li - ly fair.

That word "*Freely*" at upper left needs some explanation. The great ballad tradition of Ireland, Scotland, and England did not customarily use accompaniment. The singer could concentrate on the free flow of melody, and on getting the words and the story across, unfettered by any oom-pah-pah chords. Almost any note *could* be lengthened as the singer wanted. A folk song transcribed from the singing of a traditional singer, and then printed in a folk song book, is like a photograph of a bird in flight, in a bird book. Both were in process of change. So the written-down version is really just the most general guide to a reader. This rhythm is what's called *imperiodic rhythm* if you want to get technical.

Come All Ye Fair and Tender Ladies

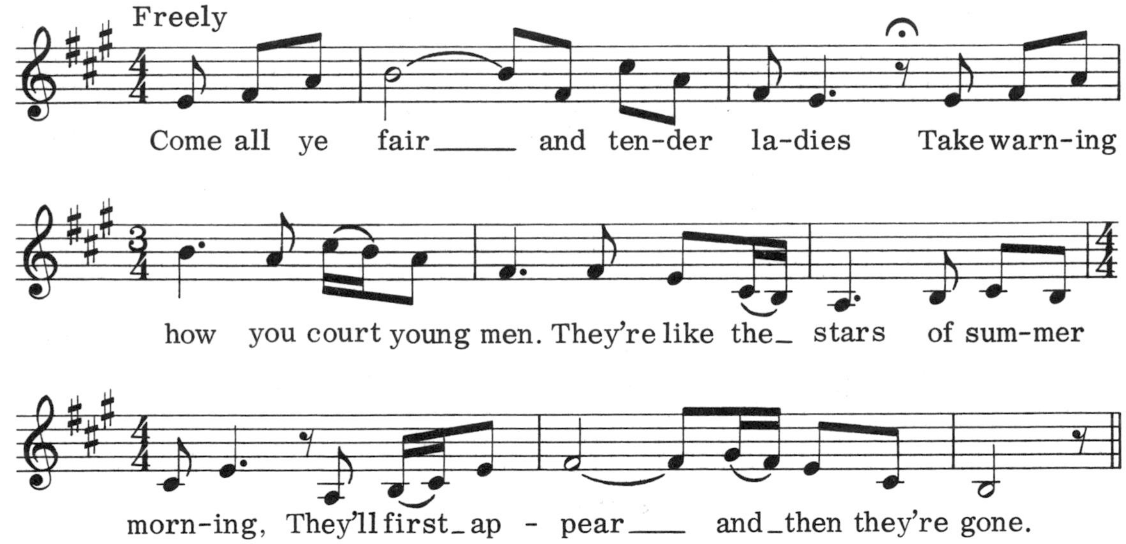
Freely
Come all ye fair___ and ten-der la-dies Take warn-ing
how you court young men. They're like the_ stars of sum-mer
morn-ing, They'll first_ap - pear___ and_then they're gone.

(That ended on the second note of the scale. The next one is in the Dorian minor mode.)

St. James Hospital

Collected by JOHN and ALAN LOMAX
from the singing of IRONHEAD BAKER

Slowly, freely
Ear-ly___ one morn - ing,___ I passed the Saint James_

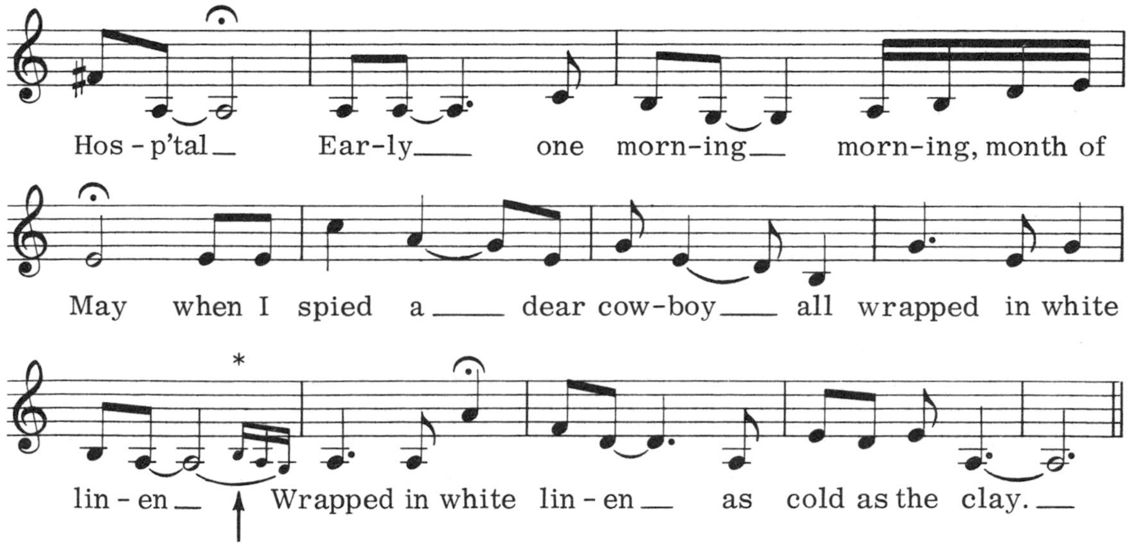
Hos - p'tal Ear-ly one morn-ing morn-ing, month of
May when I spied a dear cow-boy all wrapped in white
*
lin - en Wrapped in white lin - en as cold as the clay.

Those little notes called *grace notes* are only used when tacked on in front or in back of a regular note, and connected to it by slurs. They are so brief as not to affect the rhythm of the main notes of the measure.

Barbara Allen

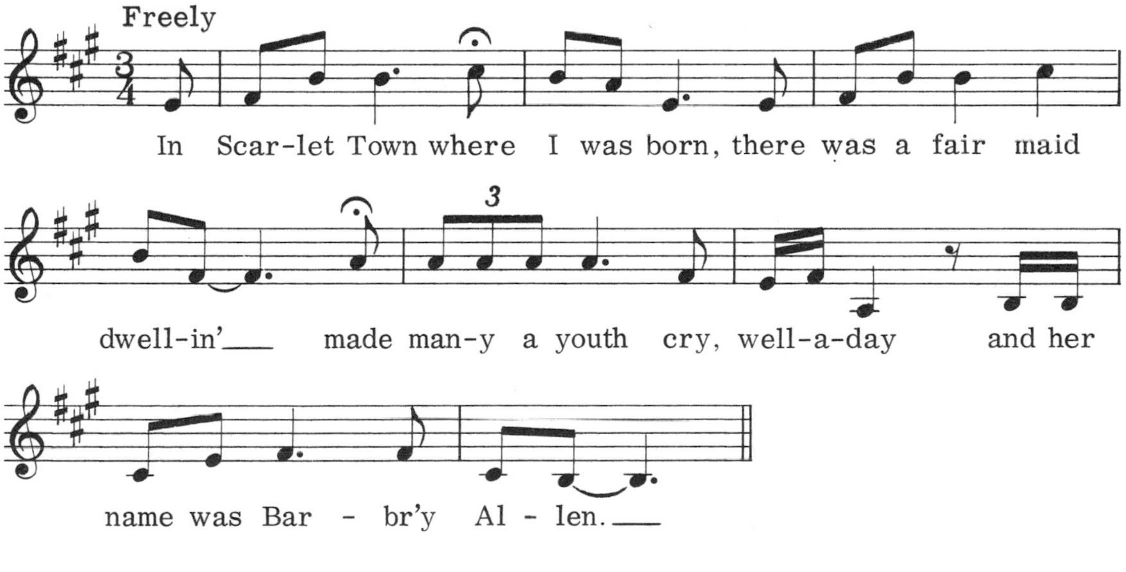
Freely
In Scar-let Town where I was born, there was a fair maid
3
dwell-in' made man-y a youth cry, well-a-day and her
name was Bar - br'y Al - len.

It's really unfair to print these ancient ballads without all their verses. They are among the greatest songs in the English language. But if any reader, in spite of the difficulty of deciphering the melodies, is encouraged to look up any of the following collections of ballads, this author will feel well repaid for writing this book.

In a library, look up the fat volumes by Bertrand Bronson, *The Traditional Tunes of the Child Ballads,* Princeton University Press.

And in the recordings and songbooks of Ewan MacColl, Jean Ritchie, and Alan Lomax, you can find many great ballads, with first-rate tunes, and advice about how to sing 'em. Deadpan, with a cadence of breathing, usually not in strict meter. It's important to hear the real ballad singing style. Too often it is hoked up, sweetened, for the stage. The real ballad singing style is like a Greek statue. It neither smiles nor frowns. Truly classic.

In North America it became customary to accompany ballads with banjo, dulcimer, or guitar. Even so, there is a tendency to hold out almost any note, sometimes for five or six extra beats. The accompanying rhythm stays regular, but the meter changes constantly from verse to verse, thus you avoid a singsong effect:

The Golden Vanity

As sung by the Carter Family

There was a loft-y ship___ and she put out to
sea___ and the name of this ship was the
Gold-en Van-i-tee,_ as she sailed up-on the low___ and_
lone-some low,___ as she sailed up-on the lone-some_ sea.__

Traditional ballad-singing style is one thing. *Bel canto* (Italian opera style) is another.

Bel canto is one of the world's great styles of singing. But it doesn't work well for Kentucky mountain ballads.

Unfortunately, many a folk song has been massacred because a schoolteacher trained in *bel canto* has read the notes of a song which was not intended to be sung in this style, and the result is neither good *bel canto* nor good American folk music.

In ballads, as in blues and spirituals and other kinds of folk songs, you want to slur notes from time to time, and purposely sharpen or flatten a note slightly. The G below the arrow should be kind of a *neutral* third—neither G♮ nor G♯.

The House Carpenter

Well met, well met, my__ own true__ love! Well
met, well met, cried__ he; For I've just re - turned__ from the
salt, salt__ sea, and it's all for the love of__ thee.

To sing the foregoing song *without* holding out some long notes would be wrong, I'd say. And this is not just for the old ballads. Woody Guthrie would keep strumming his guitar in even time, but not sing two verses the same. Sometimes long notes are shortened.

Next, an old ballad melody with some 1965 words. (Keep in mind that some of the long held notes can be shortened.)

King Henry

Tune: Traditional
Words by PETE SEEGER

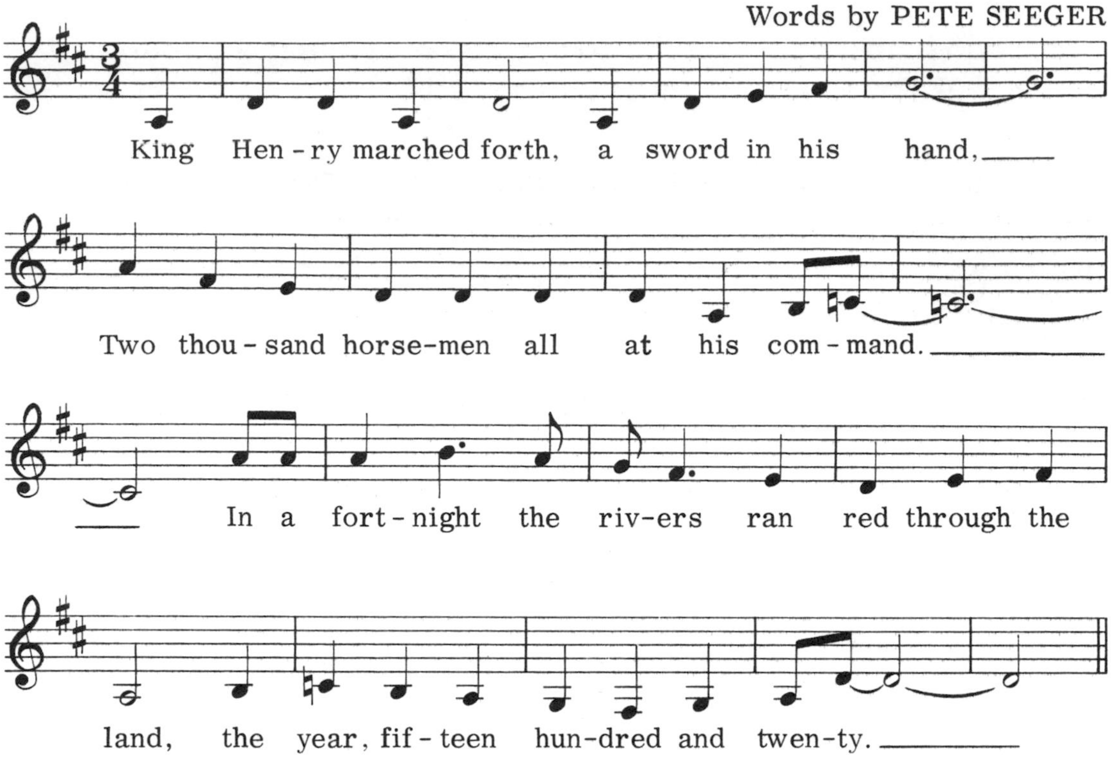
King Hen-ry marched forth, a sword in his hand,
Two thou-sand horse-men all at his com-mand.
In a fort-night the riv-ers ran red through the
land, the year, fif-teen hun-dred and twen-ty.

The year it is now nineteen sixty five;
It's easier far to stay half alive.
Just keep your mouth shut while the planes zoom and dive,
Ten thousand miles over the ocean.

Simon was drafted in sixty three,
In sixty four, sent over the sea.
Last month this letter he sent to me:
He said, you won't like what I'm saying.

He said, we've no friends here, no hardly a one.
We've got a few generals who just want our guns.
But it'll take more than that if we're ever to win.
Why we'll have to flatten the country.

It's my own troops I have to watch out for, he said.
I sleep with a pistol right under my head.
He wrote this last month, last week he was dead;
And Simon came home in a casket.

I mind my own business, I watch my TV,
Complain about taxes, but pay anyway,
In a civilized manner my forefathers betray,
Who long ago struggled for freedom.

But each day a new headline screams at my bluff;
On TV some general says, we must be tough.
In my dreams I stare at this family I love,
All gutted and spattered with napalm.

King Henry marched forth, a sword in his hand,
Two thousand horsemen all at his command.
In a fortnight the rivers ran red through the land,
Ten thousand miles over the ocean.

Not only in the English-Irish-Scottish tradition are long notes held out. You know that a mariachi band would not play two verses of the following song exectly alike:

El Rancho Grande

Fine

*Mexican mariachi bands love to hold long notes at these points—as long as their breath holds out or the guitarist wants to do some fancy picking.

D. S. al Fine

It's when the two voices in the duet are a little more independent of each other, the custom is necessary of having the tails of all the notes in one part point up and the tails for the other part point down.

Theme from Beethoven's Seventh Symphony

Likewise, when community songbooks give you the melody in the right hand of a piano part, you have to stick to the notes on top to keep untangled.

This style of piano music keeps two fingers in the right hand and two in the left hand. So a chorus of sopranos, altos, tenors, basses could also sing the parts as written.

The Battle-Cry of Freedom

GEO F. ROOT

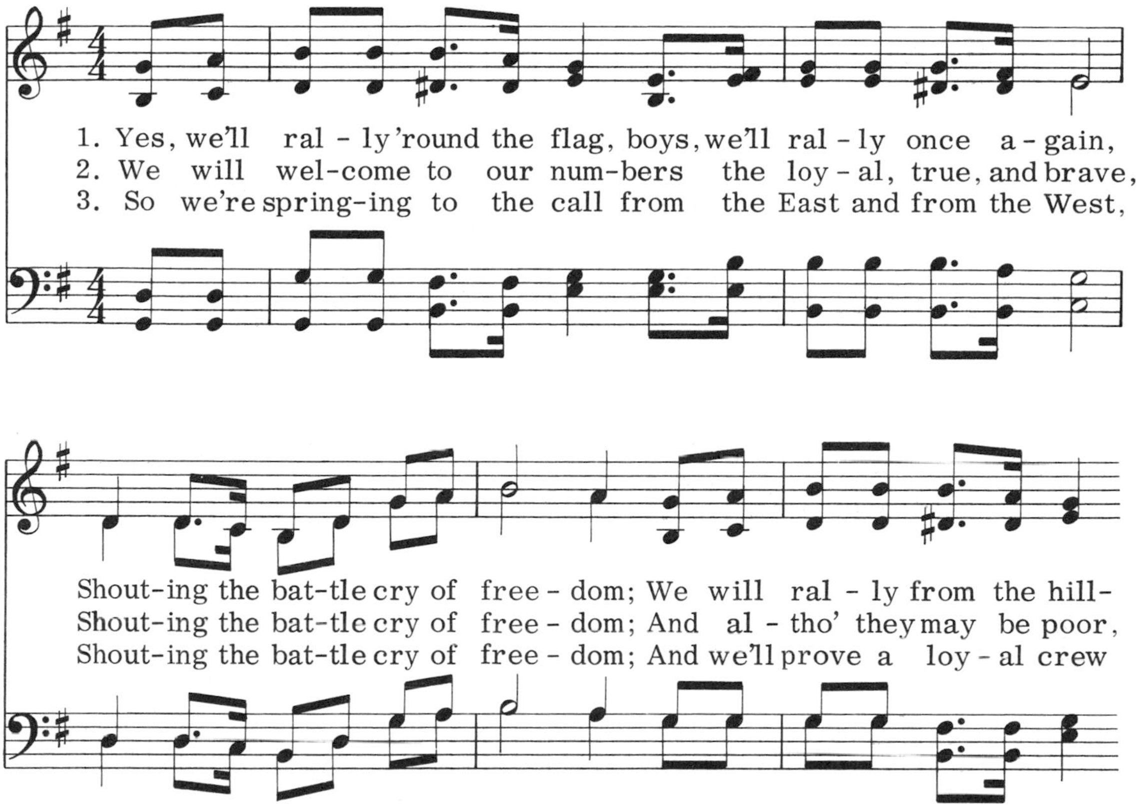
1. Yes, we'll ral - ly 'round the flag, boys, we'll ral - ly once a - gain,
2. We will wel-come to our num-bers the loy - al, true, and brave,
3. So we're spring-ing to the call from the East and from the West,
Shout-ing the bat-tle cry of free - dom; We will ral - ly from the hill-
Shout-ing the bat-tle cry of free - dom; And al - tho' they may be poor,
Shout-ing the bat-tle cry of free - dom; And we'll prove a loy - al crew

I doubt that many of you know these melodies, but see if you know any. They're all *worth* knowing.

1. Slowly

2. Have to give all of this:

3. Slowly

4. Old English Ballad sung in the southern mountains, taught me by Alan Lomax:

5.

6.

7.

3

8.

Answers

1. "Every Night When the Sun Goes In"
2. "Hills of Glenshee"
3. "Shtille Di Nacht"
4. "Johnson Jinxen"
5. "Jam on Gerry's Rocks"
6. "Devil and the Farmer's Wife" (one of 10,000 versions)
7. "Will Ye Go, Lassie, Go?" ("Wild Mountain Thyme")
8. "Maids, When You're Young, Never Wed an Old Man"

There's a thousand and one details about the subtleties of writing down and reading music, which I have not given you. I guess this book should have been titled,

"How to *Begin* to Read Music."

There's one type of irregularity which is so characteristic of American music that we'll spend the whole last chapter on it. It's a habit brought to this continent by musicians from one of the most musically rich parts of the world, Africa.

It's the tradition of keeping the basic rhythm beat steady as a clock, while the melody goes all around it, before it and behind it, under and over it. So hold on to your hats, and here we go.

Notes

Lesson 12

Irregularities: Syncopation in Blues, Gospel Songs, Etc.

Way back in Lesson 2, in prehistoric times, we used the word *syncopation* to describe what happens when your foot keeps tapping a regular beat, but the accented note of the song comes off the beat. The arrows here are the foot taps:

Da - dum - da da da

Some other songs later on had syncopation which I hope you weren't confused by:

"Lilli Marlene"	p. 70
"Tom Dooley"	p. 82
"Moonlight Bay"	p. 149
"Sly Mongoose"	p. 151
"Back Water Blues"	p. 157
"D-Day Dodgers"	p. 152–3
"He's Got the Whole World in His Hands"	p. 57

Here's a whole verse of that song:

He's Got The Whole World In His Hands

He's got the whole world_ in his hands,_ He's got the
whole wide world_ in his hands._ He's got the whole world___
___ in his hands,_ he's got the whole world in his hands._

Once you get used to the idea that any word can be sung on the beat, or ahead of it, or after it, then syncopation becomes simple. Too bad that all those tied notes look so complicated on paper. I guess the procedure should be to look at the notes and go through the song slowly, then put down the paper and see if you can feel the sway and surge of the song. So many of America's folk songs and popular songs have this same Afro-American swing that it shouldn't be too hard for you. Here's several.

One of George Gershwin's greatest:

Oh, Lady Be Good

G. GERSHWIN-I. GERSHWIN

A prison worksong sung to Alan Lomax by Vera Hall of Alabama:

Another Man Done Gone

New words and new music arrangement by VERA HALL
Collected, adapted and arranged by
JOHN A. LOMAX, ALAN LOMAX and RUBY PICKENS TARTT

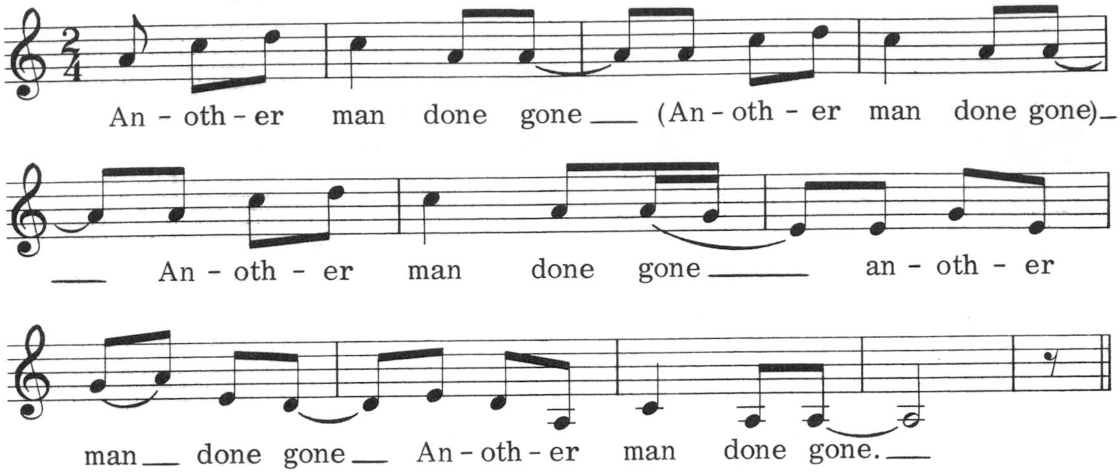
An - oth - er man done gone ___ (An - oth - er man done gone) ___
___ An - oth - er man done gone ___ an - oth - er
man ___ done gone ___ An - oth - er man done gone. ___

Many teen-age girls have harmonized on songs like this:

Once in a While

Words by BUD GREEN
Music by MICHAEL EDWARDS

From the ragtime era:

California Here I Come

JOLSON-DeSYLVA-MEYER

Jumping the gun on the third beat of the measure is so common . . .

Rock Island Line

New words and new music arrangement by
HUDDIE LEDBETTER
Edited with additional material by ALAN LOMAX

Oh, the Rock Is-land Line,_ it is a might-y good road,_ Oh, the
Rock Is - land Line,_ it is the road to ride,_ Oh, the

that some songbooks eliminate the tied note and just print a straight quarter note straddling the middle of the measure:

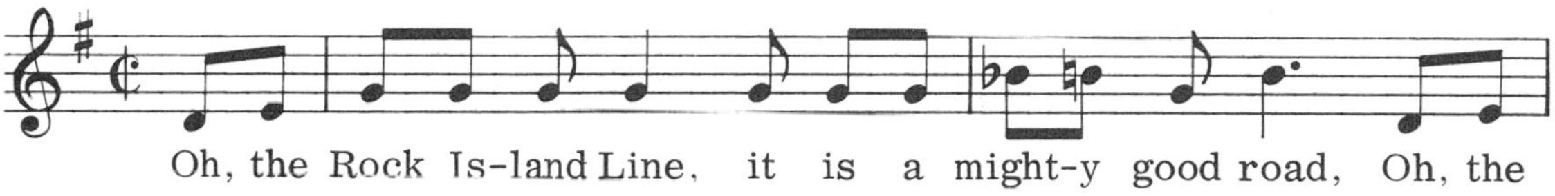
Oh, the Rock Is-land Line, it is a might-y good road, Oh, the

In Latin America, where the rhumba rhythm is commonly printed

this is often done when it is a regular pattern.

Yours

(Quiereme Mucho)

Music by GONZALO ROIG
Spanish Words by AGUSTIN RODRIGUEZ

Cuan - do se quie - re de ver - as.

Co - mo te quie - ro yo a - ti, es im - pos -
si - ble, mi cie - lo, tan se - pa - ra - dos. . .

(A beauty for two-part harmonizing. Popularized thirty years ago in the USA, composed in Cuba originally— sh-h.)

You better get used to reading it both ways.

Casey Jones
(The Brave Engineer)

Words by T. LAWRENCE SEIBERT
Music by EDDIE NEWTON

The above looks awkward and jerky on paper. Imagine how relaxed and almost conversational it would have been, done by Mississippi John Hurt.

The next song I gave you early but without all the syncopation it should have had.

Sweet Georgia Brown

This is how I gave it on p. 30.

by BERNIE-PINKARD-CASEY

etc.

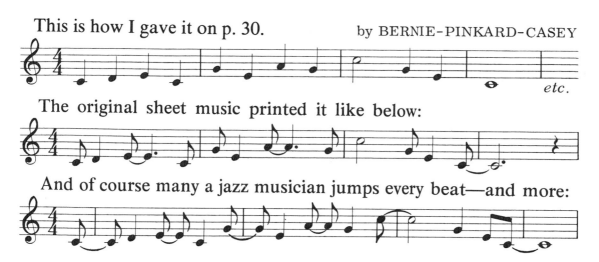

The original sheet music printed it like below:

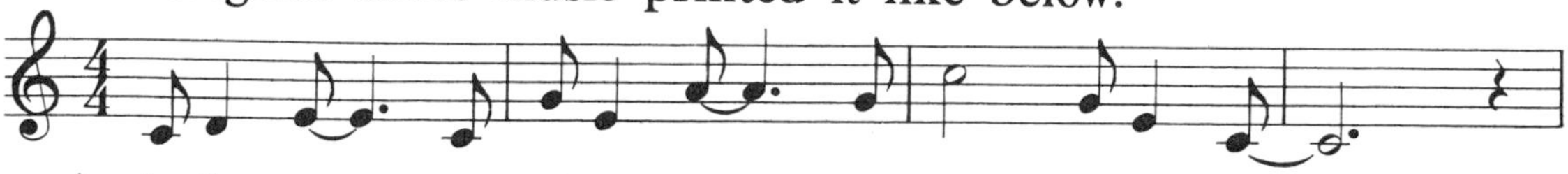

And of course many a jazz musician jumps every beat—and more:

There is probably sense in printing just the bare bones of a melody, since no two musicians would want to dress them out in the same way. The opening of the next song can be printed simply:

Michael, Row The Boat Ashore

Adaptation and new words by TONY SALATAN, LEE HAYS, RONNIE GILBERT, and FRED HELLERMAN

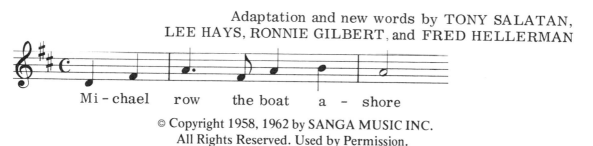

Mi - chael row the boat a - shore

Then the singer can sing it fifty different ways:

Mi - chael row the boat a - shore —

or

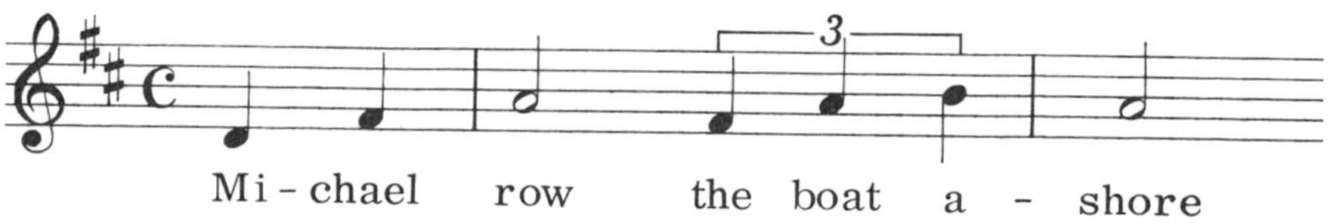
3
Mi - chael row the boat a - shore

or 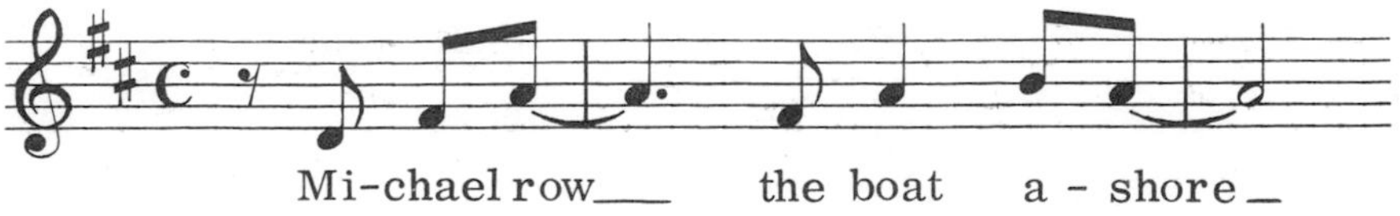
Mi-chael row the boat a - shore

or 
Mi-chael row the boat a - shore

I bet even in Olde Englande they took a song written like this:

Land-lord, fill the flow-ing bowl un - til the cup runs o - ver

And sang it more like this:

Land-lord, fill the flow-ing bowl un - til the cup runs o - ver

Not that the singer has to syncopate everything. Some do it too much, including me. In 1950, friends of mine taught me a song they'd learned from West African college students, and we sang it with many a syncopated beat:

Ev'rybody Loves Saturday Night

Words and Music by
PAUL CAMPBELL

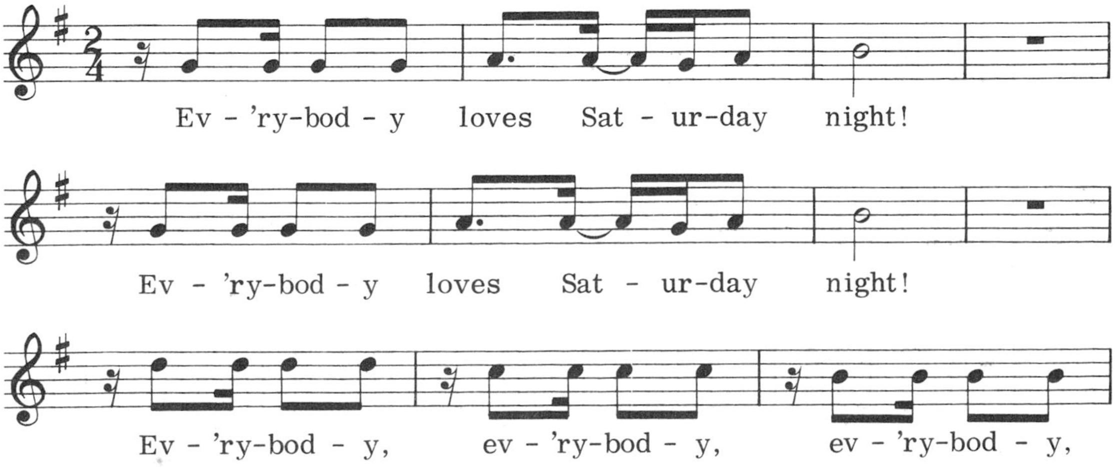
Ev - 'ry-bod - y loves Sat - ur-day night!
Ev - 'ry-bod - y loves Sat - ur-day night!
Ev - 'ry-bod - y, ev - 'ry-bod - y, ev - 'ry-bod - y,

ev-'ry-bod-y, Ev-'ry-bod-y loves Sat-ur-day night!

Years later my family and I visited West Africa and found that most people sang the song with the straightest rickety-tick beat—which brought out the unexpected humorous accent on "Saturday." Moral: If you feel a songbook has printed a song with too much syncopation, straighten it out!

Ev - 'ry - bod - y loves Sat - ur - day night!

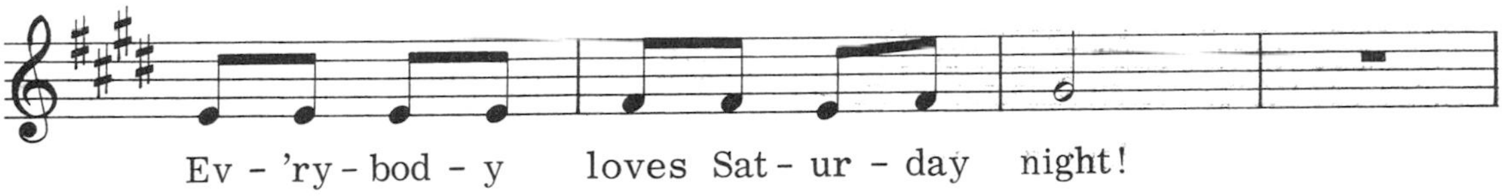
Ev - 'ry - bod - y loves Sat - ur - day night!

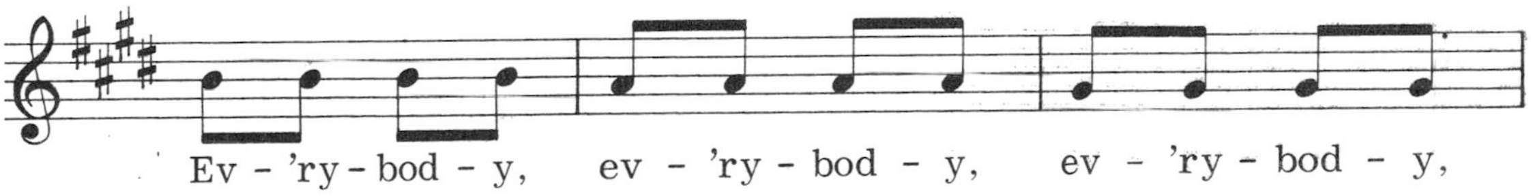
Ev - 'ry - bod - y, ev - 'ry - bod - y, ev - 'ry - bod - y,

ev-'ry-bod-y, Ev-'ry-bod-y loves Sat-ur-day night!

Yoruba words: *"Bobo waro fero Satoday!"* The song originated in the 1930's or 1940's, when Britain controlled the region and clamped a curfew on large areas, excepting only Saturday nights.

A last series of test for you.

1. (Em)

2.

3.

4.

5.

6.

7.

8. Two versions of the same song coming up now:

9.

10.

11.

Em

12.

13.

14.

15.

16.

17.

18.

19.

20.

21. The way you know the song:

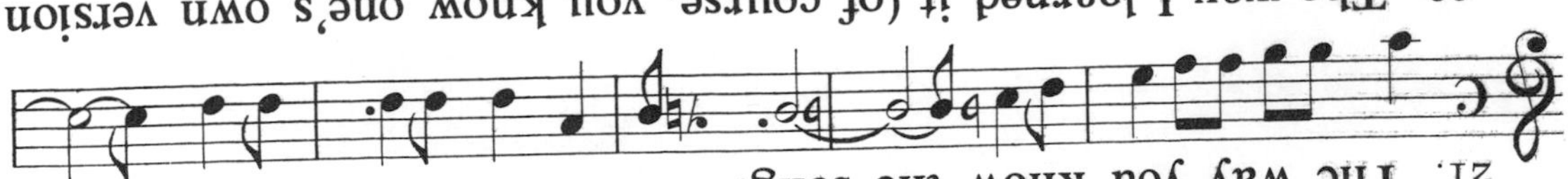

22. The way I learned it (of course, you know one's own version is always "the correct one"):

Answers

1. "Didn't My Lord Deliver Daniel?"
2. "This Little Light of Mine"
3. "Frankie and Johnny Were Lovers"
4. "Fifteen Miles on the Erie Canal"
5. "Joshua Fought the Battle of Jericho"
6. "Candy Man Blues"—Mississippi John Hurt
7. "Kisses Sweeter Than Wine," Words by Paul Campbell, music by Joel Newman

8.
9. } "New York Town," Words and music by Woody Guthrie

10. "Hold 'Em, Joe," Words and Music by Harry Thomas
11. "It's Love, Love Alone"
12. "By the Beautiful Sea," Words by Harold R. Atteridge, music by Harry Carroll
13. "Children, Go Where I Send Thee"
14. "Jay Gould's Daughter"
15. "Brown Skin Gal"
16. "Jamaica Farewell," by Irving Burgess
17. "John Henry"
18. "Follow the Drinking Gourd"
19. "Oh, Had I A Golden Thread," by Peter Seeger
20. "Woke Up This Morning with My Mind (My Mind It Was) Stayed on Freedom"

21.
22. } "All My Trials Soon Be Over"

Maybe this is as good a place as any to point out that the commercial music business being what it is, you can't always trust sheet music (or this book) to be 100% correct when it says "words and music by SO-AND-SO."

Backstage at the Grand Ole Opry the joke went around: "Can you read music?"

Answer: "Not enough to hurt my playing."

And probably for similar reasons a lot of America's best jazz musicians never learned to read music. After all, for everything you gain in this world, you lose something. What you gain with the eye can be lost by the ear.

While it's possible to play good music at the same time as looking at notes, it's a highly specialized art. Only trained actors can read a page of dialogue and have it sound as natural as it would be spoken ad lib.

In the summer of 1964 I visited one of the Mississippi Freedom Schools. Some Northern college students were helping out, teaching courses in black history, math, geography, etc. But when they spoke to their classes, their speech had none of the flow, rhythm, sonority, or poetical choice of words which their students often had. One of these black teen-agers would stand up in class, and their spoken words were a pleasure to listen to. They had spent a life of exchanging information orally and aurally, they'd heard the King James Bible in church, and "testified" on their feet. The Yankee student had got his education mainly from the printed page, and got into bad speech habits because of it.

Don't you get into bad music habits because of this book.

Here's a song that I think has never been properly appreciated because the necessary syncopation is usually ignored when printing it. In *Sing Out* magazine we had the chorus:

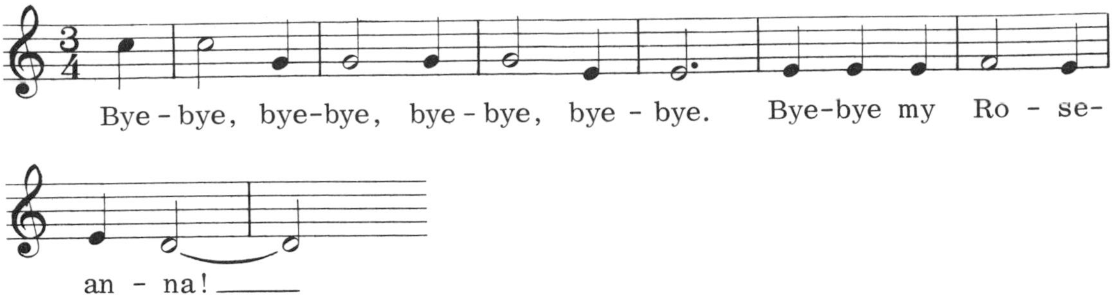
Bye - bye, bye-bye, bye - bye, bye - bye. Bye-bye my Ro - se-
an - na!

But see how it should be sung, below. Alan Lomax collected it from Negro fishermen of the Virginia tidewater country. He thinks it ranks alongside "Goodnight, Irene" as one of America's great songs for singing. I think he's right.

Sweet Roseanne

Words and Music by "The Bright Light Quartette"
(Lawrence Hodge, Arnold Fisher, James Campbell, Robert Beane, Shedrick Cain) and Alan Lomax

Oh Ro - se-anne, Sweet Ro - se-anne, Bye, Bye, my
Ro - se - an-na, I'm goin' a - way but
not to stay, and I won't be home to - mor-row,

Chorus:
Bye, bye,_ bye, bye,_ bye, bye,_ bye, bye,_ Bye, bye, my
Ro - se - an - na! ____ Bye, bye,_ bye, bye,_
bye, bye,_ bye, bye,_ and I won't be home to - mor-row.____

2. The boat is moving 'round the bend, bye-bye, etc.
It's loaded down with fishermen, and I won't, etc.

Bess Hawes, Alan's younger sister, gets her guitar classes to make up new verses to it. See what luck you have.

In all of these musical matters it is up to you, the singer, to decide which is the best way to sing a song. Over the centuries there is a continual cultural struggle going on between different forms of music, art, etc. Fortunately it is not always a war of thunder and lightning, but more often like the war going on between the roots of trees and plants in a forest. When you decide to sing a song one way or another way, a skirmish is won or lost.

Perhaps musicians can teach the rest of the human race that life is a struggle but not a war.

See if you can figure out what syncopations I have put into this transcription of one of the greatest Afro-American songs:

Down By The Riverside

*
I'm gon-na lay down my___ sword and shield,_

*A ~~ is used sometimes to show a long slur, the way a tailgate trombone ends a Dixieland phrase. It is sometimes called a smear, or glissando 

Down by the riv-er - side, down by the riv-er - side,
down by the riv-er - side. I'm gon-na lay down my
sword and shield, Down by the riv-er - side, and
stud - y war no more. I ain't gon-na
stud-y war no more, I ain't gon-na stud-y war no more,
I ain't gon-na stud-y war no more. I ain't gon-na
stud-y war no more, I ain't gon-na stud-y war no more,
I ain't gon-na stud-y war no more.
(Bass: "Stud-y war no more!")

And on that note closes Lesson 12. I've told you all I know and some I don't. If you want to learn more about reading music, get a better teacher than me. (A Juilliard grad, mebbe, or Mr. Experience.)

Extroduction

Now that you have gone through this book carefully, there are, as the sergeant said to the draftee, two possibilities:

1) Maybe you can now sing with confidence most any melody you are liable to come across.

Congratulations.

But don't get too cocky. There are many people who cannot read a note of music, but who may be much better musicians than you or me. What makes a person a good singer is often the ability to catch the swing and flow of a melody. Do you have this?

And even a good musician in one idiom or style may be hopelessly over his head in another. To know the notes doesn't mean one knows the style. A person who speaks French well doesn't necessarily know German. *N'est-ce pas? Jawohl.*

In any case, when you first decipher a tune, it will seem stiff and wooden. As long as you are staring the notes in the face, it's unlikely you can sing a song well. Get the tune in your head, put the book down. Sing it over to yourself till you get the shape of it, and your brain and muscles mold it to what you want it to be.

When I want to learn a song I scribble the words and melody on a piece of paper, carry it around in my pocket for a couple of days. I may scotch-tape it to a mike and perform the song; then I throw the paper away as soon as I can.

2) Perhaps you've found the book awfully hard going. It may be true that some people are monotones and can't carry a tune in a bucket. Just as some people are colorblind. But in my experience the problem is usually that the person was told when young, *not* to sing—so they never got practice in holding a musical pitch, or in beating a rhythm. Later on in life it was hard to learn.

Are you a parent? If you'd like your own child to be musical, start when it is a baby, with songs and rhythms and games. When they learn how to talk, they should also be learning how to sing. When they learn how to walk, they should also be learning how to dance.

When is it good time to tackle a book like this? When you already have a good repertoire of songs under your belt. When you have a sense of idiom and style and phrasing, and how to "bend" a note, and whether to accent it or throw it away. Not before.

Keeping in mind the joke I relayed to you earlier: "Can you read music? . . . Not enough to hurt my playing."—you don't want to be so dependent on notes you can't get along without them. No more than you would want to be unable to speak without a printed page before you.

But if used right, books (like TV, like tape recordings) do not have to be a substitute for our own creative activity. They can also broaden our experience so we can act more independently. Thus this book should be able to help someone gradually improve their sense of pitch and rhythm.

Practice doesn't really make perfect, but it sure as hell makes for improvement. (Who wants to be perfect, anyway? Remember Ambrose Bierce's definition: "Ach-ieve-ment: the end of endeavor, the beginning of disgust.")

Yrs. sincerely,
—still not disgustedly

Peter Seeger

Beacon NY
Nov 1971

Appendix 1

Glossary

Italian musicians had a great influence throughout Europe three or four centuries ago, so even today many composers still use Italian words to tell the performer how the piece should sound, and many music books use Italian words to describe how a song is to be sung, or an instrumental piece is to be played. Here are some of those words.

a cappella	group singing or choral music without instrument accompaniment
accelerando	becoming faster
Adagio	slow tempo, slower than ANDANTE and faster than LARGO
ad libitum	the liberty to vary from strict tempo or according to the performer's own invention
alla breve	quick double time, i.e., with the half note rather than the quarter note as the beat, indicated by the tempo mark ¢
Allegro	cheerfully, in quick tempo
Andante	walking tempo, with moderate speed
a tempo	return to normal tempo after deviations such as *ad libitum, piu lento, ritenuto,* etc.
cadenza	an extended section in free, improvisatory style, usually inserted near the end of a piece, where it gives the singer or player a chance to exhibit his technical brilliance
cantabile	singable, singing, in a singing style
crescendo	with increasing tone volume
decrescendo	with decreasing volume
diminuendo	same as *decrescendo*

dolce	sweet and soft
forte	loud, abbreviated *f*
forte-piano	loud followed by soft, abbreviated *fp*
fortissimo	very loud, abbreviated *ff*
largo	very slow in tempo, usually combined with great expressiveness
Largo	without any perceptible interruption between the notes, very smoothly
lento	slow
marcato	marked, emphasized
meno	less (*meno mosso* means less quickly)
mezzo, mezza	half (*mezzo forte* means half-loud, moderately *forte* abbreviated *mf*)
Moderato	moderate speed, faster than ANDANTE and slower than ALLEGRO
molto	very (*molto allegro* means very quickly)
non tanto, non troppo	not too much (*non troppo allegro* means not too fast)
p	abbreviation for *piano* (soft); in organ and piano music,
P	abbreviation for pedal
pianissimo	very soft, abbreviated *pp*
piano	soft; don't get this instruction to play softly confused with the musical instrument
più	more (*più allegro* means quicker, literally more quick)
Presto	fast
rallentando	gradually slackening in speed, abbreviated *rall.*
ritardando	gradually retarding or slackening in speed, abbreviated *rit.* or *ritard.*
ritenuto	immediate reduction of speed, "held back."
rubato	an elastic and flexible tempo using slight *accelerandos* and *ritardandos* which alternate according to the requirements of musical expression; literally stealing time from one note and giving it to another

scherzando	playful, playfully
sempre	always (*sempre legato* means always legato)
sforzando	a sudden and strong accent on a single note or chord, abbreviated *sfz*
subito	suddenly
tenuto	held, sustained, abbreviated *ten.*
tremolo	in singing, a slight, trembling fluctuation of pitch.
vibrato	on stringed instruments, a slight fluctuation of pitch produced on sustained notes by oscillating motion of the left hand; in singing, a scarcely noticeable wavering of the tone, to increase the emotional effect of the sound without seeming to change the pitch.
Vivace Vivamente, Vivo	quick, lively

Appendix 2 . . . A little history

Different parts of the world have developed different systems of notation independently from each other, over the past several thousand years. Usually they start with a few simple aids to memory.

In Europe, back in the Middle Ages, they tried putting little slanting lines over the hymn words, to guide the choir up or down. Then they tried putting one line, then two, then three, till they had eleven or more lines. At one time they tried writing the words right on the staff.

Development of orchestral music probably forced composers to find more accurate methods of prescribing the notes they wanted the orchestra to play. Today one could say that there are two kinds of music writing: prescriptive and descriptive. The former is what we are used to. The latter would be used by a musicologist trying to set down with utmost accuracy *exactly* what some singer actually sings—all the slurs and quavers.

Here are some examples of the many other forms of music writing which have been attempted by mankind.

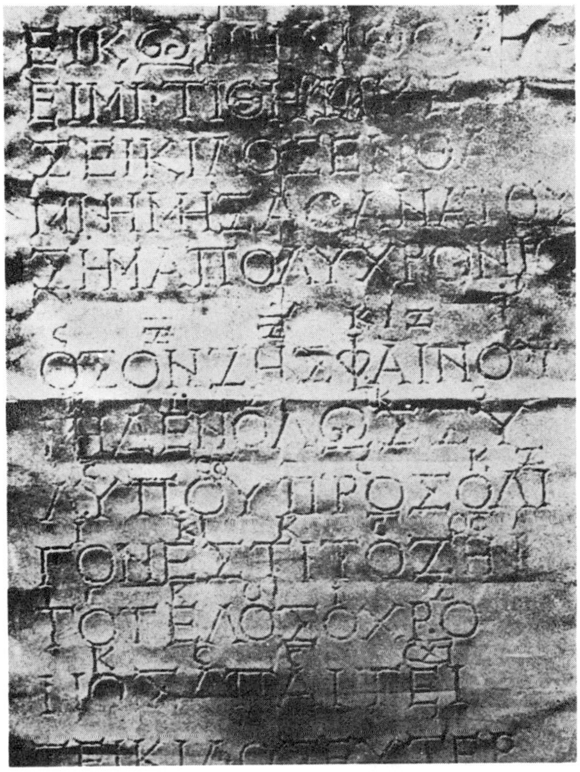

Fig. 1 is a Greek gravestone about eighteen hundred years old. The man's name was Seikilos. The words translate as, "As long as you live / shine / Don't let little things disturb you / Life is short / Time will settle all things."

Above the syllables are the notes for the melody to be sung:

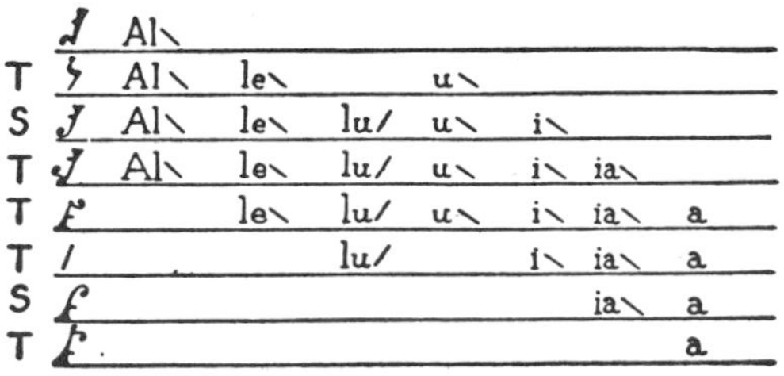
Al
T Al le u
S Al le lu u i
T Al le lu u i ia
T le lu u i ia a
T lu i ia a
S ia a
T a

Fig. 2 shows one of the early ways of writing the words on a *staff* in the Middle Ages.

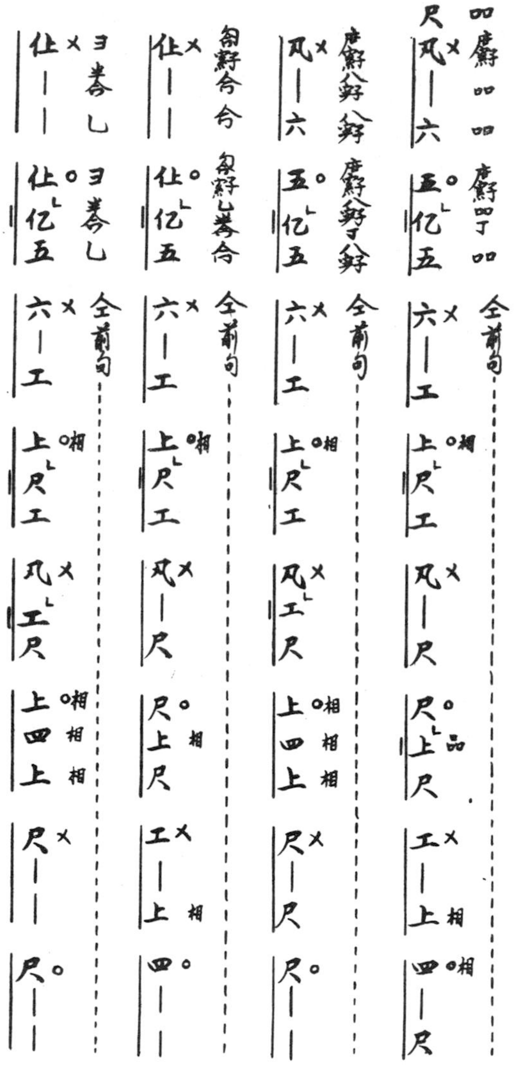

Fig. 3 shows Chinese music writing. They had written notation over two thousand years ago. This is a "modern" song, though, with directions for plucking technique on a string instrument. The tune is "Greensleeves." Start at upper right and read down.

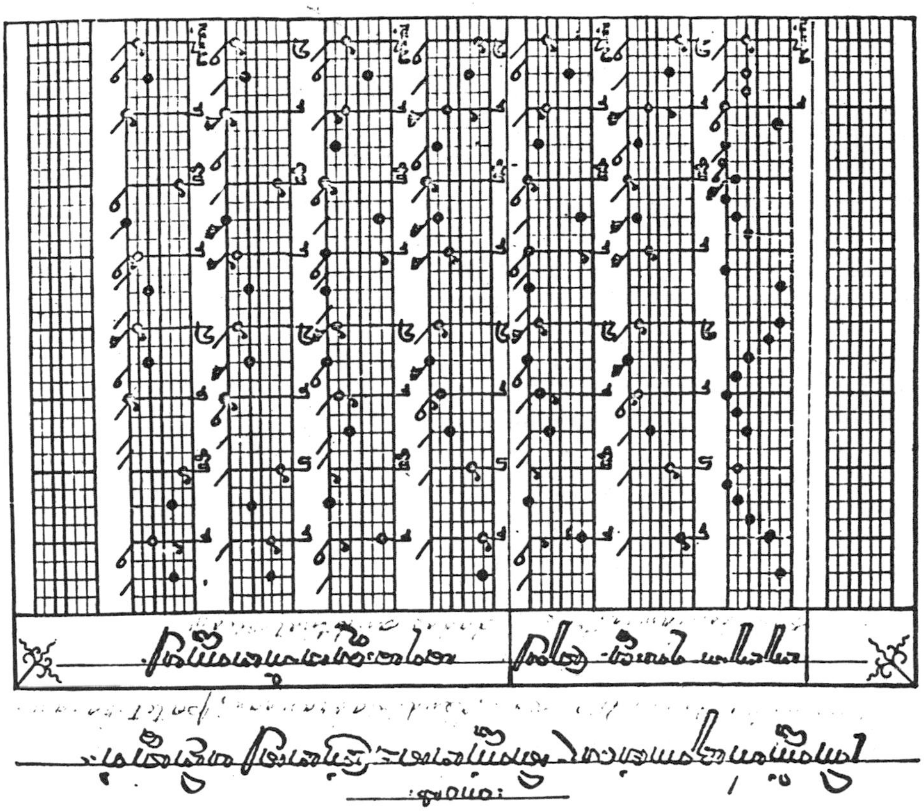

Fig. 4 is from Indonesia. The ancient gamelan orchestras of Java used such writing as a rough memory aid, but never used paper in performance. As in India, performances were full of improvisation.

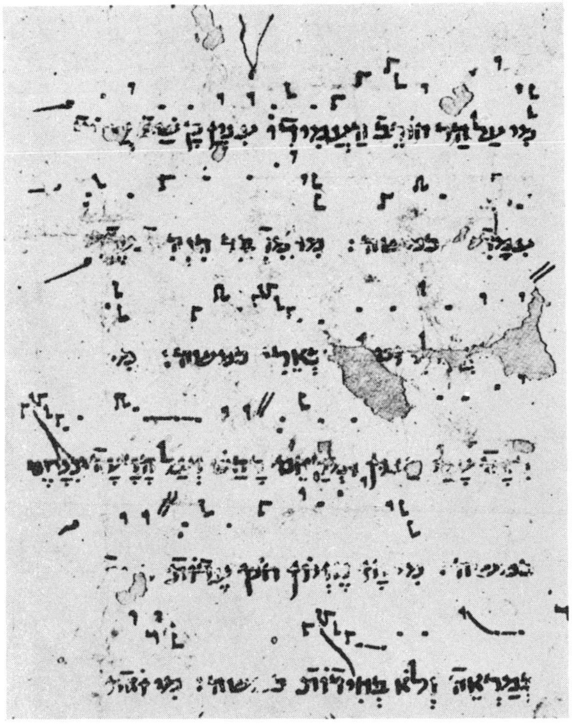

Fig. 5 is a Twelfth Century manuscript of "Obadiah the Norman." a proselyte well known in Jewish literature. Notes are above the words.

KEY E♭.

Fig. 6 shows "Tonic Sol-Fa" notation which European missionaries have taken around the globe to teach hymns. As you see, *d r m* stands for *do re mi,* no matter what key you are in, high or low.

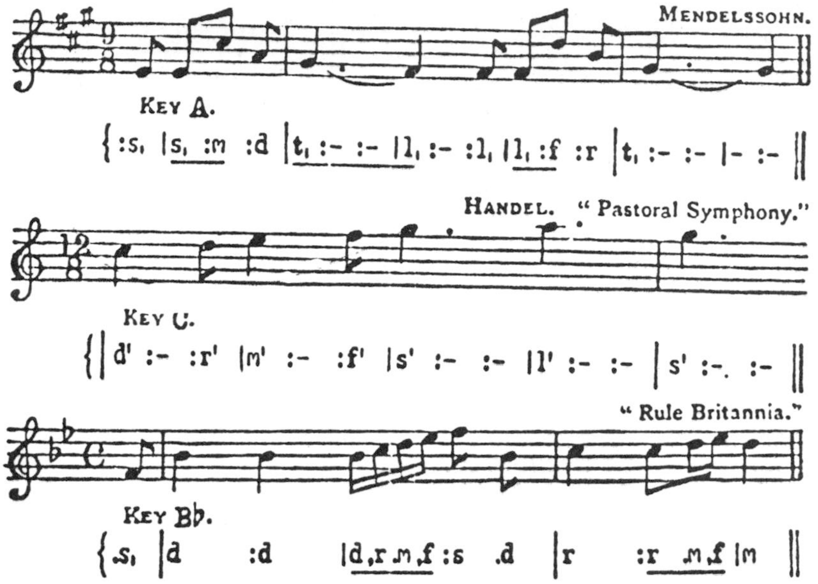
MENDELSSOHN.
KEY A.
HANDEL. "Pastoral Symphony."
KEY C.
"Rule Britannia."
KEY B♭.

Fig. 7 illustrates *shape-notes,* a style of notation still used in some country churches in the Southern states. Two singing masters in Albany, New York, introduced the idea in 1800, and it was once widely used throughout the United States. Shown here is the early four-shape system. *Do* and *fa* are triangles, *re* and *sol* are ovals, *mi,* and *la* are squares. *Ti* is diamond-shaped. Many country people could only read the shapes and were lost if they had round notes to look at. The melody is on the middle staff. High voices, male or female, took the top staff, low voices the bottom staff.

1 Amazing grace! (how sweet the sound) That saved a wretch like me! I once wa
2 'Twas grace that taught my heart to fear, And grace my fears relieved: How precious

Lastly, Fig. 8 is an example of very accurate descriptive music "writing" from the melograph machine developed by Charles Seeger and some California engineers. Any melody played into its microphone can be written on a piece of graph paper, showing exact pitch, time, slurs, vibrato, etc. This phrase is the opening line of the old English ballad "Barbara Allen" as sung by a countrysinger.

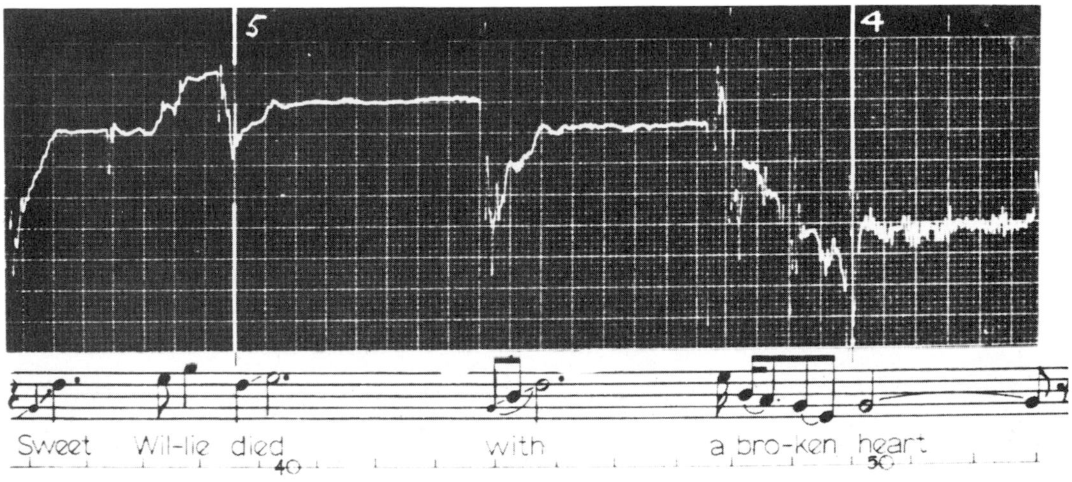
5
4
Sweet Wil-lie died with a bro-ken heart
40
50

Thanks to Charles Seeger for information on these pages.

Index of Song Titles

Reference Index